SCENE ON HUDSON AT MARLBOROUGH ABOUT 1600.

THE.

✖ HISTORY ✖

OF

THE TOWN OF

MARLBOROUGH,

ULSTER COUNTY, NEW YORK:

From the First Settlement in 1712, by Capt. Wm. Bond, to 1887.

BY CHARLES H. COCHRANE.

ILLUSTRATED.

POUGHKEEPSIE:
Printed for the Publisher by W. F. Boshart, 241 Main street.
1887.

Note: Between pages 126 and 127 are six unnumbered pages. These are referred to in the Index as 126A, 126B, 126C, 126D, 126E, and 126F, respectively.

Facsimile Reprint

Published 1993 By
Heritage Books, Inc.
1540-E Pointer Ridge Place
Bowie, Maryland 20716
(301) 390-7709
ISBN 1-55613-735-4

A Complete Catalog Listing Hundreds Of Titles On Genealogy, History, And Americana Available Free On Request

CONTENTS.

LIST OF ILLUSTRATIONS.

PREFACE.

An introduction to a work on local history is apt to be a sort of apology for what the author has left undone, for all history is of necessity incomplete, because of the lack of full records of the past. While it is true that the within sketches of Marlborough do not constitute a perfect history of the town, yet they are a more complete and conscientious collection of facts and incidents concerning the place and its inhabitants than has been attempted previously.

There are many dates or connecting links of history in this book which represent hours of labor and research. Old newspaper files, old deeds, state and county records, old account books, other histories, directories and private papers have been searched, in great numbers, to obtain all possible information concerning Marlborough and its early history. Old residents have been interviewed, and their memories stirred regarding what their fathers and grandfathers said and did.

Much valuable aid has been received from the following gentlemen: John Buckley, Nathaniel H. DuBois, Edward Anderson, H. Scott Corwin, David Craft, David Sands, Eli Harcourt, Samuel Harris, C. S. Northrip, Walter J. Caywood, Wm. C. Young, Dr. John Deyo, of Newburgh, E. A. Merritt, Earl Stone, Henry D. Fowler, of Middle Hope, Nehemiah Fowler, of Newburgh, Alexander Young of Hampton, members of families whose history appears within, and many others.

From Ruttenber's "History of Orange" many facts were gleaned, and credit is here given that accurate and faithfully-compiled work.

Rev. S. H. Jagger's "Quarter Century Discourse" has also been drawn upon largely.

Some matter has been taken from Sylvester's "History of Ulster," but the work is so notoriously incorrect that nothing could be reproduced without verification.

The files of the "Pioneer," published in Milton in 1830, furnished many valuable points and dates.

The town records, in possession of C. M. Woolsey, were drawn on to a considerable extent.

The map of the town was reproduced from old maps and surveys, new streets being inserted where they belong, and other connections made. Such streets or roads as were without names have been supplied with the name of some prominent landholder on the line, as the most convenient means of identification. The work has been faithfully done.

There is a strong tendency in writing individual histories, to exaggerate the good qualities of certain individuals, and laud them to a degree which is nauseating and ridiculous. So common has this become in numerous county histories, that the public has learned to regard such laudatory notices as amusing advertisements of the individuals in question, for which they have paid in some way or other. In order to avoid this method of making history the author of this work has used his own judgment as to what men properly deserved special notice above their fellows. This book being of limited size, doubtless some men of wisdom, virtue and ability have escaped notice. Their descendants will please pardon the omission.

No one who has not tried it, knows how difficult it is to obtain accurate information of things long dead and gone. The temptation is great to draw on the imagination to fill up gaps, and enliven dry dates and figures. While endeavoring to place events in an attractive form the writer has taken no liberties with history. Tradition has not been presented as fact, and fiction has not been substituted for tradition.

Errors there doubtless are, and a good many of them, for none can say with accuracy what was done one hundred or one hundred and fifty years ago. The record presented in these pages is offered to the public simply as the result of honest labor to bring together all that is known and believed of Marlborough, before the demise of another generation shall have carried many valuable reminiscences to the grave.

Some may criticise the book as a collection of names, and such it is to a large extent. Names are dry reading, but they are useful for reference, delightful to the descendant who sees his grandfather upon an honored roll, invaluable to the future historian, and represent the living facts without which history would not be. It is the men and not the things which make the record. God made the world, and wondrous and beautiful it is; but, without the men who inhabit it, how useless and extravagant would it appear. So this history of the men who trod the soil we tread, who saw the same hills, the same valleys, the same broad Hudson, that we see, but in a different age and generation, in less cultivated and more troublous times, is presented to the residents of Marlborough of to day, for their kindly perusal and criticism.　　　　　　　　　　　　CHARLES H. COCHRANE.

Marlborough, N. Y., Sept. 3, 1887.

ERRATA AND ADDENDUM.

PAGE 6.—Bellamont should be Bellomont.

PAGE 7.—"In 1723 it appears that Francis Harrison was a resident." This is very doubtful. Harrison, Graham, Morris, Barbarie and Wentworth were men who held official positions, and probably obtained grants of land in Marlborough through favoritism. They held them for speculative purposes. Capt. Bard and Major DuBois were probably the only original landholders who settled here. Others had to buy of the patentees or speculators.

PAGE 6.—Capt. John Evans was a man of bad political character, and appears to have gobbled up so much land in a questionable manner, that it was very proper that he should have been dispossessed. In the "Colonial History of New York" a letter is published which was written to the British authorities by those who wished to overthrow Evans' claim. This states that at that time (1701) Capt. Evans' tract (which included Marlborough) had but one house on it, and that was located near where Cornwall now is. If this be true there were no white settlers in Marlborough before 1701, and no houses here. This strengthens the probability that Capt. Wm. Bond was the first settler.

PAGE 8.—Wolvert Acker was supervisor of Newburgh in 1775, and 1777 to 1780 inclusive. He died January 17, 1799, aged 67 years, and was buried in the cemetery at Marlborough. His house was on what is now the Henry Armstrong property, not Alexander Young's, as stated. The Youngs property at Hampton, originally belonged to Gen. Leonard Smith. Acker's house is the "Wolvert Roost," made famous by Washington Irving.

PAGE 15.—James Carpenter died July, 1887.

PAGE 17.—Clementine Sands was not an ancestor to David Sands, but probably a cousin of his grandfather's.

PAGE 18.—Nathaniel Hallock died July, 1887.

PAGE 91.—Moah should be Mobury.

PAGE 97.—Robart had a ropewalk on Main street. Jasper Van Buren's store was near where Wygant's blacksmith shop now stands.

In 1877 the Y. M. C. A. of Marlborough, which flourished for about two years, issued a small paper for a few months. It was managed by H. Scott Corwin.

A. A. Bensel, of Milton, published what was styled a "History of the Town of Marlborough," in 1857. It was twelve pages in size. It contained nine pages of amusing nonsense and three pages of the precinct records from 1772 to 1779, and nothing else. Bensel had a small printing office a quarter of a mile north of Milton village.

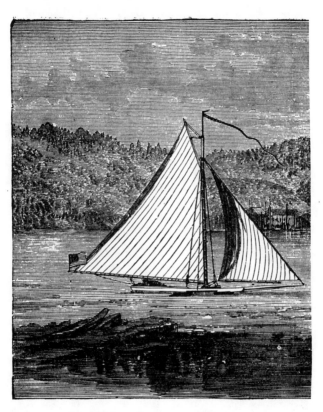

ICE BOAT OPPOSITE MILTON.

⊶ FIRST SETTLERS ⊷

HISTORIANS agree in naming Marlborough as one of the original or mother-towns of Ulster county. To convey an approximate idea of the time of earliest settlement of the town it has been necessary to refer to the early records of the county, which show that the settlers of what is now Marlborough were represented in the first legislative assembly of the colony, which met in New York in 1691. By an act of Assembly in 1743 Marlborough was embraced in the precinct of the Highlands. In 1762 this precinct was divided into Newburgh and New Windsor precincts. In 1772 Marlborough and Plattekill were set off from Newburgh as the precinct of New Marlborough, and in 1778 the precinct was dignified with the name of town. The exact date of the first settlement of the locality it is impossible to determine accurately. Many of the first settlers of the town lived at a period considerably antedating the Revolution. The earliest evidence of residence to be found is among the colonial land papers in the office of the Secretary of State of New York. The oldest of these papers is a petition of Egbert and Hendrick Schoonmaker, of Kingston, in 1697, " praying a grant for a tract of vacant land, about 600 acres, lying opposite to the high lands or thereabouts, being on both sides the Oudt-man's kill or creek, having been formerly patented to Capt. Evans, but since broken by an act of General Assembly." Whether the Schoonmakers obtained the land and settled on it does not appear, but the quantity of the land petitioned for would indicate that it was wanted for a homestead. Next come petitions of Alexander Griggs, in 1709, for 600 acres; Augustus Graham and Alexander Griggs, in 1710, for 1200 acres; Captain William Bond, in 1712, for 600 acres; Peter Johnson, in 1712, for 500 acres; Francis Harrison & Co., in 1713, for 5000 acres (mostly in what is now the town of Newburgh); Lewis Morris and others, in 1714, for 5000 acres. None of these men have left posterity among us, nor any landmarks or evidences of thrift and industry.

The vacant lands of Capt. John Evans, above referred to, were the subject of a memorable controversy, during the years 1691, 1692 and 1693, as to the right of Governor Fletcher, of the Province of New York, to grant to Capt. John Evans a large tract of land, including the present towns of Southern Ulster and nearly one-half of the towns of Northern Orange, extending to a point near Cornwall. New Marlborough precinct was at first comprehended in this tract. Evans fought stubbornly for his claim, but, for some unexplained reason, during the administration of the Earl of Bellamont, the whole transaction was declared void. Evans felt that the interference of the Earl of Bellamont was uncalled for, and being doubly assured as to the legality of the transfer, succeeded in interesting the attention of King William III, who, after hearing the argument submitted by Evans, refused to confirm the decision of the Earl of Bellamont. In 1698 the English government became aroused to the mistake of granting such large tracts of land to speculators, and annulled the patent to Capt. Evans by act of Assembly, May 12, 1699.

CAPT. WILLLIAM BOND AND SUKIE BOND.

There seems to be no doubt that Capt. William Bond was the first settler in the northern part of Marlborough, now known as Milton, and although he may not have been the first settler of the town, he is the first of whom there is an authentic record. He obtained the Bond patent from Queen Anne, June 12, 1712. His land is now taken up by the farms of Nathaniel Hallock, the Woolseys, Sears, Harcourts, Lyons and others. He also obtained a patent for 500 acres in Plattekill, in 1720. He followed the sea, but must have spent a good portion of his time in Marlborough, as he was a deputy surveyor here in 1717, and paid taxes on £15 value of land in Newburgh, in 1714, Marlborough being then attached to Newburgh.

Capt. Bond established his daughter, Sukie Bond, here, at what date is uncertain. The tradition is that he placed her in this wild spot because she refused to marry to please him. She lived in very modest style, in a little cabin on land now belonging to Oliver C. Hull, in the rear of where the old Hicksite meeting house now stands. She had some slaves to attend her, but must have led a lonely and desolate life. She and her father were buried near her cabin, but their graves are now obliterated.

Alexander Griggs paid taxes on his land in Marlborough in 1714, but there is not positive evidence that he resided here. In that year his property was rated at £35, and he paid four shillings, four and a half pence tax.

In 1717–18 the taxpayers in Marlborough were Alexander Griggs, William Bond, Mr. Gomoz and A. Graham.

In 1723 it appears that Francis Harrison was a resident, for he was given a certificate for "a certain lot of land now in his possession" (June 26, 1723). He paid taxes on this land in 1726. Other grants taken were known as the Harrison, Wentworth, Bond, Barbarie, Morris and DuBois grants. A fuller description of them will be found under the head of "Old Papers."

November 6, 1747, Samuel and Isaac Fowler purchased 500 acres, part of the Harrison patent, lying south of Marlborough, from James Alexander and Samuel Gomoz, a Portuguese Jew merchant living in New York. Jews' creek ran through this land, and was sufficiently deep for large-sized vessels and rafts of logs to float up to a saw mill on the property now owned by the Buckley family.

Isaac Fowler had a son who served in the militia during the Revolution, but Samuel Fowler must have been a Tory, for in 1788 he was arrested in Newburgh as a person of "equivocal and suspected character." He refused the oath of allegiance and was confined by the Committee of Safety. Most of the Marlborough Fowlers descended from these men. (See Fowler.)

WOLFERT ACKER.

In 1772 Wolfert Acker, or Ecker, who was the great-grandson of Jan Acker, an early Dutch settler, purchased the north part of the Harrison patent, and built a house on what is now Alexander Young's property, south of the present town limits. It was he who first established the landing at Hampton, near the site of the old dock, now known as Henderson's dock. He operated a ferry from that point to the Hudson river, passing up the Wappingers creek to very near the site now occupied by the Dutchess Print Works, in Wappingers Falls. Among his descendants is Augusta T. Ecker, wife of Rev. D. C. Niven, of Highland.

From voluminous notes left by Jonathan W. Hasbrouck, of Rondout, who had been for years collecting material for a history of Ulster county, but died before the work was compiled, the following is given concerning the interest manifested by Acker in the early struggles of the settlers:

"He entered warmly into the struggle for Independence and soon became a most valuable man for the precinct. He was chairman of the Committee of Safety for the precinct in 1775, and took an important part in the controversy in that part of the town where the strongest feelings existed in favor of the crown. His house was a favorite resort for the Whigs, who used to congregate there nearly every Sunday to talk over the progress of events."

MAJOR LEWIS DuBOIS.

Lewis DuBois, sometimes called Colonel, but more usually Major DuBois, settled in Marlborough before 1760, the exact date being undetermined.

He purchased nearly 3000 acres of land lying on both sides of the Old Man's kill. This land, or part of it, was bought from a man named Quick. The tradition is that Quick was very improvident. By some means he was given a commission in the patriotic army, but had no money to procure his uniform and outfit, so sold his patrimony to Lewis DuBois for a horse and uniform and a few dollars in ready money.

The Major lived just north of Marlborough village, in the house owned and occupied at this writing by Samuel Harris, which was built by him before 1770. He held all the land about the vicinity of Old Man's kill and the river flats in front, together with all the water privileges in the southern part of the town. He was largely interested in the milling business, operating the mill lately torn down to make room for Theodore Kniffin's large building on Landing street. He also owned and operated the woolen factory, now operated by Woolsey Wright as a grist mill. At one time Major DuBois furnished wheat to the Continental army at West Point. Of the further history of these business enterprises, a more accurate resume is given in future pages.

Lewis DuBois was supervisor of Newburgh precinct in 1763, and the most prominent man in his section. He kept several slaves, and was known as a liberal and enterprising citizen. He gave land for the erection of the Presbyterian church, and contributed largely to its support. He was a delegate to the Provincial Congress of New York in 1775, and also to the Congress which met later in the same year.

Lewis DuBois was born September 14, 1728, where is not known, but it is presumed that his father was Lewis DuBois, of New Paltz. The opinions of local historians differ as to where he spent his early life. Some claim him for New Paltz, others for Montgomery, Orange county, where he owned land. His brother, Zachariah DuBois, lived in Salisbury, near Montgomery, which has led some to think that he resided there before coming to Marlborough. However this may be, it is certain that he married Rachel DuBois, (probably his first cousin) December 17, 1756. She died young, and in 1770 he married Rachel Jansen, of New Paltz. He was established in Marlborough, and in active business, when the war of the Revolution broke out. Previously he had held the rank of major in the English militia, but he entered the " Continental Line " as a captain in James Clinton's regiment, which was recruited for the invasion of Canada—a popular craze which at that time did much to fritter away the resources of the colonists. This Ulster regi-

ment was well armed and uniformed, having gray coats with
green cuffs and facings, short breeches, long waistcoats, long
stockings, low shoes, broad-brimmed hats and old-fashioned cues! DuBois was afterwards promoted to major, in
the Newburgh regiment, and November 17, 1776, commissioned as colonel of the Fifth Regiment, under Gen. Clinton.
The other officers of the regiment were Jacobus Bruyn,
lieutenant-colonel; Samuel Logan, major; Henry DuBois,
adjutant ; Nehemiah Carpenter, quarter-master ; Samuel
Townsend, paymaster; John Gano, chaplain; Samuel Cook,
surgeon ; Ebenezer Hutchinson, surgeon's mate. Some
members of this regiment undoubtedly were from Marlborough, but who they were cannot be determined with accuracy.

Major DuBois, as he was commonly called, even after his
promotion, served with considerable distinction. Governor
George Clinton wrote of him in 1776: " Major DuBois (who
has been promoted from captain) is highly recommended to
Congress, as well by the general officers as the committee
who lately returned from Canada." Of his military career
we know that he was at Point Lacoy at the engagement with
a number of Canadians. In the spring of 1777 he was stationed in the Highlands with his regiment, and was there
when forts Clinton and Montgomery were taken in October
of that year. At Fort Montgomery they suffered severely,
the brunt of that desperate and heroic resistance falling on
Major DuBois and his troops. At this time his regiment
was mostly clad in hunting shirts, such as farmers' servants
wore, and the British thought the men to be militia, and
their dead were reported as militia on that occasion. Fifteen
or twenty of them were taken prisoners. " Missing in action " is written against the names of ninety-six of the pri-
vates, or not less than one-third of the whole strength of the
regiment at that time. These men did not run—they were
overwhelmed—falling pierced by bayonets—for no gun was
fired by the assaulting column. Many an early settler of
Marlborough found resting place in the waters of " bloody
pond," where, in the succeeding spring, arms, legs and

heads of decaying bodies were seen above the surface, presenting a monstrous and sickening sight.

Major DuBois was among the prisoners, losing his liberty in the effort to save a trumpeter from capture. Many were escaping by water, and the gallant major took a trumpeter who could not swim in tow. This delayed him so long, as he could swim but slowly with his burden, that he was captured by the British, and taken to New York, where he was detained a prisoner for nearly a year, when he was exchanged for a colonel.

He resigned his commission December 29, 1779, accepting half pay for life instead of the pay due him. During his absence in 1777 his residence in Marlborough was fired at by a British war vessel belonging to Vaughan's expedition, then on the way to the burning of Kingston. Three cannon balls have been found on the premises, which were fired at that time. One of them was picked up only thirty years ago, by Samuel Harris, lying near the surface, a few hundred yards west of Mrs. Pritchard's residence, more than half a mile from the river. Morey Wygant has preserved a tradition of what caused the British to fire at the house. The story, as given him when a boy, is that a lame man, familiarly known as " crooked-legged Jackson," saw a British vessel lying in the river opposite Major DuBois' house, and crawling down through the bushes, with his flint lock, sent a bullet into a card party in the cabin of the sloop. The red coats came out swearing, and not seeing anything but a house, adjusted their cannon and shot at that. But they didn't hit it, so " crooked-legged Jackson " was the hero of the bloodless battle.

Col. DuBois was president of a court-martial, held near Wall Kill, October 14, 1777, on a spy, Daniel Taylor, who figured prominently in colonial history, having been captured with a letter from Clinton to Burgoyne, done up in a small silver ball or bullet, which he swallowed. They sentenced Taylor to death, and he was hanged on an apple tree near the village of Hurley.

Marlborough narrowly missed becoming a port of entry

in Major DuBois' time.   An eastern company visited the
place and tried to buy land at the dock, for the purpose of
establishing a depot for whale oil.   The Major did not see
any money for him in the transaction, and the company went
to Hudson, made that a port of entry, and did a large business for years.

The names of more early settlers are found in the subscription list which was circulated to raise money to found
the Presbyterian church.   This list was started August 8,
1763, and there were then living in the place representatives
of the following old families: Carpenter, Cosman, DuBois,
Fowler, Jackson, Kniffin, Mackey, Merritt, Purdy, Quick,
Quimby, Tooker, Woolsey and Wygant.

DESCENDANTS OF MAJOR DUBOIS.

Lewis DuBois died in 1802. His second wife, Rachel, survived him five years.   He had a son Nathaniel, who died at
the age of 29 years, and his remains lie in the cemetery on Main
street.   Nathaniel was married and left a daughter Hannah.
The Major's other children were Lewis, Wilhelmus, Margaret, Mary and Rachel.   The latter died before her father,
but was married and left a daughter Cornelia.

Lewis DuBois (2d) inherited his father's business qualities
and activity.   He owned about 900 acres of land to the north
and west of Old Man's kill, and was in the milling and farming business.   He rebuilt the mill where Theodore Kniffin's
large building now stands, on Landing street.   His land
was sold in 1842, when Samuel Harris purchased the
old homestead, and 800 acres of ground, half of which was
then virgin forest.   Lewis DuBois married Anna Hull, of
Marlborough, who died in 1865, at the age of 78.   He was
father of twelve children, two of whom died in infancy.
The others were Margaret R., who married Lewis W. Young,
a merchant of Newburgh, and lives in Newburgh.   Lewis,
died in 1854, and left a son Charles, who now holds a position on a railroad in Kentucky.   Amanda Harris, married
Samuel Harris, and lived in Marlborough, dying in 1875.

THE FIGHT AT FORT MONTGOMERY, OCT. 1777.

(*Page 10.*)

Melissa, married William C. Goddard, and now living in Brooklyn. Nathaniel H., now living in Marlborough. Clementine W., married Reuben H. Rohrer, and lived and died in Lancaster, Pennsylvania. Daniel L., did business in Newburgh and Marlborough, afterwards went to St. Paul, Minn., where he died in 1862, but his remains are buried in Marlborough. Cornelia B., married the late Dr. Nath. Deyo, and lived and died in Newburgh. Anna, married Henry E. Lehman, of Lancaster, Pa., now dead. Marcus D., now living in New Windsor, Orange county, and carrying on a nursery and farming business.

Nathaniel H. DuBois, the only one of this large family of children who remained in Marlborough, was born in 1815, served as a clerk in New York and Newburgh in 1832 to 1834, after which he was called on to look after his father's affairs for several years. He then followed farming for many years. June 1, 1876, he bought the old paper mill property of Isaac Staples, and established the Whitney Basket Company, managed by his son-in-law, Oliver B. Whitney, being the largest factory in the town, and fully described elsewhere.

Wilhelmus DuBois, a son of the Major by his second wife, owned a very large tract of land, and was among the first to settle in that portion of the town known as Greaves' avenue. Asa DuBois, Joseph Greaves, Frank Carpenter, A. G. Clark and J. Ward Wygant now own farms that formed a part of the tract originally owned by him. The late Cornelius DuBois, who lived a number of years in the house situate on Orange street, in the village of Marlborough, now owned by Mrs. Sarah Bailey, was a son of Wilhelmus, and did much for the advancement of the interests of the town. Cornelius Wygant, of the west neighborhood, is a grandson of Wilhelmus.

THE CARPENTER FAMILY.

In an old burying-ground in Lattingtown (now written Lattintown) on the Odell farm, is a tombstone upon which is the following inscription: " In memory of Joseph Carpenter, first settler of this place and planter of this orchard. Departed this life July 11, 1766, aged 61 years, 3 mos. and 6 days." Although the stone is begrimed by age and the lettering almost obliterated, enough is shown to establish the fact that Joseph Carpenter was among the first to select Marlborough as his abode. The family records say that he first settled in Marlborough in 1753, and that his wife's name was Sarah. They came from Glen Cove, L. I., and settled in Lattintown, where they spent the greater portion of their lives. In 1778 Benjamin Carpenter came from England and settled near his brother in Lattintown.

Wright Carpenter was born March 2, 1749, and was the son of Joseph and Sarah Carpenter. He married Anne Smith, sister of Capt. Anning Smith, of this town, July 5, 1772, she being then only seventeen years of age. Little is known of Wright Carpenter, except that he left a good name to a large posterity. He had thirteen children: Luff, born May 4, 1773, died 1813; Asa, born May 16, 1774; Mobury, born April 25, 1775, died Jan. 1, 1851; Mary, born March 27, 1777; Leonard, born March 8, 1779; Anne, born May 15, 1780; Joseph, Aug. 22, 1781; Sarah, born May 2, 1783; Ruth, born Sept. 14, 1788, died Mar. 30, 1840; Latting, born Sept. 11, 1789, died Nov. 15, 1848; Hannah, born July 31, 1792, died Aug. 4, 1834; Julia, born Jan. 3, 1794; Leonard, born Dec. 25, 1798.

Mobury Carpenter, the third son of Wright Carpenter, left a greater impress on Marlborough than any of the elder members of the family. He was a busy man, and erected the house at Hampton, where Alexander Young now lives. There he lived while he was in partnership with his brother Joseph, in a store at the dock. He also sailed sloops to New York. In 1843 he built the store now occupied by James Carpenter & Son, and kept a general country store. He was a man of genial temperament, being universally liked· Joseph Carpenter left the store at the dock after some years, and settled in Cornwall, where he died.

Latting Carpenter married Rebecca Cahill July 10, 1816, and was father to the Leonard Carpenter, who died in 1869, and was father of Frank Carpenter, now residing west of Marlborough. He was also father of Mrs. Margaret A., wife of Gershom Thorn, now living on Bingham street, Marlborough. He died Nov. 14, 1848. The record of his family bible gives his children as follows: Hannah Jane, born April 19, 1819, died in 1853; Charlotte Eliza, born Aug. 9, 1820; Margaret Ann, born March 23, 1822; and Leonard Wright, born Oct. 22, 1826.

Leonard Wright Carpenter married Ann Matilda Fate April 5, 1849. He ran on a sloop in his younger days, afterwards went to New York city and died there.

Mobury Carpenter married Ann Merritt in 1800. His children were Leonard C., born Sept. 18, 1801, and died next year; Josiah W., born Sept. 17, 1802, died in 1843. He married 1st, Maria D. Purdy, by whom he had two daughters, Mrs. Wm. Barnes, of Middle Hope, and Mrs. Chas. M. Purdy, of Marlborough; 2d, Cecelia Caverly, by whom he left one daughter, Mrs John Oddy, of Marlborough.

Leonard S., born Oct. 28, 1804, married Eliza D. Purdy in 1832, died 1874; leaving two children, Dennis, since dead, and Mrs. Hester D. Barnes, of Middle Hope.

Alathea, born April 13, 1806, died about 1881 ; she married Michael Wygant in 1826, and had five children: Mrs. Harriet Lawrence, Mrs. Asbury Wygant, Mary C. Wygant, Edward J. Wygant and Dennis M. Wygant, all living in Marlborough at this writing.

Chas. L., born June 8, 1808, married Elizabeth Hicks in 1833, died March 15, 1869, leaving four daughters and one son, living in New York; Ann Adilia, born Jan. 30, 1811, never married and living in New York; James, born Dec. 14, 1814, keeping store in Marlborough, with his son. He married Charlotte Fowler Sept. 15, 1851, and has two children, Mary A. and James S. Carpenter.

William Carpenter, of Milton, is not closely connected with the Carpenters of Marlborough. He traces direct de-

scent to Ezra Carpenter, of Wales, England, born in 1550.
His son Richard, born in 1593, had a son Ephraim, born
June 17, 1627, in Wales. He came to America in 1678, and had
a son Ephraim, who had a son Ashmead, born Aug. 11, 1689.
Ashmead's second son was Benedict, born Jan. 11, 1715, and
lived in Westchester. Benedict was father to Elijah Carpenter, who had a son Haydock Carpenter, of Plattekill, and
he was father to William Carpenter, who came from Plattekill to Milton 34 years ago. Here he became possessor of
a fruit farm, and practiced surveying. William married a
Flagler, and his children are Caroline, who married Her-
bert Sabin, and settled at Amherst ; Mary E., who married
Chas. S. Pope, and settled in Manchester, Me.; Annie M.
married George L. Cary, of Gansevoort, Saratoga county ;
Charles M., who married Julia Wilkelow, and lives in Lloyd ;
Enoch F., who resides with his father in Milton, and carries
on fruit farming and surveying.

THE HALLOCK FAMILY.

Edward Hallock, the first of the name to settle within the
precinct of Marlborough, was a descendant of Peter Hallock,
one of the flock of pilgrims who located with Rev. John
Young in Connecticut in 1640. Edward Hallock was a sea-
faring man and owned several vessels, all but one of which
were destroyed by French cruisers in the troubles between
that nation and the English. He then brought his family
from Long Island, and December 31, 1760, came to Milton—
then New Marlborough. The party landed on a rock, which
to-day is known as " Forefather's Rock," and bears the inscription " E. Hallock, 1760." The old landmark stands on
land now owned by Christopher Champlin, on the line of
the West Shore R. R.

Edward Hallock engaged in farming and built a grist mill
and saw mill, parts of which are in existence to-day, and the
property of Nathaniel Hallock. He had a brother Samuel,
who afterwards located in New Marlborough. Samuel came
to Milton a short time after his brother Edward. He pur-

chased 1,000 acres and located above Milton, the house he built and lived in being still standing and occupied by Mrs. Conklin. His children were Elijah, Clementine, Deborah, Amy, Foster and James S. Amy married Benjamin Sands, and was the mother of David Sands, Sr. Foster married Martha Young, and their children and grandchildren are now living in town. George, son of Foster, had a son, the present George W. Hallock, living in Milton.

Edward Hallock's family was large, he having two sons and ten daughters. They first located in a little house at the head of a lane running to the river, at a point afterwards occupied by Jacob Wood's ship yard, but shortly purchased land of Sukie Bond, and erected a substantial homestead on the ground where Mrs. Phebe H., widow of Isaac S. Hallock, now resides. Edward Hallock was a Friends' preacher, and a man of more than ordinary gifts. He came of a family of preachers, and had descendants who were preachers. He died in November, 1809, aged 92 years, 5 months. His sons were Edward, jr., and James, and ten daughters, viz: Hannah, who married a Smith; Dorcas, married John Young, (coming to Milton, and locating on what is now the Lyons place, about a year before her father came); Clementine married David Sands, (a Friends' preacher of note, and ancestor to David Sands, now living on North Main street, Marlborough); Phebe, Catharine, Philena. Amy died young; Martha married John Thorn, and was mother to Mrs. John Buckley, sr.; Sarah married Henry Hull, and both were preachers in Society of Friends; Mary married Richard Carpenter. Nine of these ladies lived to a great age.

Edward, jr., lived may years in Albany, being a ship builder and a man of rare mechanical abilities. He died in 1850, near Newburgh, at the age of 96, having four sons: Edward and Jonas, who had no children; Silas and Epenetus, of Constantia, N. Y., father of David, Victor and Edward. Miss Susan Coffin, now living in Milton, is a granddaughter of Edward, jr.

James was a preacher in the Society of Friends, and mar-

ried Elizabeth Townsend, of Cornwall. He lived on the
old homestead, which he built anew in 1806. His business was
farming and running the grist mill and saw mill. He died in
1820 aged 58, and had six sons, Nicholas, Townsend, Nehemiah,
William, Edward and Nathaniel; and four daughters, Hannah, Philadelphia, Phebe and Martha. Nicholas was father
of 14 children, among them Dr. Robt. T., of New York,
James and Nehemiah, of Utica, and Samuel T., of Riceville,
of Pa. He lived in Milton, opposite Nathaniel Hallock's,
in his early and afterwards in his latter days, and his remains are buried in the Friend's cemetery in this town.
William's sons, all of whom are deceased, James, John and
William, settled in Mendon, N. Y. Of these James only is
now living. Edward was father of Valentine H. and Nicholas, of Queens, L. I., and Isaac S., of Milton. Nathaniel
was father to Thomas B., of Milton, and is now living at the
advanced age of 84 years, at his home, close to the old
homestead of his grandfather. He has been a busy man,
following farming the greater part of his life. In religion
he is a Friend, being a great admirer of Elias Hicks, the
celebrated preacher, whom he heard in his younger days.
He first attended meeting at the Friends' meeting
house on Main street, the first time the building was
used, having been built in 1806, when he was four years
old. He was also of Quaker origin on his mother's side,
his grandmother's great-grandmother having came over
with William Penn, and his great-great-grandmother being
Philidelphia Masters, the first white female child born in the
City of Philadelphia. The name of Philadelphia has been
borne by many of the Hallocks and is still in the family.
Portions of the wedding dress of the first Philadelphia are
preserved among the relics of the Hallocks. Philadelphia
Hallock, daughter of James, married James Sherman, and
has four children living: Hannah, Isaac, Townsend H. and
John.

Nathaniel Hallock is father of Thomas B., of Milton; Elizabeth H., wife of John Sherman, and Mary A., wife of Ar-

thur D. Foote. The latter is the Mary Hallock Foote, known to magazine readers as the authoress of " Led Horse Claim " and other mining stories.

Phebe Hallock, daughter of James Hallock, married John Mann, of New York, but afterwards settled in Marlborough. Her children were: the late James H., of Po'keepsie ; Sarah F., wife of Isaac T. Ketcham, Jericho, L. I.; John T., of Highland ; Anna, wife of Jacob Smith ; Capt. Nehemiah H., who was killed at Fort Royal, Va., and Martha, wife of John Hicks, Jericho, L. I.

The daughters of James Hallock all married and moved away from Milton, but the youngest, Martha, wife of David Ketcham, of Long Island, afterwards returned to this town, and still lives here, being at this writing 87 years old. She was mother to Edward H. and John T. Ketcham. Both of them lost their lives in the struggle against slavery, but have a living monument in Ketcham Post, No. 495, G. A. R., named after them, and whose survivors annually decorate the graves of the fallen heroes.

LEONARD SMITH'S DESCENDANTS.

The Smith family were among the early settlers in the northern part of the town. About the year 1762 Leonard Smith and his five sons, Anning, Luff, Nehemiah Ludlam, John and Leonard, and two daughters, came here from Long Island and purchased land north of what is now the village of Milton. Leonard Smith was at this time quite aged, and dependent on his sons. In 1763 he was chosen collector of quit rents in the patent where he lived. He was also pathmaster. The family tradition is that their progenitors in Long Island were called the " Bull Smith's," because the original settler had purchased all the land that he could ride around, on a bull's back, in one day.

All the Smith brothers were men of capacity and enterprise, though the eldest, Anning Smith, was certainly the busiest and most pushing of the family. He built Smith pond, where there is a fall of water over 120 feet in height. Here he started a woolen factory, a saw mill and grist mill, and kept a store, carried on farming and boating. He was also the first justice of the peace in Marlborough, being appointed by Gov. George Clinton. In this position he served many years. Several times he served on the Board of Supervisors. He married Eleanor Clark, of Cornwall, and had one child, when the War of the Revolution called him to serve his country. He organized a company of volunteers, was chosen captain, and saw good service. It was he who laid out the back road, running for two and a half miles through his own land, which was 1,500 acres in extent. Captain Smith was also one of the original trustees of the Marlborough Presbyterian church. He died of yellow fever in 1802.

The second brother, Luff Smith, was also a prominent man, and lived in the south part of the town. He was an enthusiastic Methodist, being a leader of the Marlborough class in the Newburgh circuit in 1798. He resided in New York city several years, and went to the state legislature from there. He died without children.

The third brother, Nehemiah Ludlam Smith, was also called upon to serve in the legislature several terms from Ulster Co., and died childless.

The youngest brother, Leonard, became a militia officer, after the Revolution. In 1798 he was a lieut. colonel, and from 1808 to 1812 he was colonel, and in 1813 brigadier general. He lived and died in Orange county. John Smith died on the Milton property, leaving a large family of children. Anne Smith married Wright Carpenter July 5, 1772. She was a daughter to Leonard and Ruth Smith, and was born Aug. 25, 1755. She was grandmother to James Carpenter, of Marlborough. The other sister married a Wood, and was mother to John and Jacob Wood. John Wood was great-grandfather to Alonzo Wood, now commissioner of roads of Marlborough. Jacob Wood was a ship carpenter.

Captain Anning Smith had five sons : Eliphalet (father of

British Gun Boats firing at Capt. Anning Smith's
residence, Milton, in 1777. *(Page 21.)*

Lewis), Nathan, Elnathan, Clark, Lewis and Anning, (father of L. Harrison); and six daughters, Lydia, who married Solomon Ferris; Sarah, who married Griffin Ransome; Phebe, who married Joseph Ransome; Ruth, who married Jacob Deyo; Catharine, who married Nathaniel W. Chittenden, and Eleanor, who married Dr. Wm. H. Gedney, sr.

When Captain Smith died his will was written by a doctor, who omitted the words "heirs and assigns" after the names of the legatees. This was discovered about twenty years after his death, and a law suit resulted, by which the younger children did not fare as well as the older. Nevertheless, Anning Smith, jr., the youngest son, acquired the old homestead, built in 1770, which had been fired on by a British war vessel of Vaughan's expedition on its trip to the burning of Kingston in 1777. Several of the cannon balls then fired are now in the possession of descendants of the family.

Anning Smith, jr., lived on the old homestead, farmed and milled, and built several sloops. He died in his 35th year.

The family is now much scattered. The Ransomes and Deyos went to Western New York, and the only one of them known in Marlborough, is the Rev. Perry Deyo, of New Jersey, who owns the old homestead in Lloyd. He is a son of Jacob and Ruth Deyo.

Lewis Smith, son of Eliphalet, lives in Marlborough, on the west end of the old Smith homestead. He married Clarissa Quick, and their children were L. Nathan, Adaline, Laura Amanda, A. J. Madison and Hannah Ellen. Adaline married Amos Dresser, and had one son, Amos. Laura Amanda married Isaac Bloomer, and her children were Melvin D., Spencer and Orrin. A. J. Madison Smith married Phebe Jane Elting, and has a son Elting. Hannah Ellen married William Woodward Cary, their children being Helen M., Adaline S., Iona and Maria. A. J. Madison is the only one of the family of Lewis Smith living at this writing. He was for many years engaged in the mercantile business in Milton.

The Smith family have always been Democrats, and always will be, as long as Democracy exists.

Dr. William H. Gedney, jr., son of Eleanor (Smith) Gedney, is a retired physician, occupying a beautiful residence
in the extreme northeast corner of the town, (part of old
Smith homestead.)

L. HARRISON SMITH,

grandson of Capt. Anning Smith, was born seventy-five
years ago on almost the very same spot on which he now
resides.   When Smith was yet but a boy he was employed
as clerk in the store of Jesse I. Conklin, at Milton village, and
here for two years he devoted his attention to the sale of
general merchandise to the villagers and farmers of the
vicinity.   But with increase of years came an ambition to
launch out in the larger world, and we next find him a clerk
in the large dry goods house of L. S. Chittenden & Co., of
New York city.   After three years' service with them he
had so commended himself to the mercantile world that he
was employed by the firm of M. E. Judson & Co., to go to
Florida to establish and manage a branch concern of that
house.   In a few years, however, we find him back in the
Metropolis of the New World, still pursuing his favorite
calling of merchandising.   For a time he was engaged in
the manufacture of gold leaf, on his own account.   Some
time in or about 1840 he returned to his native town, and
with his cousin, A. J. M. Smith, opened a store on the dock,
where for many years they did a thriving trade as dealers in
general merchandise.   The Milton of that day was far more
active and busy than the village as we find it now.   There
were three if not four stores in the village and two on the
dock.   Sands & Lockwood maintained a regular freighting
line to New York, and the steamboat "Splendid," of Millard & Mills' line, sailed daily from the place.

In the fall of 1852 L. H. Smith was the Democratic candidate for member of Assembly in the Second Assembly District, of Ulster County.   He was elected and took his seat
in the Legislature of 1853.   In those days, a generation

agone, it was considered an honor sought by the first ability in either party to become a member of that branch of the Legislature.   In the session (which will long be remembered as a turbulent one) in which the party to which our subject belonged seemed disposed to make shipwreck of its future and to drop out of existence, it is but simple truth to say that Smith was the leader on his side, and that to his political sagacity, his sterling common sense, his fearlessness and aggressive integrity, more than to that of any other member of that body, the Democratic party owes its existence in this state to-day.   And this fact was and ever since has been freely acknowledged by his party.   He has been respeatedly besought to take nominations for offices and has persistently refused—sheriff, county clerk, senator, all have been within his reach, and all have been put aside by him gently but firmly.

This may be owing in a large measure to the fact that in 1855 he formed a life partnership with Maria L. Roe, and he has found his domestic relations so pleasant that he has been unwilling to interrupt their gentle course by mixing in the turmoil, and (alas we must add in these later days) the filth and mire of active politics.   ,

The fruits of his marriage have been two sons, Fred. **H.**, now the postmaster at Milton, and L. Harry, jr., the Deputy Collector of U. S. Internal Revenue for the 4th Division of the 14th District, N. Y.   These young men have yet " their spurs to win," but, as the offsprings of such parents, they can hardly fail to secure the confidence of the general public.

In 1854 Smith was appointed Inspector of Customs, which office he retained until 1862, when a change of administration brought about, as was proper from a political standpoint, a change in the incumbency of his office.

An incident in Smith's life, while he resided in **N. Y.**, which is not generally known to his neighbors, is so characteristic of the man and so redounds to the credit of his heart, that it may be appropriately told here.   In the senatorial district of which he was a resident, a young and promising lawyer, and a personal friend of his, sought the nomination for state senator, and " Harry," or " The General "as he is frequently called by his friends, pledged him a support. When the nominating convention met, to the surprise of both Smith and his friend, the candidate, the convention nominated Smith. It was unsolicited and unexpected. He was beyond question much better equipped for the office than the candidate and far more popular in the district. But, true to his word and the demands of friendship, he declined, and when it was offered the second time he again declined, and actually forced his friend's nomination and election. The friend has since acquired a state and national reputation, and has amassed great wealth, but he can never be richer than is our friend in the proud consciousness that he was never false to his word, and has never been of those who " crook the pregnant hinges of the knee that thrift may follow fawning."

In 1863 Smith opened a coal and lumber yard at Milton landing, and continued in that business until 1881, when he withdrew entirely from business. His friends wish his health was more promising now than it is, but his mind is as vigorous, his heart as buoyant, his friendship as warm, his counsels as wise, and himself as enthusiastic and earnest in everything that is for the welfare of the general public or individual friends as ever.

MILITARY RECORD.

MARLBOROUGH IN THE REVOLUTION.

The stormy days when our grandfathers fought for liberty did not pass by Marlborough. The community was mainly loyal, though here as elsewhere Tories were found. Among those who signed the pledge of fealty to the Continental Congress and the Constitution were about 250 from New Marlborough (which included Plattekill). Among them were the following, whose names are still found among the residents of the town, showing how many residents can trace descent to the loyal of Marlborough in 1776:

Benjamin Carpenter, Lewis DuBois, Jacob Wood, John Woolsey, Michael Wygant, Richard Carpenter, Wright Carpenter, Henry Lockwood, Stephen Purdy, Jacob Kent, William Bloomer, Isaac Crepsey, Peter Barrian, Stephen Case, Annanias Valentine, Zadock Lewis, Jacob Dayton, Joseph Caverly, Samuel Mackey, Jurian Mackey, Gilbert Bloomer, Joseph Bloomer, Andrew Young, David Mackey, Nathaniel Harcourt, John Wygant, John Quick, Thomas Quick, Israel Tuthill, Jeriah Rhodes, Jonathan Woolsey, Daniel Bloomer, Job Wood, Peter Caverly, Joshua Lockwood, Thomas Quick, William Quick, William Caverly, Henry Decker, James Merritt, William Purdy, John Scott, John Mackey, Matthew Wygant, Alexander Cropsey, Andrew Cropsey, Joseph Carpenter, William Woolsey, Adam Cropsey, George Woolsey, Eneas Quimby, Richard Woolsey, Alex. Mackey, sr., Zephaniah Woolsey, Nathaniel Hull, Chas. Mackey, Nathaniel Quimby, Benjamin Woolsey, Hendrick Deyo, Nehemiah Smith, Henry Scott, David Merritt, Joseph Bloomer, Caleb Merritt, Thomas Merritt, Gabriel Merritt, Jacob Canniff, Levi Quimby, James Quimby, Thomas Wygant, Thomas Mackey, William Wygant, Josiah Merritt, Henry Cropsey, Samuel Hallock, Cornelius Wood, Nehemiah Carpenter, Leonard Smith, Jehiel Clark, Absalom Case, Anning Smith, John Stilwell, Leonard Smith, jr., Luff Smith, Joseph Carpenter.

Among the Tories whose adherence to the crown was obnoxious to these loyal men, was one Samuel Devine, whose reckless expression of opinion got him into trouble, as the following old papers show:

" Die Veneris, January 12, 1776.—In Committee of Safety, Ulster County.

" Stephen Seymour, of full age, being sworn on the Holy Evangelists this 4th day of January, 1776, saith that on Monday evening, the first instant, at the house of Daniel McGiden, he heard Samuel Devine repeatedly drink damnation to the Congress and all the Whigs; that last year was Whig year, but this would be Tory year; and likewise that all the Whigs would be hanged in the spring; and furthermore called the Whigs a pack of damned rebels; and further saith that he would not obey his officers more than he would a dog."

" Ulster County—Henry Lockwood, being of full age, etc., saith that on his way home from Newburgh, he met with some persons, among whom was a certain Samuel Devine, who there asked him if he did not know there was a reward for taking up a committee man and sending him on board the man-of-war; who there threatened to take this deponent, he being one of the committee of Marlborough precinct, and that he would have £40 in cash, or 50 acres of land for delivering him on board the man-of-war, etc."

Devine was released on this charge, but in 1777 was arrested, court-martialed and sentenced to be hung. He was pardoned under the gallows by Gov. Clinton.

Some of these Tories joined the British troops, and were with Vaughan's Expedition which fired at the houses of Major Lewis DuBois and Capt. Anning Smith, and it is supposed that they pointed out their houses to the gunners.

There are no records to show what soldiers from Marlborough fought for their country. Major Lewis DuBois and Capt. Anning Smith were the most prominent. John Wygant, David Brush, Amos Bradbury, John Rhodes, Wm. Martin, William Woolsey, Henry Cropsey, John Kniffin, Jacob Gillis, Reuben Tooker, Joseph Carpenter, Daniel Kniffin, Jehiel Clark, Daniel Purdy and George Merritt are known to have been enrolled on the side of liberty, most of them being in Capt. Arthur Smith's company, which was raised in the North District of Newburgh precinct, which territory included Marlborough and Plattekill.

Col. Hasbrouck's regiment, in which Lewis DuBois served as major, also contained a good many from New Marlborough, and during the conflicts at forts Clinton and Montgomery it is reported that the militia from Southern Ulster suffered heavily. Some of them were in service under Major Lewis DuBois at Fort Constitution in October, 1777. It is not known that any of them performed service except along the Hudson and vicinity, which demanded a large force for protection.

Major Lewis DuBois' services are enlarged on in another place. But little is known of Capt. Anning Smith's military career, beyond that his record was praiseworthy. Nehemiah Carpenter was quartermaster under Major Lewis DuBois, being commissioned Nov. 21, 1776. He was taken prisoner at Fort Montgomery in October, 1777, and afterwards exchanged and promoted to lieutenant.

Capt. Belknap's company, of Newburgh, is supposed to have received recruits from New Marlborough. On the 7th of October, 1776, the company first mustered for duty at the house of Mrs. Ann DuBois, in Marlborough.

After the War of the Revolution was over militia companies were kept up. One was organized under the command of William Acker in 1804, and continued in existence to 1838. It was composed of members in both Orange and Ulster, and saw service on Long Island in 1812-13. Capt. Acker was succeeded by Nathaniel DuBois, who served several years. The last captain of the company was Robert D. Mapes, of Marlborough.

WAR OF 1812.

Very few from Marlborough participated in this struggle, those who did being in Acker's militia company. The only names preserved are William Smith, John Kniffin, Gideon L. Keator, Daniel J. Merritt, Francis Vandebogert, Thomas Warren, Bernard Wygant, and several of the Rhodes family.

Marlborough's Representatives in the War of the Rebellion.

The following is believed to be a full list of those who represented the town in the War of the Rebellion, and is taken from the History of Ulster Co., being drawn from the muster-in rolls of the county, the census return of 1865, and the town register of 1865 :

James Anderson, enlisted Nov. 14, 1862, 156th Regt., Co. G.
Sidney Barnhart, enlisted Sept. 8, 1864, 91st Regt., Co. I.
Jacob Berrian, enlisted Oct. 15, 1862, 156th Regt., Co. G.
Reuben R. Bloomer, enlisted Aug. 6th, 1861, 6th N. Y.
Oscar B. Bloomer, enlisted 6th Regt.
James Bailey, enlisted Aug. 16, 1864, 7th Regt., Co. A.
Walter M. Bailey, enlisted Oct. 24, 1861, 7th Regt., Co A.
Chas. A. Bailey, enlisted Oct. 24, 1861, 7th Regt., Co. A.
Thomas Brown, enlisted Aug. 27, 1862, 156th Regt., Co G.
Patrick Conley, enlisted Mch. 21, 1861, 56th Regt., Co. A.
Jos. D. Cassidy, enlisted Aug. 28, 1862, 156th Regt., Co. G.
Henry Cassidy, enlisted Oct. 1862.
David C. Crossbary, enlisted Mch. 14, 1862, 20th Regt., Co. A.
John H. Crossbary, enlisted 1862, 20th Regt., Co. A, died in service.
George W. Detmar, enlisted Aug. 30, 1862. Died at Andersonville.
David Davis, enlisted Aug. 1862, 120th Regt., Co. A.
Ferris G. Davis, enlisted Aug. 6, 1862, 120th Regt., Co. A.
Daniel Davis, enlisted Aug. 6, 1862, died at Belle Isle.
Benjamin V. C. DeWitt, enlisted Aug. 27, 1862, 156th Regt., Co. G.
Peter E. DeWitt, enlisted Sept. 19, 1862, 156th Regt., Co. G.
George J. Fowler, enlisted Aug. 18, 1862, 156th Regt., Co. A, died in service.
Luther P. Hait, enlisted Aug. 6, 1861, 1st Cav., Co. H, died in Andersonville Aug. 10, 1864.
John Harding, enlisted Sept. 12, 1862, 156th Regt., Co. G.
John Kenney, enlisted Oct. 18, 1862, 5th Regt., Co. B.
Edward H. Ketcham, lieut., enlisted Aug. 26, 1862, 120th Regt., Co. A., killed at Gettysburg.
John T. Ketcham, lieut , enlisted Feb. 4, 1863, 4th Regt , died in Libby prison Oct. 8, 1863.
John McVay, enlisted Aug. 20, 1862, 156th Regt., Co. G.
Wm. Miller, enlisted Sept. 2, 1862, 156th Regt., Co. G.
George H. Miller, enlisted Feb. 23, 1864, 20th Regt., Co. G, died in service.
John McCarty, enlisted May 5, 1862, 1st Regt., died of wounds.
John H. Mackey, enlisted Aug. 12, 1862. 120th Regt., Co. A, died in service.

Charles Lee Mackey, enlisted Sept. 1, 1864, 128th Regt., Co. H.

David F. Mackey, enlisted Sept. 20, 1862, 156th Regt., Co. G.

Morris Lee, enlisted Aug. 10, 1862, 120th Regt., Co. A.

Wm. J. Purdy, lieut., enlisted Nov. 14, 1862, 156th Regt., Co. G.

Peter V. L. Purdy, enlisted May 3, 1861, 5th Regt., Co. E.

Alonzo S. Petit, enlisted Nov. 1861, 5th Regt., Co. E.

Stephen J. Power, enlisted Aug. 15, 1862, 6th Regt., Co. I, died in service.

George W. Quimby, enlisted Sept. 20, 1862, 156th Regt., Co. G.

John D. Quimby, enlisted Sept. 19, 1862, 156th Regt., Co. G.

Thos. Elliot, enlisted Aug. 15, 1861, 73rd Regt., Co. H.

Chas H. Free, enlisted Aug. 15, 1862, 6th Regt., Co. I, died of wounds received at Cedarville.

George Palmateer, enlisted Jan. 5, 1864, 156th Regt., Co. E.

Stephen Rhodes, enlisted Sept. 3, 1862, 156th Regt., Co. G.

George Ryer, enlisted Aug. 27, 1862, 156th Regt., Co. G.

Reuben H. Rose, enlisted Aug. 8, 1862, 6th Regt., Co. I.

Aaron Rhodes, enlisted Mch. 11, 1862, 20th Regt., Co. A.

Theodore Rhodes, enlisted Aug. 1862, 156th Regt., Co. A.

Walter Rhodes, enlisted Aug. 1861, 20th Regt.

George W. Smith, enlisted May 1, 1862, 19th Regt., Co. I.

Henry Scott, enlisted Aug. 6, 1861, 6th Regt.

Isaac Lewis, enlisted April 19, 1861, 3rd Regt., Co. B.

Phineas H. Smith, enlisted Sept. 2, 1862, 156th Regt., Co. G.

Isaac Theals, enlisted April 21, 1864, 98th Regt., Co. C.

Peter Terwilliger, enlisted Aug. 22, 1862, 156th Regt., Co. G, died in service, July 30, 1863.

Jeremiah Terwilliger, enlisted Aug. 7, 1862, 120th Regt., Co. A.

James Terwilliger, enlisted Sept. 18, 1862, 168th Regt.

Matthew Terwilliger, enlisted Sept. 30, 1862, 156th Regt., Co. G.

Daniel Tuthill, enlisted Nov. 1861, 5th Regt., Co. E.

Samuel Valentine, enlisted Aug. 3, 1864, 16th Regt., Co. M.

John H. Valentine, enlisted April 14, 1861, 3d Regt., Co. B.

David M. Weed, enlisted Sept. 6, 1862, 156th Regt., Co G.

James N. Whims, enlisted Sept. 12, 1862, 156th Regt., Co. G.

James B. Williams, enlisted Jan. 27, 1864, 156th Regt., Co. G.

John Wordin, enlisted Sept. 12, 1862, 156th Regt., Co. G.

Isaac Fletcher Williams, enlisted Sept. 8, 1862, 156th Regt., Co. G.

Charles C. Wygant, enlisted Aug. 20, 1862, died at Salisbury Prison, Nov. 30, 1864.

John S. Wood, enlisted Aug. 1863, 15th Regt., Co. B.

Chas. L. Woolsey, enlisted April 23, 1861, 5th Regt., Co. E.

C. M. Woolsey, lieut., enlisted Oct. 6, 1864.

William York, enlisted Aug. 3, 1862, 120th Regt., Co. A.

John H. Dingee, enlisted July 25, 1862, 124th Regt., Co. A.

Wm. H. Duncan, enlisted Aug. 10, 1862, 120th Regt., Co. A.

James C. Brewster, enlisted Sept. 20, 1862, 156th Regt., Co. G.

James M. Benson, 120th Regt., Co. A.

R. F. Coutant, enlisted Aug. 22, 1861, 156th Regt., Co. G.

Cevonia Lounsbery, enlisted Jan. 19, 1863, 98th Regt., Co. B.

John Hendrickson, enlisted Aug. 24, 1864, 10th Regt., Co. A.

Lewis Hornbeck, enlisted Sept. 20, 1862, 156th Regt., Co. G.

Isaac N. Hornbeck, enlisted Sept. 15, 1862, 156th Regt., Co. G.

Augustus Clark, Jesse Lyons, Jonathan M. Staples, W. H. Dimsey, John B. Ball, Alexander Coe, Geo. Rowley, James B. Ellis, Andrew S. Ward, James P. Giddes, John C. Ward, James I. Fitzgerald, Andrew Mundt, Thomas Morron, Jacob Rightmag, Eli Dark, Joseph Todd, Abram Alexander, Andrew Helehan, Calvin Parker, Robt. Thornton, Jesse W. Staght, W. A. Clark, Wm. Buckley, Thomas O. Brien, Hugh McGingh, George Goldsmith, Nehemiah Frear, Jerome Scouten, Moses Mundleson, George Holmes, Reuben P. Taylor, James Grach, Daniel Sullivan, Sison D. Trew, Frederick Lewis, Alfred DeDonnel, Wm. I. Phelon, Wm. Husker, W. A. Palmer, Joseph Fearen, James Carney, W. I. Reed, Thos. McArtney, Wm. Fleming, Chas. Chatt, James Martin, Carl Kample, Thos. Hevey, Oscar Lutz, John Decker, George T. Fland, Chas. Partridge, Patrick McBecker, Samuel Myer, Wm. Tee, John Miller, John Stakley, James Dunn, Joseph Colnell, Wm. Duffy, Thomas Brown, James Debricina, Frederick Stearns, James Morris, Chas. M. Sanley, Wm. Minner, Daniel Sarlie, James Riley, Henry Marcy, Walter Sharp, Geo. E Terin, George Pendleton, James Smith, Thomas Ryna, James Many, Wm. Stillwell, John Kelley, John O'Brien, John Ryan, Oscar Collier, Thomas Marr, Patrick Murphy, James Dryer, Robert Burke. Daniel Nevins, enlisted Oct 18, 1861.

Daniel B. Martin, enlisted Aug. 9, 1862, 120th Regt., Co. A.

Hezekiah Martin, enlisted Aug 11, 1862, 120th Regt., Co. A.

John Margison, enlisted Aug. 7, 1862, 120th Regt, Co. A.

Wm. York, enlisted Aug. 11, 1862, 120th Regt., Co. A.

Elmore Terwilliger, enlisted Aug. 1, 1862, 120th Regt., Co. A.

Wm. L. Dougherty, enlisted Aug. 1, 1862, 124th Regt., Co. A.

Jesse E. Knapp, enlisted Aug. 13, 1862.

Oliver Lawson, 2d lieut. 1st Mtd. rifles, enlisted Aug. 5, 1862.

James A. Hyde, capt , enlisted Aug. 22, 1862, 120th Regt.

George Duncan, enlisted 1861.

Wm. Duncan, enlisted 1861, 12th Regt.

Isaac Sims, enlisted April, 1861, 3rd Cav.

NAVY.

Cornelius Atherton, enlisted Sept. 5, 1864, ship " Grand Gulf."

David Johnson, enlisted Aug. 16, 1864, ship "Clamatus."

Horace B. Sands, enlisted Sept. 7, 1862, ship "Mohegan."

John W. Williams, enlisted Sept. 7, 1862, ship " Mohegan."

Martin Fisher, enlisted Aug. 16, 1864, ship " Columbus."

It is impossible to give any history of what these men did, as they were so scattered that their record would embrace a complete history of the Rebellion.

OLD PAPERS.

Major DuBois' Will.

L. S. { THE PEOPLE OF THE STATE OF NEW YORK, BY THE GRACE OF GOD, FREE AND INDEPENDENT:

ALL to whom these presents shall come, or may concern, Send greeting: KNOW YE, That at Ulster County, on the first day of February, instant, before Joseph Gasherie, Esq., Surrogate of our said County, the last will and testament of Lewis DuBois, deceased, (a copy whereof is hereunto annexed) was proved, and is now approved and allowed of by us, and the said deceased having, whilst he lived, and at the time of his death, goods, chattels, or credits within this State, by means whereof the proving and registering the said will, and the granting administration of all and singular the said goods, chattels and credits, and also the auditing, allowing and final discharging the accounts thereof, doth belong unto us; the administration of all, and singular the goods, chattels and credits of the said deceased, and any way concerning his will is granted unto Lewis DuBois, junior, Johannis T. Jansen and Johannis Bruyn, executors in the said will named, they being first duly sworn well and faithfully to administer the same, and to make and exhibit a true and perfect inventory of all and singular the said goods, chattels, and credits, and also to render a just and true account thereof when thereunto required. In testimony whereof, we have caused the seal of office of our said Surrogate to be hereunto affixed. Witness, Joseph Gasherie, Esq., Surrogate of the said County, at Kingston, the eighteenth day of February, in the year of our Lord, one thousand, eight hundred and three, and of our Independence the twenty-seventh.   JOSEPH GASHERIE,

Surrogate.

In the name of God! Amen! I, Lewis Dubois, of the town of Marlborough, in the County of Ulster, and State of New York, being in health, and of sound mind and memory, (Blessed be the Lord) Do, this nineteenth day of November, in the year of our Lord Christ, one thousand, seven hundred and ninety-five, make and publish this my last will and testament, in manner following: Imprimis, I order all my just debts and funeral charges to be paid out of my personal estate, in as short a time as the same may be conveniently done after my decease; Also I give unto my beloved wife, Rachel, the Northwest room in my present dwelling house, also the room to the East thereof, called the stoveroom, also one of my cellars in the same and as much garret room and as much of the gardens as she may stand in need of, and also of the water, and privilege of the bleach yard, together with a free and uninterrupted privilege of passing and repassing thro' the other part of my said dwelling-house, with her servants and attendance, as often as she may think proper. Also the privilege of taking as many apples or other fruits out of the orchard, and as much of the cyder, when made, as she may have occasion for her family's use, all which is to be at her command during her widowhood, also I give unto my said wife, Rachel, two feather-beds, with the bedsteads and all the furniture thereunto belonging, together with her choice of my negro-wenches, also my best cow, two iron pots, one pair of hand irons, one fire shovel and tongs, one tramel, one tea kettle, one set of tea cups and saucers, my best cupboard, with all the linen therein, as well as all the linen brought with her when I married her, together also with all her wearing apparel, also my best looking-glass, half a dozen common chairs, my best table, one trunk, one-half a dozen of table knives and forks, one dozen pewter plates, my dresser with the glass doors, also one of my best horses. Also, I give, devise and bequeath unto my son Lewis all that part of the tract of land whereon I now dwell, granted by letters patent bearing date the fifth day of June, Anno Domini 1712, unto Augustine Graham and Alexander Griggs, which part of the said tract hereby devised to my son Lewis, Begins at a walnut tree, formerly marked with three notches on four sides, for the Northwest corner of the said tract, standing where two stone fences meet; thence along the Westerly bounds thereof, as the magnetical needle pointed in the year 1786, South twenty-nine degrees and thirty minutes, West twenty-five chains to a stake and heap of stones; then along a line of marked trees, South sixty-nine degrees, East fifty-three chains and thirty links to a black oak sapling, marked three notches on four sides, standing about two chains Southwesterly from a small pond of water; then, as the needle now points South twenty-three chains and seventy-two links to a tree marked on the North bank of the Old Man's Kill, and so continuing the last mentioned course, two chains and forty links further, to a stake and stones put upon the South side of the public road, leading westward from the town of or village of Marlborough, along the said Old Man's Kill; then South sixty-eight degrees and fifteen minutes, East eleven chains and twenty-four links to a stone formerly set in the ground, for the rear lots of said town; then South sixty-two degrees, East eight chains and sixty-three links to the Northwest corner of lot number 8 of said town; then, along the Northerly bounds thereof, South eighty-five degrees and fifteen minutes, East four chains to the stone set for the Northeast corner thereof, also a corner of the lot by me leased to Thurston Wood; then, along the last mentioned lot, South thirty-seven degrees, East two chains and three links to a stone set in the ground; then South fifty-one degrees and a half, East along the Southwest side of the lot distinguished by the name of Crown Hill, by me leased to Henry Decker, to the Southerly bank of the Old Man's Kill, aforesaid; then, along the said Southerly bank, down the stream, as the said bank turns and winds, to a certain point of land at the North side of the South branch of the said Old Man's Kill, being the place of beginning mentioned in the said letters patent, and runs thence, along Hudson's River, Northerly as it runs, to the North bounds of the said tract, being on a direct line, one hundred and two chains;

thence, along the North bounds of said tract, the needle
pointing as in 1786, South eighty-six degrees and thirty
minutes, West one hundred and twenty-six chains and a
half, to the place of beginning. Containing eight hundred
and twenty-four acres, be the same, within the bounds
aforesaid, more or less.

Also I give and devise, unto my said son Lewis, all the
right, title and interest which I hold of, in and to two
water lots lying between the channel and the West bank of
Hudson's River, adjoining on the East side of the above devised lots, so as the said two water lots have lately been surveyed at my expense, by Henry Livingstone, of Poughkeepsie, a map and return of which survey, is now lying under
the consideration of the land office of this State. Also I give
and devise unto my said son Lewis a certain lot of land adjoining the town or village of Marlborough, aforesaid, being
bounded by the Northeast thereof by the said lots by me
leased to Thurston Wood and Henry Decker, and the line
of the first lot herein devised to my said son Lewis, and
bounded to the Southward thereof by a line drawn on a
South, eighty-three degrees. East course, the needle pointing as in the year 1785, from the Southeast corner of the lot
number six in the said town or village, and is to extend from
the fronts of the lots number six, number seven and number
eight, eastward, between the aforesaid line drawn and the
fronts of the said lots leased to Thurston Wood and Henry
Decker, and the said line of the first lot herein devised so
far, untill it contains one acre and a half of land, which said
four lots of land, hereby devised, with the rights, members
and appurtenances thereunto belonging, with the rents, issues and profits thereof are to be holden unto my son Lewis
and to his heirs and assigns forever, in fee simple, subject,
nevertheless to the devise hereinbefore mentioned, in favor
of my said wife, and I do hereby order my said son Lewis,
his heirs, executors or administrators to provide and bring
to the door of my said wife, all the firewood which she may
have occasion of for her fuel, also provide good keeping for
her horse and cow, both in winter and summer, or for such

time and so long as she may incline to live in my present
dwelling house or on the above described premises and remains my widow, and I do hereby make that part of my estate hereinbefore devised unto my said son Lewis, chargeable with the provision and delivery thereof unto my said
wife ; Also I give unto my said son Lewis, one good cart,
one waggon, one plow, with the irons thereunto belonging,
one yoke of oxen and three horses, two milk cows, all my
chains and all my gears and tackling for furnishing of teams,
my potash kettle, my weaving loom and all my reeds and
gears and appurtenances thereunto belonging, my fanning-
mill, all my sleds, my croebars and all my ironwork belonging unto my saw mill, my screen and all my tools and implements belonging or commonly made use of in my grist
mill, together with all other farming utensils and implements
of husbandry whatsoever not hereinbefore mentioned ; Also
twelve sheep, one featherbed and bedstead, with all the
furniture, one saddle and bridle, my gun and silver-hilted
sword, my writing-desk and my clock now in my dwelling-
room ; also my negro man named Tite.

Also I give and bequeath and devise unto my son Wilhelmus all that Southerly part of the said tract, being bounded
as follows, to-wit : Beginning at the North side of the old
Man's Kill, aforesaid, at a certain point of land between the
said branches, being the place of beginning mentioned in the aforesaid letters patent, and runs from thence,
along the South bounds of the said tract, as the needle
pointed Anno Domini 1786, South eighty-five degrees and a
half, West one hundred and forty-eight chains to the South-
ermost corner of said tract, being a walnut tree, formerly
marked with three notches on four sides, then, along the
West bounds of said tract, North twenty-nine degrees and
thirty minutes, East ninety-eight chains and a half to a stake,
a heap of stones put up for the Southwesterly corner of the
first lot hereinbefore devised unto my said son Lewis, then,
along the same, as it is bounded, on the Southerly sides, with
the several courses thereof to the place where the last described lot, devised to my said son Wilhelmus, first began.

Containing six hundred and sixty-two acres, be the same, within the bounds aforesaid, more or less. And the reversion and reversions, rents, issues and profits thereof, (excepting, nevertheless, the lot of one acre and a half hereinbefore devised to my son Lewis, which is comprehended within the bounds of the last described lot.) To hold the said lot of land, with the rights, members and appurtenances, unto my said son Wilhelmus, for and during his natural lifetime, and at and after the decease of my said son Wilhelmus, I give, devise and bequeath the same to the children, lawfully begotten or to be begotten by my said son Wilhelmus, ' to hold the same to my said grand children, and to their heirs and assigns forever in fee simple unto each of my said grand children, males and females, each of them an equal share thereof, respectively, as tenants in common ; Also I give, devise and bequeath unto my said son Lewis, and to his heirs and assigns forever, in fee simple, the Southerly, equal half part of my lot of land in Stuben township, in the State of New York, conveyed to me by Thomas Machin, by two certain deeds, one bearing date the thirteenth day of October, 1787, the other bearing date the thirtieth day of July, 1788, which lot is distinguished in a map of the division of said township, filed in the Secretaries office of said State, by lot number 14 and contains six hundred and forty acres, and I order that the said Southerly half part of said last mentioned lot shall be separated from the Northerly half part thereof by a line, running Easterly and Westerly, through the middle thereof, parallel to the Northerly and Southerly bounds thereof ; Also I give, devise and bequeath unto my said son Wilhelmus the Northerly half part of said lot, number fourteen, so to be divided as aforesaid, to be holden unto my said son Wilhelmus, for and during his natural lifetime and, at his decease, I give and devise the said Northerly half part of the said lot number fourteen unto my said grandchildren, begotten, or lawfully to be begotten of my said son Wilhelmus, and to their heirs and assigns forever unto each of my said grandchildren, males and females, an equal share thereof as tenants in common, also I give, devise and bequeath unto my daughter, Margaret, the Southerly half part of my lot of land in Woodhul township, in the State of New York, which lot was conveyed to me, by the aforesaid Thomas Machin, by deed bearing date the thirtieth of July, 1788, and contains six hundred acres, and is known and distinguished in the map and division of the said township of Woodhul, by lot number thirty-six, and I order that the Southerly half part of the said last mentioned lot shall be divided from the Northerly half part thereof by a line running through the middle thereof, from the Easterly to the Westerly bounds thereof, parallel to the Northerly and Southerly bounds of the same, and that the said Southerly half part so divided shall be and remain unto my said daughter Margaret and to her heirs and assigns forever. Also I give, devise and bequeath unto my two granddaughters, to wit : Hannah (only child of my son Nathaniel, deceased) and Cornelia (only child of my daughter Rachel) the Northerly half part of said last mentioned lot number thirty-six, so to be divided, to hold the said last mentioned Northerly half part of the lot No. 36 unto my said two granddaughters, their heirs and assigns forever, each of them an equal share thereof, as tenants in common ; Also I give, devise and bequeath unto my daughter Mary, all the certain lot of land, lying in the town of Montgomery, in Ulster County, within a tract called the eight thousand acres, which lot is distinguished by lot number 15 in the third allotment of the last division of the said tract made by Thomas Moffat, Christopher Tappen and Cornelius Schoonmaker, Esquires, Commissioners, appointed for that purpose in pursuance of the act for the partition of lands, which said lot contains one hundred and fifty-one acres, as by the field books and maps filed in the Secretary's office of this State, and in the Clerk's office of Ulster County, reference unto the said division there being had, will fully appear, which said last mentioned lot of land, I give and devise unto my said daughter Mary, during her natural life time, and, at her decease, I give, devise and bequeath the same unto the children, lawfully to be

begotten and now begotten of my said daughter Mary, and
to their heirs and assigns forever, each of my daughter
Mary's children, males and females, an equal share therein,
as tenants in common; also I give and devise unto my
daughter Margaret, all that lot known by the lot *number
twelve* in the first allotment of the said division made of the
eight thousand acre tract, containing one hundred and two
acres and one tenth of an acre, as, by the said maps and
field books, will also appear, to hold the said lot *number
twelve* unto my said daughter Margaret for and during her
natural lifetime, and at her decease, I give and devise the
said lot *number twelve* unto all the children now begotten or
to be begotten of the body of my said daughter Margaret,
and to their several and respective heirs and assigns forever, each of my said last mentioned grandchildren, males
and females, an equal share therein as tenants in common, in
fee simple; Also I give, devise and bequeath unto my said
granddaughter, Cornelia, (only child of my daughter Rachel,
deceased) all the residue of my lands in the said eight thousand acre tract, being part of the old division of part of the
said tract, and in that part of lot *number twelve* in said old
division, which Andries Le Fever, released to me by indenture, bearing date 14th day of June, Anno Domini 1790, and
contains ninety-five acres and one-third of an acre, as, by the
said release remaining of record in the Clerk's Office of Ulster County, reference being thereto had, will appear; to
hold the said residue or lot of land hereby devised unto my
said granddaughter Cornelia, her heirs and assigns forever,
in fee simple; Also I give and bequeath unto the children
begotten and to be begotten of the body of my said daughter Mary, the sum of five hundred pounds, lawful money of
New York, to be paid unto him, her or them (if more than
one) in equal shares, after my said daughter Mary's decease,
as the children shall or may, after said decease, arrive or be
of age. And I order that my executors hereinafter named,
shall put the said sum of five hundred pounds out upon interest, with good security, at discretion, and that they
pay the interest from time to time thereof, as it may

come into their hands, unto my said daughter Mary, as a maintenance and support for her, during her life time, after which the principal sum to be paid, as before directed, unto her children; Also I give and bequeath unto the children now born, or to be born, lawfully, of the body of my said daughter Margaret, the like sum of five hundred pounds, lawful money of New York, to be paid to them respectively, by my said executors, after the decease of my said daughter Margaret, in like manner as I have hereinbefore directed the like sum to be paid to the child or children of my daughter Mary. And I also impower and order my executors to put out the said sum of five hundred pounds at use, on good security, at their discretion, and that they pay the interest of the said last mentioned sum, from time to time, as it comes into their hands, unto my said daughter Margaret, as a maintainance and support for her, during her life ; also I give and bequeath unto each of my said two granddaughters, Hannah and Cornelia, the sum of two hundred and fifty pounds, lawful money aforesaid, which said sums of two hundred and fifty pounds shall be paid by my executors unto my said last mentioned granddaughters, respectively, as they shall respectively arrive of full age, and, if any one or both of my last mentioned two granddaughters shall happen to die without lawful issue of her or their bodies begotten, before she or they may respectively arrive to the age of twenty-one years, then and in such case, the legacy hereby given unto them or such of them so happening to die without issue as aforesaid, shall be equally divided among my other children, to wit: my sons Lewis, Wilhelmus, and daughters Mary and Margaret and to their respective heirs and assigns forever ; Also I do hereby order and direct my said executors, out of the monies which I may have at use at the time of my decease, to keep or retain, or set apart the sum of five hundred pounds, New York currency, and my said executors shall annually pay the interest of the last mentioned sum unto my said wife Rachel during her widowhood as a further support for her. And if, at any time after my decease, and during her widowhood it should

appear to my said executors that the interest of the said sum
of five hundred pounds, together with other provision made
in this will, unto my said wife, should not be adequate to afford a reasonable and decent support for my said widow
then, and in such case, it shall be lawful for my said executors, and upon the request of my said wife, from time to
time and at discretion to take part of the said last mentioned
principal sum, and to appropriate such part towards the better maintenance and support of my said widow. All my
other estate, both real and personal, that shall remain after
payment of my debts and funeral expenses, and the legacies
hereinbefore devised, I give, devise and bequeath the same,
together with the last mentioned sum of five hundred pounds
or the Residue thereof, after my wife's decease or Day of
Marriage, unto my said four children, Wilhelmus, Lewis,
Mary and Margaret, my wife Rachel, and my two grand
daughters Hannah and Cornelia, that is to say, unto my
said son Wilhelmus, and to his heirs and Assigns forever,
one sixth part thereof, and unto my said son Lewis, his Heirs
and Assigns forever, one sixth part thereof, unto my said
Daughter Mary, her Heirs and Assigns, one sixth part
thereof unto Margaret, one sixth part as aforesaid unto my
said two Grand Daughters the one sixth part thereof, as
aforesaid, and unto my beloved wife, Rachel, one other sixth
part of the said Residue. It is however to be understood
that the said last mentioned sum of five hundred pounds, or
the residue thereof, after my said wife's Widowhood shall
expire, shall be divided only among my said two sons, and
two Daughters, and my said two Grand Daughters, each of
my said Sons and Daughters one fifth part thereof, and the
remaining fifth part thereof unto my two grand daughters,
Hannah and Cornelia. All the Legacies and priveleges, by
my this my Will given unto my wife, I give unto her in lieu
of her right of Dower. And Lastly I do hereby make, ordain, Constitute and appoint my son Lewis, my good Friends
Josiah Merritt and Johannis Lefever, Esq., my brother-in-Law
Johannis T. Jansen, and Cornelius DuBois, Junr., and Johannis Bruyn, and the Survivors of them to be executors of this

my Last will and Testament. And I do also Nominate my said Son Lewis and my said brother-in-Law, Johannis T. Jansen, to be and act as Guardians to my said Grand Daughters, Hannah and Cornelia, and to have the care of their Estate.

IN WITNESS WHEREOF I have hereunto Set my hand and Seal, the Day and Year first above written.

LEWIS DuBOIS. (L. S.)

Signed, Sealed, published and declared by the Testator as his last Will and Testament, in presence of us, who Signed our Names hereto as Witnesses in this said Testator's presence, and of each other—page 2d. the words *South sixty nine degrees, East* Interlined in the 12th. line, *East* in the 23rd.-*four* on Razure in the 28th. (in the third page, the words *one* in the 11th. line on Razure) page 6th. the word *Grand* wrote on the *blot*, 26th. line (page 8th. last line, *Daughters* interlined page 9th. *to wit*, on razure in the 27th. line and *be* in the third line) 10th. page, 16th. line, *I* on Razure, the last page, 18th. line, the letter *U* in the word Guardian, Interlined.

ANDREW ELY,   JOSIAH MERRIT,
JOHANNIS T. JANSEN,   JOHANNIS BRUYN.

Ulster County, ss : Be it remembered that, on the first day of February, in the year of our Lord, one thousand, eight hundred and three, personally came and appeared before me Joseph Gasherie, Surrogate of the said County, Johannis T. Jansen and Johannis Bruyn, of the town of Shawangunk, in the said County, yeomen, and Andrew Ely, of the town of Marlborough, yeoman, and being duly sworn, on their Oaths declared that they and each of them did see Lewis DuBois sign and seal the within written instrument purporting to be the Will of the said Lewis DuBois, bearing date the Nineteenth day of November, one thousand, seven hundred and ninety-five, and heard him publish and declare the same, as and for his last Will and Testament that, at the time thereof, he, the said Lewis DuBois, was of sound disposing mind and memory to the best of the knowledge and belief of them, the deponents, and that they, the said deponents, together with

Josiah Merritt, subscribed the said Will, as witnesses there-to, in the testator's presence. And that Lewis DuBois, Junior, Johannis T. Jansen and Johannis Bruyn, Executors named in the preceeding will, likewise appeared before me and were severally sworn to the true execution and perfor-mance of the said preceeding will, by taking the usual oath of an executor. JOSEPH GASHERIE, Surrogate.

The preceeding is a true Copy of the original will of Lewis DuBois, deceased, and also of the Certificate of the proof thereof—Note the words *said* in page 8, the 16th line, *respective*, page 10, the 3rd. line, *Son*, same page, the 27th. line, *daughters*, page 11, in the 10th. line being interlined.

JOSEPH GASHERIE, Surrogate.

THE BOND PATENT.

Anne, by the grace of God, quene of Great Britain, France and Ireland, defender of the faith, etc., to all whom these presents shall come, or may in any wise concern, greeting: Whereas, our living subject, William Bond, Esq'r, his hum-ble petition presented to our trusty and well beloved Robert Hunter, Esquir, Captain Generall and Governour-in-chief of our provinc of New York and territory depending thereon in America, and Vic Admirall of the same in Council hath prayed Our grant and confirmation of a certain tract of Land in the County of Ulster, being part of the Land formerly granted to Captain John Evans, now vacated and reserved: Beginning on the West side of Hudson's river, in the line of the South bounds of the land of Mr. John Barbarie, it runs with the said Line up into the woods North sixty-one degrees, West one hundred and seventy chains, thence South three degrees, East fifty-one chains, thence South sixty-one degrees, East one hundred and fifty chains to Hudson's river; thence up the river Runs to the place where it first begun, containing in the whole six hundred acres English measure, being bounded Northward by the said land of the said John Barbarie, Westward by land not yet surveyed, Southward by land not yet surveyed, and Eastward by Hudson's river aforesaid, the within petition we being willing to grant.

KNOW YE that of our especiall grace certain knowledge and meer motion we have given, granted, ratified and confirmed and by these presents do for us, our heirs and successors give, grant, ratify and confirm unto the said William Bond, all that the said grant of land and premises above mentioned and described with the hereditaments and appurtenances thereunto belonging within the limits and bounds aforesaid, together with all and singular woods, underwoods, trees, timber, feeding pastures, meadows, marshes, swamps, ponds, pools, water, water tours, inert or in action, runs and streams of water, fishing, fowling, hawking, hunting, mines and mineralls, standing, growing, lying and being to be used had and Enjoyed within the Lands and bounds aforesaid, and all other profits, benefits, privileges, libertys and advantages, hereditaments and appurtenances whatsoever, unto the said tract of Land and premises and any part and parcel thereof belonging or in any wise appertaining, and all our estate, right, title, interest, benefit and advantage, claim and demand whatsoever, of, in, or to the said tract of land and premises with the hereditaments and appurtenances aforesaid and every part and parcel thereof, and the reversion and reversions, remainder and remainders, together with the yearly and other rents and profits of the same tract of land and premises and of every part and parcel thereof except always and reserved out of this Our present grant unto Our heirs and successors all such firr trees and pine trees of the diameter of twenty-four inches at twelve inches from the ground or root as now are or shall be fit to make masts for Our royall navy, and also all such other trees as are or shall be fitt to make masts, planks or knees for the use of our navy aforesaid only which now are standing, growing and lying, and which hereafter shall stand, grow and be on and upon the said tract of land and premises or any

part and parcel thereof with free liberty and license for any
person or persons whatsoever (by us Our heirs and successors thereunto, to be appointed under our sign manual), with
workmen, horses, wages, carts and carriages, or without to
enter and *come* into and upon the same tract of land and
premises or any part thereof, hereby granted them, to fell,
cut down, root up, hew, saw, rooe, have, take, cart and carry
away the same for the use aforesaid (and also except all gold
and silver mines), *To have and to hold* all that, the said certain tract of land and premises with its hereditaments and
appourtenances hereby granted aforesaid (except as before
excepted only) unto the said William Bond, his heirs and
assigns forever to the sole and only proper use, benefit and
behoof of the said William Bond, his heirs and assigns
forever.

To be holden of us our heirs and sujects in fee and conion
soccage as of our manors of East Greenwich in the
County of Kent, within our realm of Great Britain, *yeilding*
rendering and paying therefore yearly and every year unto
our heirs and successors from henceforth forever at our custom house in New York to our, or their collector or receiver
(stationed) there for the time being at, or upon the feast day
of Saint Michael the Archangle (commonly called Michal-
mas day), the yearly rent or sum of two shillings and six-
pence current money of our province of New York for every
one hundred acres of land of the before mentioned track of
land of six hundred acres hereinbefore granted and confirmed in lieu and stead of all other rents, dues, duties, services, and demands whatsoever. *Provided* always and these
presents are upon this condition, that the said Wm. Bond,
his heirs and assigns, some or one of them shall and do within
the space of three years now; next ensuing the date hereof
settle there and make improvements of three acres of
land at the least for every fifty acres of the said tract of land
of six hundred acres hereinbefore granted, and in defalt
thereof the said Wm. Bond, his heirs or assigns, or any of
them or any other person or persons, by his or their consent, order or procurment shall set on fire or cause to be set

on fire and burn the woods on the said tract of land hereinbefore granted or on a part or parcel thereof to sear the
same, that then, and in either of these cases this our present grant and every clause and article herein contained shall
cease, *dertermine* and utterly void anything herein contained
to the contrary thereof in any wise notwithstanding. *And* we
do and hereby will and grant that these our letters patent
or the record thereof in our Secretaries office of our said
province, shall be good and effectival in the law to all in-
tents and purposes notwithstanding the not true and will
reciting and mentioning of the premises or any part thereof,
the limits and bounds thereof of any former or other letters
patent or grants whatsoever made or granted of the same
six hundred acres of land and premises or of any part thereof
being, or any of our progenitors unto any other person or
persons whatsoever, body politic or corporate or any law
or other restraint, uncertainty or imperfection whatsoever
to the contrary in any wise notwithstanding.

In testimony whereof we have caused the great seal of our
said province to be hereunto affixed and these presents to be
recorded in our said secretarie's office. *Witness*, our trusty
and well beloved Robert Hunter, Esquire, Captain General
and Governor-in-Chief of our said province of New York
the province of New Jersey and the territories depending on
them in America, and Vice Admiral of the same in council
at our fort in New York this twelfth day of June, in the
eleventh year of our reign.

[L. S.]

To this interesting old document is appended Queen
Anne's seal, a tremendous affair of wax, three and a half
inches in diameter.

The Bond patent is the oldest existing title to land in
Marlborough, and was granted to Captain William Bond,
the first white settler within the town limits, of whom there
is any record.

CALENDAR OF N. Y. COLONIAL MSS. INDORSED "LAND
   PAPERS," IN THE OFFICE OF THE SECRETARY OF
        STATE OF NEW YORK, 1643 to 1803.

1697—NO DATE; VOL. II.—Petition of Egbert and Hendrick Schoonmaker, of Kingstowne, praying a grant for a tract of vacant land, about 600 acres, lying opposite to the highlands or thereabouts, being on both sides the Oudtman's Kill or Creek (Marlborough landing?), having been formerly patented to Captain Evans, but since broken by an act of General Assemby (town of Marlborough, Ulster Co.) Page 268.

1709—AUG. 18; VOL. IV.—Petition of Alexander Griggs, of the County of Ulster, praying a grant for 600 acres of land in said county, lying on the West side of Hudson's river, beginning on the South side of Old Man's creek and running up the river to a point called Old Man's Hook, together with 6 acres of meadow, lying at a certain place called Ye Dance-Chamber. Page 182.

1710—FEB. 23; VOL. V.—Petition of Augustine Graham, Surveyor General, for a patent to him and Alexander Griggs, for 1,200 acres of land at ye Old Man's creek, being part of the resumed lands formerly granted to Capt. John Evans.

1712—APRIL 7; VOL. V.—Petition of Augustine Graham and Alexander Griggs, praying a patent for a tract of land in Ulster Co., being part of the land formerly granted to Capt. John Evans, now vacant and resumed, lying at the Old-Man's Kill. Page 88.

1712—May 3; VOL. V.—Petition of William Bond for a grant of 600 acres of land adjoining John Barberie's, on Hudson river, in Ulster Co., being part of Capt. John Evans' patent, now vacant and resumed. Page 100.

MAY 13.—Report of S. Staats and others of the Council to whom the foregoing petition was referred. Also on the 15th of May, Warrant to the Surveyor General to lay out for William Bond the land prayed for in the above petition. Page 100.

JUNE.—Description of a survey of 600 acres of land on the

West side of Hudson's river, in Ulster Co., laid out for Wm. Bond. Aug. Graham, Sur. Gen'l, with a Draft. Page 100.

JUNE 6.—Petition of Wm. Bond for a warrant to the Attorney General to draught letters patent for 600 acres of land, in the County, granted upon a former petition.

1712—JUNE 12 ; VOL. V.—Petition of Peter Johnson for a grant of 500 acres of land lying to the Northward of a small run of water, which runs into Hudson's river, to the Southward of the Dance Chamber, being part of the lands formerly granted to Capt. John Evans. Page 113.

1713—July 13.—Petition of Francis Harrison and Company, praying for a patent for 5000 acres of land. Page, 167, Vol. V.

1714—JULY 10; VOL. VI.—Certificate of Land Board to Francis Harrison and others for a certain tract of land in Ulster Co., bounded on the North by Andrew ffolks' land and ye nine Germans families, on the West and South by land unsurveyed, and on the East by Hudson's river, containing 5000 acres. Page 48.

JULY 10.—Warrant for a Patent to Francis Harrison and others for the land last described.

1713—JULY 10.—Petition of Francis Harrison and Company, praying for a patent for 5000 acres of land. Vol. V, page 170.

1713—VOL. 6; PAGES 6, 8, 9.—Petition of Francis Harrison and others for a warrant to the Surveyor General to survey 5000 acres out of the resumed lands formerly granted to Capt. John Evans, with (Nov 23) Report of A. D. Peyster and others of the Council to whom the foregoing petition was referred, recommending the same be granted, and on April 10, 1714, Warrant to the Surveyor General to survey and lay out the land.

1720—MAY 26; VOL. VII.—Petition of Francis Harrison and others for a warrant to survey and lay out for them 5000 acres of land in the County of Ulster, being part of the resumed land of Capt. John Evans, beginning at the S. E. corner of the tract of 10,000 acres lately granted to Jeremiah Schuyler, on the West side of Paltz creek. May 31, report of A. DePeyster, of the Council to whom it was referred. June 2—Warrant of a survey for the same.

1723—JUNE 26; VOL. IX.—Certificate to Francis Harrison for a certain lot of land now in his possession, being his share in an allotment of 5000 acres granted him, in company with Mary Tatham and others, beginning on the West bank of the Hudson river, and containing 1000 acres, together with an undivided fifth part of ye meadow ground called the Dance Chamber, and 315 acres adjoining the West bound of aforesaid tract for highways.

1714—AUG. 26; VOL. VI.—Warrant to the Surveyor General to lay out for Lewis Morris and others 5000 acres of land, lying on both sides of Old Man's creek, in Ulster Co., near Hudson's river, being part of ye lands formerly granted to Capt. John Evans.

1715—JUNE 30; VOL. VI.—Petition of Servus ffleraboom, on behalf of Johnnes Johnson and others, children of Peter Johnson, deceased, for 300 acres of land lying North of a small run, which comes into Hudson's river South of the Dance Chamber, being part of the tract formerly granted to Capt. John Evans, lying with the bounds of the land of Francis Harrison and Comp'y, but excepted and reserved out of his patent.

1717—NOV. 20.—Description of a survey of 300 acres of land lying within the patent granted to Francis Harrison & Co., on the West side of Hudson's river, in the County of Albany (evidently Ulster) near the Dans Chamber, being part of the resumed lands of Capt. John Evans, laid out for the children of Peter Johnson, deceased, by Wm. Bond, Deputy Surveyor, with draught. 179.

1719—AUG. 27; VOL. VII.—Petition of Melcher Gellis, praying a patent for 300 acres of land, being part of the re-assumed land of Capt. John Evans, lying on the West side of Hudson's river, near the Dans Chamber, the said land being comprehended within the limits of the tract granted to Francis Harrison & Comp'y, but excepted and reserved out of their patent. With, Oct. 1, Report of A. D. Peyster and others, a committee to whom the same was referred. 68.

Oct. 8.—Warrant for a patent to Melcher Gellis for the above mentioned 300 acres, near the Dans Chamber.

1767—Feb. 9; Vol. 33.—Caveat by Gilbert Purdy against granting any lands in the South part of Ulster Co., between or near the patent of Francis Harrison or James Alexander, to Thomas Palmer, Samuel Fowler or Henry Smith, until the others are heard. Page 28.

Feb. 14; Vol. 33, Page 35.—Petition of Henry Smith, the elder, Samuel Fowler and Isaac Fowler, all of the precinct of Newburgh, in the County of Ulster, praying a grant of all the land above 5600 acres within the bounds of a certain tract granted Francis Harrison and four others in the said county.

1769—April 18; Vol. 25, Page 113.—Petition of John Belfield, of the precinct of Newburgh, in the County of Ulster, Matthew Van Cura, of Dutchess county, praying the privilege of keeping a Ferry over Hudson's river opposite their respective dwelling houses in Ulster and Dutchess County, to the exclusion of all others, for the distance of 5 miles.

1775—Dec. 22; Vol. 35.—Return of survey for Christopher Duyckinck, James Downes, Wm. Butler and William Kennedy, of sundry lots, containing 3275 acres of land in the County of Ulster. (Plattekill and Marlborough, Ulster Co.)

1786—Feb. 21.—Affidavit of Thomas Palmer and Frederick Rhinelander respecting the claim of Solomon Simpson, and his associates to lands in New Marlborough, Ulster Co. Page 54, Vol. 41.

1787—Nov. 19; Vol. 45.—Abstract of letters patent issued to Lewis Morris, Augustine Graham, Symon Clarke, Henry Wileman, Wm. Bond, Henry Rainer and Alexr. Griggs on the 10th Feb'y, 1714, for 3600 acres of land in the County of Ulster, Marlborough. Page 120.

1791—Caveat of Anthony Rutgers against granting to any person Wm. Butler's part of lands formerly surveyed for James Lendabetter, Charles Gyles, F. Rhinelander and others in New Marlborough, Ulster Co. Page 71.

1793—Jany. 26.—Return of survey of 1841 acres of land for Daniel Graham, Marlborough, Ulster Co. Vol. 55, Page 113.

1793—JANY. 3.—Notice by Lewis DuBois that he intends to apply for grant of a water lot in New Marlborough, Ulster Co. Vol. 60, Page 154.

1791—JANY. 31.—Petition of Lewis DuBois for a grant of land under water at New Marlborough, Ulster Co. Vol. 60, Page 156.

1793—MARCH 19.—Petition of Lewis DuBois for a grant of the flats in Hudson river, opposite his property at Old Man's Kill, in New Marlborough, Ulster Co.

NOV. 20.—Certificate of certain inhabitants named, of the neighborhood of New Marlborough, in favor of the above application. Vol. 60; 157.

Description of the land covered by water of Hudson's river, opposite to the farm of Lewis DuBois.

APRIL 22.—Return of a survey for Lewis DuBois of 28 acres of land under water at New Marlborough, and map of the above land. Vol. 60, Page 159.

1796—Feb'y 12.—Certificate of undersigned inhabitants of the town of Marlborough, in favor of granting the above water lot to Lewis DuBois. Vol. 60; 160.

FEB'Y 16.—Claim of Lewis DuBois for bounty land, as Colonel in the line of this State and in the Army of the United States. Vol. 60; 161.

1767—NOV. 2; VOL. 24.—Return of survey for Samuel and Isaac Fowler of the surplusage of land contained in a lot now in their possession, being part of a tract of land granted to Francis Harrison and others in the County of Ulster (Newburgh.) [Note.—Sam'l and Isaac Fowler purchased 500 acres, part of the Harrison patent, from Samuel Gomoz, Nov. 6, 1747. Gomoz was a Jew merchant in New York. The creek that runs through Fowler's and Wolfert Acker's land was called Jew's creek. Ruttenber's Hist. of Newburgh.]

1786—VOL. 41.—Copy of John Barbarie's patent for 2000 acres of land, on the West side of Hudson's river, being part of the lands formerly granted to Capt. John Evans, dated March 24, 1709, Marlborough, Ulster Co. Page 45.

1787—NOV. 19; VOL. 45.—Abstract of letters patent issued

to Lewis Morris, Augustine Graham, Symon Clark, Henry
Wileman, Wm. Bond, Henry Rainor and Alexr. Griggs on
the 10th Feby, 1714, for 3600 acres of land in the County of
Ulster, at Marlborough.

1791—AUG. 15.—Proposal of Dan'l Graham to pay 2 shilling an acre for 2400 acres of land in the township of New
Marlborough, in the County of Ulster.

1792—JAN'Y 23.—Proposal of Dan'l Graham to pay 3
shilling an acre for a tract of 2400 acres of land in New
Marlborough, Ulster Co.

1793—JAN'Y 14.—Letter of Dan'l Graham to the Commissioner of the land office explanatory of his proposal to
purchase 2000 acres of vacant land in Ulster Co.

JAN'Y 26.—Return of survey of 1841 acres of land for
Dan'l Graham, in Marlborough, Ulster Co.

BILL OF SALE OF A SLAVE.

The following is a copy of a bill of sale of a slave to Josiah
Merritt, grandfather of J. C. and P. E. Merritt. The slave
referred to was the mother of Figaro Milden, and grandmother to Jacob and George Milden, of Marlborough.

KNOW all men by these presents that I Joseph Sherwood
of the Town of New Burgh County Ulster and State of New
York for and in Consideration of the sum of twenty pounds
of Current Lawful money to me in hand paid by Josiah
Merritt of the Town of Marlborough County and State
aforesaid HAVE granted bargained and sold and by these
Presents DO grant bargain and sell unto the sd Josiah Merritt one Negro Girl Named Syl Aged Seventeen years To
have and to hold the said Negro unto the sd Josiah Merritt
and his Executors Administrators and Assigns for and during the Natural life of Her the sd Girl. And I the said
Joseph Sherwood for myself my Executors and Administrators unto the sd Josiah Merritt his Executors Administrators and Assigns against me the said Joseph Sherwood

my Executors Administrators and Assigns shall and will Warrant and Defend by these Presents; In witness whereof I have hereunto set my Hand and Seal this twenty-eighth day of March one thousand seven Hundred and ninety-three.

JOSEPH SHERWOOD, [L. S.]

Sealed & Delivered }
 in the presence of }

Sarah Mory,
Jacob Degroot.

Deed from Charles Brown to Benjamin Harcourt.

The following extracts from an old deed show how cheap land was in Marlborough in 1828, and give the location of lands owned by several old residents:

This indenture made the twelfth day of April in the year of our Lord, one thousand eight hundred and twenty-eight, between Charles Brown and Margaret, his wife, of the town of Marlborough, in the county of Ulster and state of New York, of the first part, and Benjamin Harcourt of the same town, of the second part, witnesseth that the said parties of the first part, for and in consideration of the sum of ten thousand dollars lawful money of New York, to them in hand paid, etc., etc., the land described as follows:

Beginning at the west side of the road leading to Lattin-town, and running thence along the land of Frederick Barnard, North eighty-seven degrees, East forty-nine chains and forty links to the Northeast corner of the lands hereby intended to be conveyed, thence along other lands of the said parties of the first part, South three degrees, West twenty-four chains and seventy-five links to the lands of Guernsey Smith, thence along lands of the said Smith, Allen Lester and John Crook, South eighty-seven degrees, West one hundred and forty-six chains to the lands of Josiah Lockwood, thence along the lands of the said Lockwood, John Kniffin and John Cornfield North nineteen degrees. East thirty-

four chains and forty links to the lands late of James Butterworth, thence along his lands North seven degrees, East
eighty-one chains to a point, thence South nine degrees,
East three chains, eighty-six links, thence South sixty-one
degrees, East three chains and ten links, thence South
eighteen degrees, West one chain and seventy-five links to
the place of beginning, containing four hundred and seven
acres and one-half of land, be the same more or less, etc., etc.

CHARLES BROWN.

MARGARET ^{Her} x BROWN.
<small>mark</small>

Signed, sealed and delivered)
    in the presence of   }
       A. D. SOPER.

DEED FROM DRAKES TO MATTHEW WYGANT.

These extracts from an old deed give a few points as to
old settlers in Lattintown :

This indenture, made the sixth day of October, in the
year one thousand eight hundred and one, between William
S. and Samuel Drakes and Rebecker and Mary Drakes, of
the town of Marlborough, in Ulster county, and state of New
York, of the first part, and Matthew Wygan', of the same
place, of the second part, witnesseth, that the said partys of
the first part, for and in consideration of the sum two thous-
and and sixty-two dollars and fifty cents, etc., etc., all that
piece or tract of land situate lying and being in the town,
county and state aforesaid, being part of a tract of land
known and distinguished by the name of the seven patenteen ;
being the most southerly division of lot number four ; beginning at the Southeast corner thereof of chestnut stump,
standing in the fence and stones around it, from thence
North thirty-four degrees, East twelve chains and eighty
links to a heap of stones set in the line when the said tract
was divided by Charles Clinton, Esq., from thence West as
the compass pointed when the said tract was first divided,

one hundred and fifty-five chains to the line of the West end of the said tract, thence along the line Southwest about twelve chains to the Southwest corner of said lot, thence along the line thereof, East one hundred and fifty-three chains to the place of beginning, containing one hundred and seventy-three acres of land, reserving the publick road that leads through said lands, that leads from Lattintown to Newburgh, and also one rod in breadth on the North side from Benjamin Ely's Southeast corner to the main road, which Joseph Mory now uses as his private road. The aforesaid lands are bounded on the East by Joseph Mory, on the North by Joseph Mory, Dr. Benjamin Ely and Levi Quimby, on the West by lands granted by letters patent to Daniel Graham, deceased, and on the South by the lands of Elisha Purdy and Hannah Connell, widow, and Joshua Lounsbury and Silvenus Purdy, etc., etc.

WILLIAM S. DRAKE.

SAMUEL DRAKE,

REBECKER ^{Her} x DRAKE,
^{mark}

MARY DRAKE.

Sealed and delivered in)
 the presence of)
  JOSEPH MORY.
  MICHAEL WYGANT, JR.

AN ELEGY

On the death of Capt. Annanias Valentine, Thomas Pinkney Isaac Elliot, Jacamiah Cropsey and Leonard Merritt, all respectable citizens of the town of Marlborough, who where unfortunately drowned on the flats in front of the town in attempting to go on shore on Friday morning, December 12, 1800, in a violent storm of wind and rain.

This poem will be recognized by many old residents as one which attained considerable local celebrity in their younger days.

Come all ye good people, of every degree,
And listen with attention one moment to me,
For a sorrowful story I mean to relate,
Of a mournful disaster that happened of late.

Oh, Marlborough! tremble at this awful stroke.
Consider the voice of Jehovah, that spoke
To teach us we're mortals, exposed to death
And subject each moment to yield up our breath.

Oh, reader! these coffins exhibit to view
A striking example that's mournfully true
To show thee that death will be thy certain doom,
That shortly the body must enter the tomb

On Friday, the twelfth of December, so cold,
In the year eighteen hundred, as I have been told,
The wind blowing high and the rain beating down,
A vessel arrived at Marlborough town.

The anchor being cast and their sails stowed away
All hands for the shore prepared straight away.
Down into the boats soon all did repair,
And unto the shore were preparing to steer.

But, mark their sad fortune, mournful indeed!
Yet no man can hinder what God has decreed,
For the councils of heaven, on that fatal day,
By death in an instant called a number away.

A number of men in their health and their prime
Called out of this world in an instant of time.
For their boats turning over plunged all in the deep,
And five out of seven in death fell asleep.

A vessel at anchor was lying near by,
The men in the cabin heard their piercing cry:
To grant them relief they hasten with speed,
And two of their number from the water were freed.

These sorrowful tidings were carried straightway
To their friends and relations without more delay.
But, Oh! their lamenting no tongue can express,
Nor point out their sorrow, great grief and distress.

Three wives widowed, left in sorrow to mourn
The loss of their husbands, no more to return;
Besides a great number of orphans, we hear,
Lamenting the fate of their parents so dear.

Also a young damsel left mourning alone
For the untimely death of her lover that's gone:
For the day of their nuptials appointed had been
In the bonds of sweet wedlock these lovers to join.

Yet, alas! their lamentings are all in vain.
Their husbands are drowned, they can't them regain.
Their friends and relations came now too late,
The council of heaven had sealed their fate.

Their bodies being found were all conveyed home
And the Sabbath day following prepared for the tomb.
Their bodies in their coffins were laid side by side
In Marlborough meeting house alley so wide.

A numerous concourse of people straightway
Attended with sorrow on that mournful day,
To see the remains of the neighbors so dear,
And join their relations in a friendly tear.

A sermon was preached on the occasion also,
While the people attended with a solemn awe,
To see such a number by death snatched away,
Who all lay before them as lifeless as clay.

The sermon being ended the corpses were conveyed,
And in the cold caverns of earth they were laid,
Where now we must leave them to molder to dust
Until the resurrection of the just and unjust.

To the widows and mourners o'erwhelmed with grief:
May you all trust in God, who will grant you relief.
He'll ease all your sorrows and soothe all your pain,
And finally take you to glory to reign.

Come all that are living and know you must die,
I pray you take warning by this tragedy,
That when death shall call you and close up your eyes,
Your souls may be happy with Christ in the skies.

PRECINCT MEETINGS.

The following extracts from the early records of the Newburgh Precinct meetings, will be of interest, as Marlborough was then included in the territory, and a number of first settler's names will be found in the record:

At a Precinct meeting at the house of Capt. Jonathan Hasbrouck, for the precinct of Newburgh, the first Tuesday in April, in the year of our Lord one thousand seven hundred and sixty-three, according to an act of Assembly for that purpose.

Samuel Sands, Clerk.

Capt. Jonathan Hasbrouck, Supervisor.

Richard Harker, Jesse Windfield, Samuel Wiatt, Assessors.

David Gidney, Constable.

Henry Smith, Collector.

Joseph Gidney, Benjamin Woolsey, Poor Masters.

John McCrary, John Wandal, Burras Holmes, Isaac Fowler, Humphrey Merritt, Thomas Woolsey, Path Masters.

Nathan Purdy, Isaac Fowler, Fence Viewers and Appraisers of Damages.

Lenard Smith chose to collect the quit rent, the patent he now lives on.

Then adjorned to the house of Capt. Jonathan Hasbrouck.

1764.—The town officers were:

Samuel Sands, Clerk.

Lewis DuBois, Supervisor.

Nehemiah Denton, Henry Tarbush, Peter Ostrander, Assessors.

Samuel Winslow, Constable and Collector.

Daniel Thurstern, Michael Demott, Poor Masters.

Cornelius Wood, Martin Wygant, Leonard Smith, Henry Smith, Gilbert Denton, Edward Hallock, Benjamin Carpenter, Path Masters.

Samuel Sprague, Henry Smith, Jehiel Clark, David Purdy, Isaac Fowler, Pounders.

1767.—Silas Wood, Constable, to take his fees from Isaac Smith's house.

1768.—It is agreed on by Stephen Case and Micajah Lewis, candidates for Constable, than whoever of them is chosen Constable for the year ensuing, that they will appoint two deputies to serve under them, such as shall be agreeable to the inhabitants, such deputies to have full fees for what they serve, and shall be obliged to give the Constable surety, etc., and shall serve his turn in tending our General Court.

1769.—Voted, at annual meeting, that the sum of £30 be raised for the support of the poor for the year ensuing. That Martin Weygant be Pounder for the German patent and all adjoining.

1771.—Rule first, voted, as an encouragement to all succeeding Poor masters, the more faithfully to discharge their duty in their office, by preventing all unnecessary charges and needless costs on the inhabitants of the Precinct, and also a reward for their good service, we freely vote them the sum of £110 each, etc.

Rule Third.—That no Poor master for the time being shall for any cause whatever, relieve or cause to be relieved, or made chargeable, any person or persons whatever, that may by law be transported, or any private person can be made accountable for according to law, on pain of perjury, and making themselves liable to pay all such charges, and forfeit to the use of the poor twenty shillings and charges of prosecution, to be recovered before any of his Majesty's Justices of the Peace, etc.

1772.—And it is voted, that the Assessors shall have for their serving the sum of £14 each, provided they go to every man's house and make the enquiry of their substance, and they are not excused of working on the road.

£30 voted to support the poor.

1773.—Voted that £50 be raised to support the poor, and Poor masters have £210.

1777.—Voted £100 be raised for the poor.

1778.—Voted that any person that shall take cattle to keep on the commons of this Precinct, from persons out of another Precinct, shall be subject to be assessed for them, etc.

Voted that the donations collected in this Precinct be applied to such poor whose husbands or parents were either killed or taken prisoners at Fort Montgomery, etc.

Town Meetings.

The precinct of New Marlborough was set off from Newburgh March 12, 1772, and the precinct became a town by act of the legislature March 7, 1788. Consequently the meetings were called precinct meetings between those dates, and since then town meetings. Plattekill was represented at these meetings prior to 1800. The first precinct meeting was held at the house of Henry Deyo, April 7, 1772. At this meeting Abijah Perkins was chosen clerk; supervisor, Lewis DuBois; Assessors, John Yonge, Jacob Wood, Marcus Ostrander; poormasters, Robert Merritt, Joseph Mory; commissioners, Richard Woolsey, Durmee Relyea; pounder, Silas Purdy; fence viewers, Caleb Merritt, Richard Carpenter; pathmasters, Gabriel Merritt, James Quimby, Jacob Wood, Samuel Merritt, Henry Deyo; constable, William Martin.

The second precinct meeting was held at Richard Carpenter's, April 6, 1773. At this time the first road districts were laid out. These original districts were again divided in 1779.

In 1776 the precinct meeting was held at Silas Purdy's inn. The first meeting after the precinct became a town was held April 7, 1778, when £125 were voted for the poor, and "also to collect this year for the last two years Rearages," amounting to £70. At this meeting it was also "Voted that John

Davis, last year's collector, be paid sixteen pounds for bad money he lost in the county treasury, out of the poor fund."

At the town meeting held in Lattintown April 4, 1780, it was voted that collector this year be paid a bad thirty dollar bill out of the first spare poor money.

In 1785 the meeting voted that road No. 2 from Lattintown "somewhere along by Moses Quimby's, up to the Paltz precinct, be known as No. 26."

The easy manner in which collectors were remunerated for bad bills, seems to have caused several dishonest freeholders to try to take advantage of the easy methods, and swear they had paid their tax when such was not the case, for May 29, 1790, the following was passed: "Voted, that the town in general shall pay no taxes for any individual in particular who pretends to have paid theirs twice over."

The town granted its first liquor licenses in 1792, the price being £2 each. The following took out licenses: David Merritt, Jacob Powell, Thomas Mott, Daniel Crawford, Chris. Ostrander, Ebenezer Foote, Caleb Merritt, William Ostrander and Rich'd Lewis.

April 2, 1793, it was "Voted, unanimously, that the dog tax be finally disannulled."

In 1794 David Merritt was town clerk. He was the first to hold that office who wrote a respectable hand, and his penmanship in the town records is very good.

April 7, 1795, the town "Vouted that the supposed wife of and is not the wife of Robert Gilmore to be transported and not t) be chargeable any more to the town of Marlborough."

April 5, 1796, at the town meeting, "Voted, that all innholders of the town or tavernkeepers shall pay the excise moneys down or No 1 be permitted to retail Spiritus Lickwor." Also "Voted, no liquor shall be sold at the next town meeting and no Hors racing shal Be don under the Penalty of five pounds fine."

In 1799 it was "Voted, that our next annual town meeting be held at the house of Benajah and Samuel Wright, in Pleasant Valley, and by an agreement between the people on the West side of the mountains and those on the East side, the town meeting is to be held alternately on the West and East side," the Supervisor to be chosen from the side where held.

This agreement was not of long duration, however, for the following year Plattekill was set off as a town by itself, and held its town meetings independently.

On May 1, 1800, an election for Senator was held in town. Eighty-four votes were cast for fifteen candidates. There do not appear to have been any party nominations for most of the names voted belonged to residents of Marlborough.

MANUFACTURING.

___

MARLBOROUGH FACTORIES.

Grist mills and saw mills were the first manufacturing industries carried on in Marlborough village. Major Lewis DuBois ran two grist mills, one where the large manufacturing building of Theodore Kniffin now stands, corner of Main and Landing streets, and the other the mill now occupied by Woolsey Wright.

There was also a grist mill on Buckley's creek, built by Charles Millard, afterwards run by a man named Angell. It subsequently became the property of John Buckley, and Gabriel Merritt used to run it fifty or sixty years ago.

A saw mill was located on this creek, back of the cemetery, and logs were floated up there. Gabriel Merritt also attended to this saw mill.

___

JOHN BUCKLEY AND HIS MANUFACTORIES.

From Sylvester's "History of Ulster County" we take the following account of John Buckley's manufacturing enterprises, which was obtained directly from his descendants, and is authentic:

John Buckley, of Marlborough, was among the early manufacturers of this state. He was born in Jaffray, N. H., May 3, 1786, and educated at the public school in his native town. Having a decided liking for mechanical operations, he learned the trade of a wheel-wright and machinist. In 1805 he was employed by Almy & Brown, of Providence, where he became acquainted with Samuel Slater, the father of American manufacturers, who was then engaged in manu facturing and building cotton machinery in Pawtucket. It is said that most of the manufacturing establishments erected in different parts of the country from 1791 to 1808 were built by men who had directly or indirectly drawn their knowledge of the business from Providence or Pawtucket. Mr. Buckley was employed over three years in the extensive machine shops of Almy & Brown, where he acquired a thorough knowledge of his business. In 1809 the Pleasant Valley (Cotton) Manufacturing Company, in Dutchess County, was incorporated, when he was engaged to superintend the construction of their water-wheel and running gear, and the greater part of their machinery. After this was completed, and the mill in successful operation, he was invited to join the "Cornwall Cotton Manufactory," recently chartered (1811), in which he was a stockholder, where he superintended the building of their wheel and machinery. At this time there was an increasing demand for all kinds of domestic goods, and a large amount of capital was invested in cotton and woolen manufactories. During war of 1812 this capital was very productive, but at its close the British manufacturers, having large quantities of goods on hand, adapted and originally intended for the American markets, poured them into this country to an amount far beyond the wants of the people or their ability to pay, with a double view of vending their goods and ruining the rival establishments of this country. These goods were forced on the market and sold at auction at such ruinous prices that most of the manufacturers were obliged to stop their works, and many of them failed. Mr. Buckley was not discouraged; feeling confident that manufacturers would soon be protected by a judicious tariff, he purchased in the spring of 1815 the carding and spinning-mill which had been established in Marlborough about 1810-11. He also purchased a farm. Here he commenced carding and spinning wool for the farmers in Orange and Ulster Counties. Soon after he added several looms and began making cloth. This enterprise was so successful that he enlarged his mill. In 1822 he entered into partnership with his brother-in-laws, James and John Thorne, under the firm of Thornes & Buckley. The mill was again enlarged, and known as the "Marlborough Woolen Factory." At this time they commenced making broadcloth and satinets. Most of the operatives engaged in woolen factories were Englishmen; the foremen in the different departments commanded high wages, and sometimes it was difficult to get good and experienced men, especially dyers. Mr. Buckley was obliged to take this department under his especial charge. He soon established a reputation for durable and brilliant colors, which the mill enjoyed as long as the firm continued business. Their cloths were regularly exhibited at the fairs in New York, where in 1823 they received a premium of a silver pitcher for the best piece of blue broadcloth manufactured from American wool. After the "American Institute" was organized there were frequent exhibitions of these cloths, and the firm always received the diplomas of the institution. For many years their cloths were sold by Thomas Dixon & Co., an English commission house on Pine street.

Mr. Thorne used to relate with particular satisfaction a little incident that showed how prejudiced the leading fashionable tailors were in favor of English cloths. He had tried several times to sell an invoice of his goods to a Broadway tailoring establishment. The senior partner spurned at the idea of their making up American cloths. Happening to meet the same man at Mr. Dixon's store, he called to Mr. Thorne, and said, " Mr. Thorne, here is the kind of cloths we want. Your American manufacturers can't give your cloths such a finish as these have." Mr. Thorne observing that they were his own goods, made no reply, and turned quietly away.

The firm was dissolved in 1830. Mr. Buckley continued the business until 1855, when he converted his factory into a cotton mill, making twine and cotton warps. This he continued until the commencement of the Rebellion, in 1861, when he ceased manufacturing. A few years afterward he sold all the machinery in the mill and retired from business. He died in Marlboro, June 1, 1870, in the eighty-fifth year of his age. For more than fifty years he had been actively engaged in manufacturing, giving employment to a large number of operatives, never having any difficulty with any of them, and always retained their confidence and esteem.

OTHER OLD FACTORIES.

The first carding machine in the town was erected on Old Man's Creek, as early as 1810–11. It stood near Woolsey's ice house. Another was soon after establised by a man named Longbotham.

The first fulling mill was owned by Lewis DuBois, and built about 1806.

In the year of 1826 a fulling mill, on Old Man's Creek, was operated by David Waters. He was followed by a man named Stratton, who commenced the manufacture of broadcloths. Joseph Hepworth and James Longbotham followed in turn. In 1830 Hepworth moved up to the Greaves' mill, where he and Cornelius DuBois operated a woolen mill for a great many years. The mill was subsequently leased to Joshua Bailey, who ran it as a shoddy mill until the dam was carried away in the freshet of 1855 or 1856.

Curtis Wright, father of Woolsey Wright, had a cooper shop in Marlborough for a number of years.

On the site of the Stratton mill Kirk & Bower carried on business for a time. It is now a grist mill, operated by Woolsey Wright.

In 1862 a paper mill was built by Nathaniel Adams, on the present site of the Whitney Basket Co.'s works. To this day old buttons can be picked up in the ravine below, where they were thrown by rag sorters in the mill. Miles J. Fletcher had an interest in the mill, and it was operated by Robert Beebe & Co., until Fletcher made an assignment. Later the property was owned by Augustus Clark, and H.

H. Holden. The manufacture of hymn-book paper was the principal work of the mill. Subsequently Hensebeck, Slee & Collingwood, of Poughkeepsie, bought it, and made a failure. Then the Rahway Glue Co. ran it as a glue factory, which was not successful, and the property was taken by the mortgagee, Isaac Staples. June 1, 1876, Nathaniel DuBois bought it, and established the Whitney Basket Co.

The lower grist mill, operated now by B. B. Apgar, was built by Robt. B. Minturn about the same time as the paper mill. The old DuBois mill, now torn down, was operated in 1826 by William Seabring and Jeremiah Clark.

The shoddy mill above the old property site, operated by Sheard & Gibson, was erected as a grist mill by Matthew T. Berrian. Joshua Bailey subsequently engaged there in the manufacture of blankets and carpets. A paper mill just below was owned by David Munn, and run by Patten & Beebe.

George Archer had a machine shop at Marlborough village at quite an early day, where DeWitt Kniffin's cup factory is now located.

William S. Clark & Son have in successful operation a large flouring mill on Old Man's Creek, above Marlboro village. It formerly belonged to John Kniffin, and was run by him for many years. It was at one time operated by Cornelius W. Wygant.

On Jews Creek Andrew Oddy operated a rag machine at an early day, and continued in the business for a great many years.

————

THE WHITNEY BASKET FACTORY.

This large and prosperous concern had its beginning at Milton in 1853, when John F. Whitney started to manufacture fruit baskets. In 1862 he took his son, Mr. Oliver B. Whitney, into partnership, under the name of John F. Whitney & Son. In June, 1876, the present factory was built on the site of the old paper mill, the property of Mr. Nathaniel H. DuBois, who united with Mr. Whitney under the style of The Whitney Basket Co.

The main portion of the new factory is 160 feet long, and there is a wing 42 feet in width, all three stories high, with basement. Back of the factory is a large building used as a storehouse, dwelling and wagon house. This is 30x60 feet, and has four floors, including the attic and basement. An additional drying house, 30x55 feet, was built in 1885.

There are also two steam drying chest on the first floor, capable of containing 150,000 baskets each.

At the east end of the factory is the blacksmith shop.

In the basement of the main factory is placed the shafting which transmits power to the machines above, consisting of planing and slitting machines, gang saws, cutters and two rotary veneer machines. These are remarkable pieces of mechanism. They receive a big log, somewhat after the manner of a lathe. The log revolves against a stationary knife, which peels off sheets a twentieth of an inch (or more) in thickness. During each revolution the log is gradually raised one-twentieth of an inch, by which means is preserved a uniform thickness of the sheet. Other knives divide the wood into proper widths, while some merely cut one-half through, for convenience in bending the corners of the baskets.

This industry is the largest and most valuable one established in Marlboro, and is kept running the year round, although the season for selling is of course confined to the summer months. Thirty men and sixty women and girls are employed at the factory, the pay roll amounting to $500 per week. They use very good wood in their baskets—beech, birch and basswood—none of which affect the flavor of the fruit, as is the case with pine and some other woods. The logs are cut in lengths of four and a half to five feet, (used green and soft) and placed in a steam vat 28 feet long, and capable of containing 25 logs at a time. There they soak 48 hours or more, and are then turned over to the veneer machine.

The baskets are made up on the second floor, a former being used, over which the wood is bent, and held in place by an iron band while the rim is tacked on.

The Company manufacture more of the square quart baskets than any other kind ; also a great many " Jumbo " gift baskets, they being especially in demand because they do not have to be returned to the shippers. More than a million square quarts are made annually, and nearly as many of the gift crates. Next come peach baskets, strawberry, American quart, Centennial, round quart, Paragon, Beecher, verbena, snides, etc. The total output is nearly 5,000,000 a year.

An idea of the immensity of the business may be gathered from the fact that forty kegs of one kind of tacks constitute an ordinary purchase. They are made of Swede's iron and barbed to prevent their pulling out of the wood.

The manufacture of crates is a large part of the firms' business. The gift crate, gotten up by Mr. N. H. DuBois some half dozen years ago, has a very large sale, being used in connection with the gift baskets, which were designed by Mr. O. B. Whitney. The gift crates hold 50 pounds of grapes, and are very neat and simple in construction.

The rapidity with which baskets and crates are made up is astonishing. Often a log is taken from the dock in the morning and goes down the river in the evening in the shape of crates and baskets filled with fruit. When there is a rush for a particular kind of crate or basket, frequently a long string of wagons may be seen at the factory waiting until more are made, and they do not have to wait long either.

A thirty-horse turbine wheel and forty-horse engine supply the power at the factory, the engine being used more or less as the water is scarce or plenty to supply the turbine. The Company avails itself of every modern contrivance for assisting the manufacture of its goods, in fact most of its machinery was designed here, as this is the leading basket factory in the country.

The Western Union Telegraph Co. has an office in the building so that the Company can receive orders from New York as quickly as from Marlborough.

WHITNEY BASKET FACTORY—ERECTED 1876. (Page 68.)

SHEARD & GIBSON'S WOOLEN MILL.

Thomas Sheard and John H. Gibson established their mill
in Marlboro in April, 1875, in a very modest way, in a 24x34
building. Their special business is the manufacture of bed
and horse blankets. Their trade has grown materially, and
they now occupy the commodious factory building north of
the village, close to Western avenue. Their main structure
is 105x34 feet. Five smaller buildings in the vicinity are
used for picking, dyeing and drying, and one is the engine
and boiler house. The firm also operate the old Bailey mill
half a mile up the stream.

On the first floor of the main factory are two large rooms,
styled the fuller and finishing rooms. Above is the spinning and carding department, and on the third floor the
weaving is done.

The full capacity of the factory is forty hands, of both
sexes, and 800 to 1000 blankets a day. The machinery used
is expensive, and there is a great deal of it. The power is
furnished by a thirty-six horse water wheel, and with the
aid of the steam engine the force can be increased to one
hundred horse power. In 1883 some $17,000 worth of new
machinery was added, and the total value of the plant is now
over $30,000.

The present year (1887) arrangements are being made to
enlarge their facilities, land being acquired for new buildings
and for the enlargement of the dam.

A brief description of the methods of manufacture may be
of interest. The material is first brought in from the pick-
er's department, where it has been prepared for the cards.
Next it goes to a spinning machine, where it is made ready
for the loom; then to the weaving room, the fuller, and to
the masher to be cleaned. A hydraulic extractor is used to
drive out the water. This machine is a very interesting
study. The soft, mashy compound is whirled around at a
tremendous speed, driving out the water by centrifugal force.
The coloring and finishing processes follow, and the blankets
are ready for the cutter. The spinning mule is self-adjust-

ing, and extends the entire length of the second floor. Here the yarn runs in and out in a manner very complex to the uninitiated observer, finally winding on to bobbins for the loom. On the third floor the looms are used to make up the blankets, and here they are stored until sold.

GREAVES' DYE AND CARPET WORKS.

Joseph Greaves' dye manufactory was started in May, 1860, in a two-story frame building, near the present factory at the lower end of Greaves' pond. The firm was originally composed of Joseph Greaves and William Reed, but after a time Reed withdrew. Their factory was destroyed by fire about four years ago, when brick buildings were substituted. These have been constantly increased in size and number until now there are five substantial buildings in the factory proper, and two tenant houses and Joseph Greaves' handsome residence on the premises. The factory is largely devoted to the manufacture of aniline dyes, many of which have no counterpart in the country, and no visitors are allowed in portions of the factory in order that the secret may be preserved. The business is large and permanent.

Joseph Greaves, jr., carries on the manufacture of ingrain carpets, which forms a considerable portion of the business. Only the very best grades of goods are manufactured. The capacity of this branch of the business has been increased recently, and business booms. The establishment of the Messrs. Greaves has been and is a material advantage to Marlborough.

Greaves' pond is a sheet of water, nearly half a mile long, formed by the damming of the Old Man's creek. It furnishes power for the dye and carpet factory, and some day in all probability will furnish the water supply for Marlborough.

DeWitt Kniffin started a berry cup and fruit crate factory about 1867, adjoining the Methodist church. About ten years later he removed to his present location on Western avenue. He employs about a dozen hands, and manufactures all varieties of cups and crates, his trade being mostly local.

MILTON FACTORIES.

Just a statute mile above the Milton R. R. station on the West Shore, juts out into the river a small square dock, in a dilapidated condition, at present, that has been for a long time a landmark. Its history dates back to 1770 or previous, when it was built by Capt. Anning Smith, who had a woolen mill there. The old road leading to it was known as the King's highway, and there can be but little doubt but that it was among the first roads opened up for the convenience of settlers at a distance from the great water-way. At present the structure is known as the pin factory dock. About forty-two years ago a company from Poughkeepsie, whose projectors were Messrs. Jewett, Howard, Moseley and Van Vliet, leased the water-power formed by a small stream which comes foaming to the river over a very steep ledge of rocks, descending almost one hundred and thirty feet, while making an advance of less than three hundred toward the Hudson. Upon the land leased in connection with the power a brick structure was erected, and the manufacture of solid-headed pins was commenced and continued for a few years, when the company sold its machinery and the rights in such improvements as it had made upon them in the mean time to a company in Waterbury, Conn., whose patents they had infringed. Previous to the erection of the pin factory it was known as the "old dock." A store house used to stand near it, and some portions of the old foundations were upturned when the railroad cutting was made. Sloops were built and launched near it. Just upon the edge of the bank, at the top of the fall, the Indians buried their dead. Tradition has it that the places of sepulture were plainly seen when the land was first occupied by the whites. It would also seem that for a long time the red men's bones were allowed to rest in peace. Not only so, but the place was honored, for just at the west, and almost side by side with the remains of the forest children, the earliest settlers laid their loved ones to sleep. Here nameless graves are seen in abundance, indicated by common, flat, mossy stones at the head and foot. Nearly an acre of land is thus completely covered. East of this plot and about half way down the river bank by the brook's side is the old mill seat. The foundations have been removed recently, and the presence of two worn mill stones alone indicates the fact that Anning Smith's flour mill once stood there. At an early day this mill-seat was deemed too valuable to be disposed of, as was much of the land about here, and rights in it were reserved for the purpose of sawing the plentiful supply of timber growing near. Forty acres of land were duly surveyed and described and held in common with the mill privilege.

In 1844 Sumner Colman started a wheelbarrow factory at the pin factory dock, which was burned out in 1852. New buildings were then constructed near the dock and the manufacture was carried on in a much larger scale, John Newman coming from Newburyport, Mass., in 1854, to take charge of it. In 1861 he bought the factory, and in 1864 he took John H. and S. O. F. Colman into partnership under the style of John Newman & Co.

In 1870 the factory was again burned, but rebuilt much larger in dimensions. In 1875 Mr. Colman withdrew, and the business was carried on under the name of John Newman & Son. John Newman was paralyzed in 1881 and gave up active business, dying March 23, 1884. John H. Newman continued the business until his death Sept. 30, 1885, when the business was closed up by his son, Frank Newman, and the property disposed of to H. H. Bell & Sons and converted into a plush factory.

The power at Smith's pond was used before the war for the making of corn mills for the Southern trade. A prosperous business was carried on for several years, but the breaking ont of the war destroyed the market, and caused the closing of the factory.

James Hall and Jacob Rowley ran auger factories in Milton at an early date.

In 1822 Moses Birdsall ran a hat factory, which closed up in 1830. William A. Field conducted a hat factory after that date.

The Bell Manufactory of Knit Goods, Etc.

In 1880 Henry H. Bell, and his two sons, Winslow M. and Arthur E., moved from Long Island and started a plush and glove-lining factory at the old pin building, below Smith's pond. Their business grew steadily, and in 1886 they bought the wheelbarrow factory near Milton depot and landing, altering it to suit their increasing trade.

Henry H. Bell has practically retired from the management of the business, and his sons have run it since 1884. They have spent several thousand dollars in improving their new factory, which now contains about 17,000 sq. feet of flooring. It is four stories high and built in fire-proof compartments that can be closed up in case of fire.

The process of manufacture is full of interest. They purchase their wool and cotton in large quantities, already wound on paper bobbins, called caps or tubes. These are taken by girls and wound by winding machines on to large wooden spools, each containing two pounds of yarn. These spools are then taken to the knitting machines, which are automatic wonders. Imagine a great cylinder of cloth a yard in diameter rising from a machine, with hundreds of little wheels and threads, each performing its important work. If a thread breaks, or a hole is made in the cloth, the machine stops automatically for the operator to adjust the difficulty. Over a million stitches are made per minute on these machines.

The cloth is then taken to the menders, who mend all holes and crochet the drop stitches; thence to the wash house where the oil and dirt is taken out.   After cleansing, the goods are dyed in different tubs, according to the color desired, and afterwards wrung out in a machine called the "Hydraulic Extractor." This is a large cylinder into which the wet goods are packed.   It revolves at the rate of three miles per minute and the centrifugal force drives out the water leaving the cloth almost dry. The remaining moisture is taken out by hot-air drying machines.

The cloth is then cut longitudinally and wrapped on rollers for the brushing machines.   These raise the nap and finish the goods.   Afterwards they are measured and examined in the finishing room.

This factory gives employment to a number of men and girls, and is one of the permanent institutions of Milton.

Walter Millard's Sons' Lumber Trade.

The history of the rise and growth of the great lumber and coal firm of Walter Millard's Sons' properly belongs to Marlborough, although the main offices are now in Dutchess county.

In 1802 Charles Millard, grandfather of the present members of the firm, was living on what is now the Buckley property, and established and ran two saw mills on Jews creek.

From an advertisement in the "Political Index" published in Newburgh in 1809, is obtained the following description of the mill seat: It was located "within half a mile of the Meeting-House, containing about twenty-three acres of good land, with a handsome grove of timber, and a young orchard of the best ingrafted fruit, and a variety of other fruit trees. The situation is very pleasant.   There is on the premises a good dwelling house, a barn with other outhouses, also a never-failing run or rill of water within a few feet of the kitchen, and a good well. Also a grist mill and a saw mill, so constructed as to take the logs out of the water without any expense of land carriage. It will cut eight or ten hundred logs in a year. The buildings are all well finished. There is also a convenient place on the premises for a fulling and plaister mill."

At these mills Charles Millard made a specialty of sawing white pine lumber, such as is generally used for sash doors, finishing, siding and flooring. This business he continued until 1824, assisted by his sons John, James, Charles, William and Walter.

His trade grew steadily, extending over in Dutchess Co. even to the Connecticut line, and a considerable distance up and down the river. Most of the lumber was shipped in winter by teams over the ice, the bulk of the trade coming from the east side of the Hudson, owing to the manner in which Marlborough is shut in from the west by the mountains. During the summer timber was received in rafts from Glen Falls, Fort Edward and the neighborhood of Lake Champlain. In 1824 the Champlain canal was opened. The same year Charles Millard removed his residence to New Hamburgh, establishing a lumber yard at that place. Most of his lumber after that time came from head waters of the Hudson and Lake Champlain. 1829 Charles Millard died. Walter, his son, succeeded him in the lumber business attending to that business alone until 1834. In that year he connected himself with the freighting business, running the sloop Melan. The year following he built the barge Lexington to do the freighting, taking in as partner, Uri Mills, who had one-third interest.

In 1844 they purchased the dock property at Marlborough of the DuBois estate. A freighting business was immediately established in connection with that at New Hamburgh. The same year the steamboat Splendid was purchased and ran from Marlborough and New Hamburgh on Mondays and Thursdays.

A lumber business was also established at Marlborough. In 1851 the partnership with Uri Mills was dissolved. Freighting business was continued in name of W. Millard & Co. In 1854 W. Millard retired from freighting business, continuing the lumber business at both places.

John P. Millard, nephew of Walter, and H. H. Holden, succeeded to the freighting and steamboat business, and in 1857 put the propellor Wyoming on their line. Holden soon withdrew and Samuel N. Millard took his place, the style of the firm being J. P. Millard & Bro. They carried on the freight and lumber business at Marlborough and freighting business at New Hamburgh.

In 1863 Wm. B. Millard became a partner with his father in the lumber business, the firm being then W. Millard & Son. In 1880 Walter Millard died, and the business was managed by Wm. B. Millard and his executors until 1884, when the present firm of Walter Millard's Sons was formed.

The immense trade which this firm enjoys has been the gradual growth of years, but received its greatest boom at the outbreak of the civil war. In 1861 the popular opinion was that great commercial depression would immediately prevail, and values decrease. Walter Millard thought differently and went to the wholesale lumber district, buying up all the lumber he could find, at low rates. The stock then laid in was sufficient to last the firm three or four years, with its already great trade. The wisdom of his course was soon apparent. Prices advanced steadily. He was able to sell at the lowest wholesale price. From that day to this, the impetus which the business then received has increased.

The dock property in Marlborough, familiarly known as the "lower dock," is but a small branch of this great firm's possessions. They have other branches at Wappingers Falls and Stormville, while their headquarters are in New Hamburgh. They do their own freighting in their own vessels—two steamboats, a sloop, flat-bottomed boat and canal boat. Their purchases are about all direct with the mills in Michigan, Maine and Canada, and in some instances taking the full cut of one mill for a year.

The firm deal in everything necessary in the construction

of a house, making contracts as far as the furnishing of materials for fifty houses to one party. The business is largely wholesale, although they supply the local retail trade. About fifty men are employed. The present office was erected in 1881, of fine brick, and finished in hard wood. There are various other structures in New Hamburgh, for the storing of doors, blinds, sash, mouldings, etc. A complete hardware establishment, with paints, building paper and mason's materials, is on the premises.

The name of Walter Millard's Sons has become known all along the Hudson, and in lumber circles over the whole country. Their fame is deserved, as it is the result of energy, integrity and business sagacity. Their success has done much to aid the progress of this section, and will do more in the future.

MILTON IN 1830.

As Seen Through the Columns of the "Pioneer."

Daniel S. Tuthill published The National Pioneer in Milton, in 1829, and for several years subsequently. It was issued every Wednesday, at "$2 per annum, payable quarterly, or two dollars and fifty cents at the end of the year." This price was for village subscribers and those who got their papers through the post rider. Mail subscribers were charged half a dollar less, having to pay their own postage. Advertisements of one square or wider were inserted three weeks for one dollar, and twenty-five cents for each subsequent insertion. The paper had agents in the surrounding places, as follows : New Paltz—Jacob J. Schoonmaker, John Benson, Simon Deyo, and J. O. Hasbrouck ; Plattekill— Samuel Morehouse ; Shawangunk—John C. Mastin, Samuel Johnson, Esq., and Cornelius Schoonmaker ; Marlborough Village—Barnabas M. Mapes ; Lattintown—Thos. S. Warren. The following heavy motto appeared under the heading of the Pioneer : "Let it be impressed upon your minds, let it be instilled into your children, that the liberty of the Press is the Palladium of all your rights."

There were four pages of six columns each. The first was devoted to miscellany ; the second to foreign and United States news ; the third to market reports and advertising ; the fourth to miscellany, a bank note table, and patent medicine advertisements. Like all papers of its day, its best places were devoted to foreign news, the idea seeming to be that those events which transpired at the greatest distance must necessarily be of most interest. This policy excluded all local news—on the principle that people must know that anyway—and it is to be regretted that these papers tell us so little of what Milton was at that time.

In the issue of September 1, 1830, occurs the following death notice :

DIED.—On board the sloop Beekman, Capt. King, of Milton, Mr. William Monger, aged 51 years. His death was occasioned by a blow he received while getting the vessel under weigh from New York.

From the advertising columns of the Pioneer more is to be learned about Milton than from the reading matter. Advertisements appear from David Brower, tailor, in Milton village ; Anson St. John, manufacturer of cabinet ware and fancy chairs, also painter ; C. S. Roe, general storekeeper, agent for threshing machines, real estate agent, dealer in rye, oats and corn, and owner of a tow boat ; Mrs. M. B. Taylor, milliner, of Marlborough ; Charles Field, hat manufacturer ; Longbottom & Co,, announcing the retirement of James Kinworthy ; and many others of more or less interest. From one of these we learn that the proprietor of the paper, D. S. Tuthill, also kept a store at New Paltz landing, (Highland). Here he sold goods at "reduced prices," just as the modern merchant does.

Daniel S. Tuthill, or Selah Tuthill, as he was commonly called, was a man of considerable ability and business enterprise. He is remembered by David Sands, of Marlborough, who, when quite a small boy, used to go into the Pioneer office after copies of the paper, and recollects seeing the hand-press, operated by a big lever.

From the files of the Pioneer we learn that Cornelius Polhemus kept a public house in Marlborough in 1830, as witness the following advertisement :

" For Sale. The house and lot on which the subscriber now lives, situate in the village of Marlborough : it has been occupied as a public house for many years, and affords as great advantages for the business as any other location in the vicinity. The buildings are in good repair and conveniently arranged ; there is a variety of fruit trees on the premises, all of which are of the best quality. The above property will be sold at a great bargain, and terms of payment made accommodating to the purchaser. Apply to the subscriber on the premises.

CORNELIUS POLHEMUS.

Marlborough, April 7th, 1830."

Benjamin Hulse kept a public house, at the same time as Polhemus, in Milton, as we find sales of property advertised to take place at his inn.

Cornwall S. Roe was one of the most prominent men in Milton in 1830, if his advertisements in the Pioneer prove anything. In one copy of the paper he had no less than sixteen advertisements of various kinds. He kept a general store, where were sold dry goods, groceries, crockery, hardware, lumber, tar, plaster, salt, fish, pork, etc. He bought grain and flaxseed at " highest cash prices," and purchased patent rights for agricultural machinery in order to have the exclusive sale in his section. He also speculated in land. In one place he advertises that the ladies of Ulster county can be supplied with Navarino Hats, either in the flat or made up in the neatest manner at short notice. In another place behold: " The Tow boat Atalanta, Capt. C. S. Roe, now performs her passage with all regular speed ; and to meet the economical views of all, passengers are taken at the low rate of Four Shillings, who find themselves ;— Six shillings and found. She arrives both ways before day-light. C. S. ROE.

Milton, April 7, 1830."

Where the boat ran to is not stated.

We copy other interesting advertisements :

Cabinet and Chair
Manufactory.

Anson St. John, respectfully informs his friends and customers that he continues the above business at his new stand in the village of Milton, where he keeps constantly on hand a general assortment of Cabinet Ware, consisting of Tables, Bedsteads, Stands, Secretaries, Bureaus, and Sideboards, of every description, which he will sell at reduced prices, and on reasonable credit,   He has also a general assortment of Fancy Chairs, consisting of Fancy Bamboo, and Cain Seat Windsor and Common Rush Bottom Chairs. Painting of every description, done with neatness and at the shortest notice.

Dec. 23, 1829.

Tailoring.
David Brower

Respectfully announces to the public that he continues to carry on the tailoring business, in all its various branches and fashions in Milton villiage, where he will be happy to attend to his customers. From his long experience, and employing none but superior hands in his business, he can assure the public that his work will be done in style equal to that of any person of his profession either in Newburgh or Po'keepsie, therefore hopes to meet and receive a share of public patronage.

Cutting and Basting done according to the order of his customers.

Milton, Feb. 10th, 1830.

NOTICE.

The Subscriber has discontinued his business at the New-Paltz Landing, for the purpose of closing his concerns. All Persons indebted to him are respectfully informed that his Books are now arranged for settlement, and he wishes them to call on or before the 15th day of June next, and settle the same, as all notes, bonds and accounts, due and unsettled at that time, will be placed in the hands of proper officers for collection. Persons having claims against the Subscriber will please present them for liquidation.

John Benson,

May 26th, 1830.   New-Paltz.

Charles Field,
Hat Manufacturer,

Returns his grateful acknowledgments to his friends and the
public, for the very liberal patronage he has received from
them, and solicits a continuance of the like favors. Being
desirous of their further patronage, wishes to inform them
that he has opened a Hat Store, in the City of New York,
at No. 36½ Bowery, which will enable him to have his hats
finished in the city, according to the latest fashions, and furnished to his costomers, at reduced prices.

The business in future will be conducted by his son William A. Field, at his old establishment, in the village of Milton, a few doors south of Jacob P. Townsend's store. All
persons having unsettled accounts with him, are requested
to pay immediate attention to the same. The books of
accounts are left with William A. Field, who is fully author-
ized to collect and settle the same.

Milton, 4th mo. (Apr. 14), 1830.

New Goods.
Cornwell S. Roe

Would respectfully inform his friends, and the public, that
he has just received at his store, in addition to his former
stock, an extensive assortment of Dry Goods, Groceries,
Crockery, Hard and Hollow Ware, Etc. Etc. Also, Nails,
Lumber, Coarse and Fine Salt, Tar, Plaster, Fish, Pork all
of which will be sold at reduced prices, and upon favorable
terms. The highest price in cash will be paid for all kinds
of grain.

Dec. 23rd, 1829.

Tow-Boat Atlanta.
Captain Cornwell S. Roe,

Urged by a sense of duty by his numerious friends announces
the uninterrupted prosecution of his Towing Business, and
assures the public that there is no difficulty now, even re-
mote in appearance; he makes this notice for the express
purpose to settle the agitation of the public in relation to
the steam boat accident, some time since, by running against

a sloop. Also in relation to a mercantile misfortune with which he is in no way connected, he regrets the folly that some have now, as past, circulated any idle tale, to impede the regularity of his business. Wanted Rye, Oats and Corn —at fair prices—Cash on delivery.   C. S. Roe.

Milton, May 19th, 1830.

Steam Boat Notice.

The Hudson River Steam Boat Line is now plying between New-York, and Albany, leaving New-York at 5 o'clock, P. M. every day, (except Sunday) when they leave Albany at 10 o'clock A. M.

The Steam Boats arrives at Milton from New-York, every night between eleven and twelve o'clock. From Albany, they arrive at Milton between three and four o'clock every afternoon. The boats will land and receive passengers at the Steam Boat Landing, Milton.

Peter Quimby.

Milton, May 3rd, 1830.

Notice.

The copartnership existing under the firm of James H. Longbottom & Co. was desolved by mutual consent, on the 15th day of December last. James Kinworthy retires from the concern. The business will be continued as usual by James H. Longbottom.

Feb. 6th, 1830.

Tailoring.

Mr. Charles H. Taylor announces to the public that he has commenced the Tailoring Business in all its various branches and fashions, in Marlborough Village, over the store of Barnabas M. Mapes, where he will be happy to attend on his customers. He can assure the public that his work will be done in first New York Style, equal to that of any person of his profession, therefore hopes to merit and receive a share of public patronage. Marlborough, June 29, 1830.

N. B. Cutting done in fashionable style and at short notice, and on reasonable terms; all kinds of country produce taken in payment.

Millinery.

Mrs. M. B. Taylor respectfully informs the public, that she has recently established the business of Millinery and Dress Making in Marlborough Village, nearly opposite the store of Mr. Fletcher, where she will be happy to accommodate customers in the above branch, upon the most moderate terms.

Marlborough, June 29, 1830.

List of letters remaining in the Post Office, at Milton N. Y., October 1st, 1830.

Robert Brown	Cornwell S. Roe
William Brown	John Sheffield
David Brower	Benjamin Sands
Rev. Jones Hobbs	Albert Stewart
Louisa B. Meech	James Stewart
Henry Perkins	Elisyabeth Woolsey
Ann Maria Ransome	John Worall

A. D. Soper, P. M.

Threshing Machine.

The subscriber, having purchased the interest of the Patentees, for this country, in two new invented Threshing Machines, offers the same for sale, at Milton Landing. The machines will either be furnished, or rights sold to farmers empowering them to construct the same. Town rights will be disposed of to mechanics, or others upon reasonable terms. Certificates of the most respected farmers in the county, confirming the great advantages of these machines are in the possession of the subscriber at his store, where the machines may be seen at any time.

Cornwell S. Roe.

Milton, Dec. 23, 1829.

Salt and Tar.

Sack salt of the very best quality and quantity, constantly for sale at the lowest prices. Also, Tar by the barrel.

C. S. Roe, Milton, April 7, 1830.

PRESS

On which Daniel S. Tuthill printed the "Pioneer" at Milton, in 1830. (Page 84.)

Stocks at Silas Purdy's Mill, Marlborough, in 1773.

(Page 86.)

OLD CUSTOMS.

———

The manners and methods of our grandfathers were different from our own. From various sources information has been gleaned as to the ways of the early residents of this town.

Those who could afford it, kept slaves, and each owner put a mark upon his black servants, and registered the same with the town clerk, in order that runaway slaves might be the more easily traced. For instance the mark of Matthew Wygant was "a square notch or ha'penny on the upper side of the left ear." This was previously Abraham Deyo's mark, but in purchasing Deyo's slave or slaves, Wygant evidently adopted it to avoid re-marking the poor blacks.

As a rule the slaves seem to have been well treated, though there is an instance on record of one owner having shot his man slave and killed him, for which he was never punished, the irregular times of the Revolution enabling him to escape prosecution.

About 1800 the residents began to give their slaves freedom. Many were allowed their liberty on the death of their old masters. John J. A Robart owned five, named Mongo (also called Louis Supreme), Figaro and his wife Althea, Charlotte and Olivette. He gave these their freedom in 1813. Figaro Milden, an aged colored man residing on Western avenue, was named after the Figaro above mentioned, and was himself a slave when a boy.

October 10, 1804, Benjamin Ely abandoned a black child to the state, being evidently the progeny of one of his slaves, whom he did not care to be at the expense of bringing up, foreseeing that all would have to be freed in a few years' time.

In 1773 stocks were set up at Silas Purdy's mill, where W. S. Clark & Son's mill now is, and there minor offences were punished in the traditional manner. One pound was voted at the town meeting that year, to pay for the stocks.

The pound was a very necessary institution during the latter part of the seventeenth century. Two were established in the town, one at Silas Purdy's, the other at Robt. Everett's. Many settlers were in the habit of feeding their stock along the roads, and the animals were always getting away and trespassing on other people's ground. The sheep seem to have been particularly annoying, and a heavy fine was imposed at one time on stray rams, and anyone finding one and not reporting to the town clerk, to have the " stray " registered (so that the owner might be fined) was liable to a fine of eight shillings. The hogs came in for their share as nuisances, but were allowed to roam if well yoked together. It was customary for anyone finding a stray animal to go to the town clerk with a description of it. The clerk entered this on the town book, which was supposed to "advertise " the finding. When the owner turned up he had to pay the clerk two shillings for advertising, and settle with the man who had found and fed his stock.

The methods in vogue in dealing with the poor were somewhat odd. On one occasion, in 1782, "a poor boy, named Liba Herrington, was sold at vendue, to Uriah Mackey. for 7 £, 8 shil., and he to have him bound by the poormaster until he is 21 years old, to have meat, drink, washing and lodging, and reading, writing and cyphering, and two suits of clothes when of age, one for holidays and one for common days."

In 1778, " Joseph Webb, the only person chargeable to the precinct, was sold to the lowest bidder for £87, for one year's boarding, exclusive of clothing, on this condition—if any person in the precinct of Newburgh will keep him for a smaller sum they are to have him." He was sold to John Scott. There must have been a cheerful prospect before a poor pauper who was disposed of in this fashion !

In 1789 there was a pauper known as old Relyea, to whom

the town had been giving aid, while his sons were really able to support him. The fact came up at the town meeting Sept. 5, 1789, and it was "Voted, that the poormaster immediately prosecute the children of old Relyea for his maintenance by the town." Evidently the poormaster did not get anything out of the sons, for the same thing was voted the next year, accompanied by wrathy resolutions.

During the Revolution it was the custom for men to take the oath of allegiance to the Continental government, and have the clerk enter the same on the town records. Many men who had Tory sympathies, when they found themselves becoming the objects of scorn and persecution, made the best of it, and swore in with the new government.

OLD HOUSES.

The residence of Samuel Harris, on North Main street, was built by Major DuBois about 1770, perhaps sooner. It was the best house in town.

The Exchange hotel, Samuel H. Kniffin, proprietor, is supposed to be nearly if not quite as old as the DuBois mansion.

James Carpenter's residence has withstood the storms of nearly a century.

The house adjoining, where J. E. Woolsey lives, is nearly as old.

The old stone house where Isaac Hall lives, formerly occupied by J. J. A. Robart, dates back to the Revolution.

The small house at the corner of Main and DuBois streets, property of Dr. E. P. Bailey, was there over seventy years ago, and is supposed to have been built during the last century.

The old building adjoining J. C. Merritt's store was formerly used as a weave shop by Spence & McElrath. Robert Moses worked in it, and it stood further to the east.

C. E. Reynold's shop on Main street was originally built

for John B. Wygant, for a wagon shop, also shoe and paint shop. Barnabas Mapes leased it at one time.

The Thomas Marvin house, nearly two miles north of the village, on Main street, was built by Eli S. Woolsey's grandfather, before the Revolution.

The Milden house, on Western avenue, is supposed to be over one hundred years old.

In Milton the old houses are—the red house at the head of Sears' lane, where the first town meeting was held in March, 1789. The Hallocks lived there, when they arrived in Milton in 1760, previous to building the old homestead.

The Hallock homestead, now occupied by Mrs. Phebe Hallock, was built about 1762.

The old house occupied by Mrs. Conklin, north of the Presbyterian church, was built by Samuel Hallock, some time in the sixties. It was afterwards bought by Benjamin Sands, and was fired at during the war of the Revolution, by Vaughan's expedition. David Sands, jr., picked up an iron cannon ball near the old house some years ago.

The Anning Smith house was built in 1770, and also got a dose from the British gun boats in 1777.

The Hepworth house, half way between Milton and Marlborough, was built shortly after the Revolution, and was kept as a hotel by William Holmes.

The Bingham house on Bingham street was built in 1795.

In 1820 Adam Cropsey's house stood just south of Dr. A. H. Palmer's present residence. South of where the brick house now is were two little houses, occupied by two old ladies, Mrs. Havens and Mrs. Plumstead. Henry Cropsey lived about where the brick house now stands. Where Henry Carpenter lives a Miss Wilson then resided. At this same date a little house with a rear basement was next to McMullen's hotel on the south. Van Buren's grocery store came next.

Chas. E. Reynold's carriage shop was formerly a part of the hotel building. Barnabas Mapes leased part of the hotel grounds, and built a portion of the present structure.

OLD ROADS.

The old post road, running through the town, at a distance of about half to three-quarters of a mile from the river, is undoubtedly the oldest road in the town. It probably dates back one hundred and fifty years. There are several dwellings on this road which are more than one hundred years old, and it formed the natural route for land travelers between New York and Albany.

The back road from Milton was built by Capt. Anning Smith some time near the Revolution. He laid it out entirely through his own land.

The road from Lattintown to Newburgh is also an old road, and reasonably straight, a virtue which has been shamefully avoided in laying out the town.

The Farmers' turnpike was ordered built by the town in 1790, to run from Lattintown to the river. Westward it ran to Wallkill, and afterward to Modena.

Hampton turnpike was laid out about 80 years ago. It ran in a straight line from Hampton to Plattekill. The direction of the road through Marlborough was close to the southern boundary of the town, crossing the county line just south of Chas. G. Velie's residence. The road was built so straight over hills and down valleys that it was nothing but steep grades. Teamsters were not long in finding out that it was more easy for their horses to draw a load around than over these hills. As a consequence the turnpike was little used. After a time Thomas Fyfe, who owned the place now belonging to Alex. Young, shut off an unused portion of the " pike," having given other land for the public use. John C. Storms later shut off still more of it, and Alexander and Wm. Young closed off other portions on their property, and to-day there is not much left of the Hampton turnpike.

The old Huckelberry turnpike is now known as Bingham street. About 18 years ago it was put through in its present shape, by the efforts of Dr. E. E. Taylor.

The following were the road districts in 1772 :

1–Caleb Merritt's line, on the road that comes from Wolvert Acker's, to Louis DuBois' north line.

2–At DuBois' north line, to run to Lattintown road.

3–From the last mentioned to the Paltz line.

4–From Elijah Lewis' dock to John Caverly's line.

5–To run from the last mentioned to Jo. Hicks' westward, and South to Capt. Gale's North line.

6–From the last mentioned southward to the river road.

7–To begin at the new bridge by Silas Purdy's mill to run southward to Dr. Perkins' South line.

8–To begin at the last mentioned, to run to Newburgh.

9–To begin at the Jew's house, to run westward to J. Russell's.

10–To begin below Samuel Townsend's, to run West out of the precinct.

11–To begin at Deyo's bridge, to run to Nathaniel Quimby's house.

12—From Silas Purdy's mill northward to Lattintown road.

13–From Mr. Brush's log house to Jonathan Hicks'.

14–From the last mentioned to the pine swamp.

15–Still westward to the precinct line.

16–From the Plattekill to Capt. Terpanney's.

17–Still southward to Newburgh line.

18–To begin on the road from Lattintown, to run on the Everitt line southward to Newburgh.

19–From John Duffield's to the sixth district west.

20–From the East district to the Newburgh road at Mr. Megmin's.

21–From the Lattintown road to the Paltz line.

OLD VESSELS.

Shortly before the Revolutionary War there was a dock and storehouse at Smith's pond, from which Capt. Anning Smith ran a vessel to New York twice a week. Another dock was built after the war, just below the present dock, and Capt. Hall ran a sloop from that point. A little further to the South during Jefferson's administration, about 1804, a dock was built from which Thomas Powell, of Newburgh, ran a vessel to New York. He also kept a store there, and it was from his wife that the fast and famous steamer Mary Powell derived her name.

The original landings for vessels at Marlborough were in Jew's creek, one being at the junction with what is now called Buckley's creek and the other about half way between that point and the Ravine Falls. A road used to run from these landings to the main road, at a point just south of the cemetery.

The sloop Stranger was run from DuBois' dock in 1822 or 1823, and the Thomas Hoyt was run by Moab Carpenter at about the same time. These vessels proved too small for the trade, and about 1825 Mowbray Carpenter and Josiah Lockwood sailed two sloops between Marlborough and New York, named the Victory and Robert Minturn. They carried flour, hay, butter, wood, live stock and farmers' produce of various kinds, the captains selling the cargoes, for want of modern commission men. Mr. E. A. Merritt used to run in the Victory in 1833 and 1834. Also James Carpenter.

In 1836 a stock company placed the steamboat Fannie on the Marlborough route, and ran to New York twice a week. Jacob H. Tremper (now widely known as the captain of the steamer Baldwin) commanded this early steam craft, which was run two years, and then sold because the business did not pay.

The steamer Splendid, owned by Millard & Mills, accommodated the town's traffic about 1845. A barge from Milton, the Lexington, Capt. Roe, also stopped here regularly, and a boat run by horse power, from New Hamburgh, connected with it at Marlborough.

The propeller Wyoming was put on the line in 1857, and was run by J. P. Millard and H. H. Holden from Millard's dock. Samuel Millard afterwards purchased Holden's interest. The Wyoming did a prosperous business for several years, carrying as much as 300 bags of flour a week during the busy season.

N. Woolsey Wright at one time ran a sloop to Haver-straw, largely for convenience in shipping flour from his own mill. A sloop styled the Abe Jones, was also used in the coal trade.

With the growth of the fruit industry, a daily line of boats became necessary, and the Marlborough vessels disappeared, the trade being carried on by the steamers of the Pough-keepsie Transportation Co. and Cornell Steamboat Co.

RAVINE FALLS, MARLBOROUGH, AS THEY APPEARED IN 1800.

(Page 93.)

REMINISCENCES.

THE RAVINE FALLS.

The Marlborough of to-day is a very different-appearing place from the Marlborough which is described in other pages. It is emphatically a live town, and during the summer season receives a large increase of vigor and business from the fruit industry and the visits of pleasure seekers. The tired occupants of the city, or the wealthy who travel for pleasure, come here in increasing numbers every year. The attractions are lovely scenery, a moderate temperature in "dog days," and fruit not surpassed in flavor by any grown in any portion of the world.

Perhaps the most interesting natural curiosity within the town limits is the fall of Old Man's Kill or creek into the Sucker Hole, a tumble of about 235 feet. The body of water running over is not large, but the height is so great, and the fall so little broken as to constitute a waterfall to see which is worth many miles to travel.

The Sucker Hole either derives its name from the sucking of the water in and out or because sucker fish are caught there. Every high tide the Hudson sends its waters into the creek almost to the foot of the falls. The precipitous sides of the hole are densely clothed with verdure, preventing a good view of the falls from the railroad or the river, but a trip down the rocks well repays the labor of the returning climb. The prospect obtained from the top of the precipice, from the rear of residences on Main street, may be compared to an infantile Yosemite. The picture is framed on either hand by walls of rock half hidden among dark cedars and a variety of foliage. In the depths of the foreground Jew's creek winds its way to a cove, which is crossed by the

West Shore R. R. tracks.   Beyond is the blue Hudson, with
the shores of New Hamburgh, and the entrance to a tunnel
in the distance.

The precipice on the west side of the Sucker Hole has
been the cause of many accidents, though it is not known
that any lives were lost there.   About seventy years ago a
carpenter shop stood where the stables of McMullen's hotel
now are located.   During a lively little hurricane it blew
over into the chasm, and the fragments were scattered far
and wide.   Among other things a saw was blown to the
point where Buckley's creek connects with the Old Man's
Kill, a distance of almost half a mile from where the shop
stood originally.

A little over thirty years ago a boy named Polhamus fell
over the precipice while returning from Sunday school.   He
remained there all night, although searchers were out with
lanterns looking for him.   He was found in the morning,
not fatally injured, nor was he crippled in consequence.

Some years since a young man named Birdsall, a relative
of the late Hosea Birdsall, slipped over while cutting slip-
pery-elm bark, but was not seriously hurt.

Later, a reckless young fellow, whose name is lost to history, went down on a bet after a set of false teeth.   He
climbed down most of the way, and jumped the rest, but
failed to break his neck.

In 1885 Willie Burke, son of Edward Burke, about six
years old at the time, fell over while in pursuit of a ball.
He went from the top clear to the bottom, and broke a
thumb, but was not injured otherwise, beyond a few scratches.

In 1886 a tramp, who was somewhat the worse for liquor,
rolled over, but stopped on a ledge of rock about seventy
feet from the top.   He was badly cut about the head, but
tramped out of town the next day, as though uninjured.

Probably others have fallen over this dangerous precipice,
but it is not likely that any one could have been killed here,
and no record preserved of the accident.   It is astonishing
to think that five persons could fall a distance of from seventy
to two hundred and thirty-five feet, and none of them be

killed, but their immunity is generally ascribed to the mass of soft rubbish which has accumulated at the foot of the declivity. This has operated as a spring mattress to break the fall of those who took the terrible tumble.

––––––

FACTS AND INCIDENTS.

Some fifty years ago a man named Pell lived on the Isaac Hall place, on Main street, in a tenant house. His wife died, and he went crazy with grief. He was not confined, and one night the poor man dug up his wife's body, and was found attempting to feed her.

Previous to 1830 or '35 large brick yards were located back of the present Knickerbocker Company's ice house. There was another where J. W. Keveny now owns, about a mile north, which was owned by Young & Moore. Nathaniel Adams built the first brick yard in Marlborough about 1825, but the clay all ran out inside of ten years.

Singularly enough, Marlborough supplied Newburgh with coal one winter twenty or thirty years ago, before the railroads were through. The supply in that city gave out, and the Millards being well stocked, sent coal down in carts all winter.

The sand bank to the north of Landing street used to come all the way to the dock store. To William C. Young belongs the credit of digging away a large part of it.

Seventy-five years ago wolves went plenty in the Marlborough mountain, and committed frequent depredations.

Lewis DuBois owned a fulling mill, when the 18th century was in the small figures, which he seems to had some difficulty in keeping employed, for over date of August 6, 1810, he advertised in the Newburgh " Political Index " the following :

"A Clothier Wanted, at the mill of the subscriber; one who can come well recommended, either on shares or otherwise. The stand is one of the best in the country, it being ten miles distant from any other Fulling Mill. The mill is new and calculated for carding also.

LEWIS DUBOIS."

The clothier secured by this advertisement could not have been satisfactory to DuBois, for on February 4, 1811, appeared the following notice:

"Dissolution: the public are informed that the partnership of Lewis DuBois and Nathan Tupper, in the Clothier's business, was dissolved on the first of December last.

LEWIS DUBOIS."

Sept. 15, 1817, the mill was again advertised to let, for a term of years.

Letters for Marlborough went to the Newburgh post office previous to 1809, and were advertised if not called for. Under date of July 1, 1807, were advertised letters for Alexander Cropsey, Josiah Merritt and Charles Millard, all well known residents. Either they were negligent about getting their mail, or these were letters with heavy postage due on them, which they did not care to redeem.

A good many farms were offered for sale during the war of 1812 or previous. Among others Mary Quimby advertised a farm of 150 acres, about a mile West of the Hudson, John Van Wie wanted to sell a farm of 137 acres, and it is probable that he sold as it is the only mention of his name in any record concerning Marlborough. David Merritt advertised his Lattintown farm, and Charles Millard tried to sell his mill property.

In 1818 post coaches ran through Marlborough three times a week, the line being between Albany and New York.

Jew's creek was navigable up to within about fifty years. In 1812 several vessels were run up in the creek for shelter

from British gunboats, which they feared were in pursuit.
John and Andrew Cropsey owned the creek about that
time (possibly a few years later) and ran sloops up as far as
Buckley's point.

It is a curious fact that Marlborough was not settled as
soon as surrounding towns because the soil was supposed to
be so poor. The New Paltz patentees came here before loca-
ing at the Paltz, and looked over the ground, deciding that
it was too rocky. The first white settlers of Dutchess county
also paid a visit to Marlborough on a like errand. and voted
that the land was of little or no value. Now, that our soil
has been proven the most valuable fruit land of the fertile
Hudson valley, this estimate of our ancestors seems amusing.
The unpromising rocks and stones retain the moisture so
necessary and valuable to the production of fine fruits.

STORES AND STOREKEEPERS IN MARLBOROUGH.

John Conger kept a store, where John Badner is now located, about 1810 or 1815. He afterwards removed it to the
dock.

John J. A. Robart kept a store in a shed-like structure
near where Isaac Hall lives, on Main street, about 1810.
This building was afterwards used as a school house, and
later moved to the site of Carpenter's present store, where it
was used by a hatter. All the oxen in the vicinity were required to move the building. The hat shop was run by
Reuben Drake, father of Wm. Drake, of New Hamburgh.

John DeSilvia had a store on Main street in 1816.

Joseph Lockwood kept a grocery on the dock about 1819
or '20. After that Joseph Carpenter kept store there, subsequently removing to Cornwall.

Jasper Van Buren kept a store where Mrs. Hinsdale's
house stands on Main street, in 1821.

James Whitmore had the store, vacated by John Cruger,
for some years. He was a brother-in-law of Gabriel Merritt.

Robert Spence and Wm. McElrath kept a store where J. C. Merritt is for a number of years. They also ran a woolen mill in the building now used by Woolsey Wright as a grist mill, employing fifteen or twenty hands. They came here young men and lived together, in the same house where Figaro Milden now lives, until Spence got married. The woolen mill was afterwards run by a man named Stratton, and later by one Longbotham. Joseph Hepworth, grandfather of J. A. Hepworth, also ran the mill for a time.

Wm. McElrath succeeded Spence & McElrath, and built the store now occupied by J. C. Merritt, about forty-five years ago.

Miles J. Fletcher kept a store at the location of S. Corwin's Sons fifty years ago.

Mowbray Carpenter was also one of the early storekeepers.

John Polhemus kept store here about 1830.

Lewis W. Young had a store at the dock for a number of years.

Recollections about Milton.

The South line of the Bond patent remains as a landmark to the present day, never having been crossed by subsequent sales and divisions of property. An old rock near the residence of C. S. Northrip is yet pointed out in the village, which was cut to mark this boundary.

It may be of interest to note that the price of land in Milton changed but little between 1753 and 1775. The price was but little over one pound per acre. Some of these acres are now very valuable. Every timber tree twenty-four inches and over in diameter, twelve inches from the ground, or that attained that size while the individual possessed the land, was reserved for use in the British navy for masts. Rights in any mines of gold or silver that might be discovered were reserved by the crown.

In 1862 a young ladies' seminary, boarding and day school, was carried on in Milton by Rev. E. W. Clark, below the Methodist church, on Church street. The town proved to be too small to support such an institution.

'Rev. P. C. Oakley formerly set type beside one of the Harper brothers, in New York city.

The Milton Savings Bank was organized June 1, 1871. Leonard S. Carpenter, president; Jesse Lyons, 1st vice-president: William H. Gedney, 2d vice-president; Ethan Parrott, secretary. No business was ever transacted by the organization.

About seventy years ago a ferry known as Lattimer's was run across the Hudson at Milton, from the old stone house. It is stated that when Gen. Washington had his headquarters at Newburgh, gold was sent to him from Boston to pay off the troops, and was brought across the river at this ferry.

The first meeting house in Milton was a store, located on the corner near the old Hallock homestead. Here the Friends worshipped prior to 1806.

A number of years ago Smith Mackey had a hay press where H. H. Bell & Son's plush factory now stands. He did a thriving business.

Milton has always been favored by steamboats as a landing, though only a village, but in the days when steamboat racing was fashionable, before the people learned that it was dangerous, captains often refused to stop, and row boats were sent out, and packages would be tossed back and forth in quick fashion.

C. M. Woolsey has in his office the commission of his ancestor, Wm. Woolsey, as ensign, dated July 4, 1778, and bearing the autograph of George Clinton, the first colonial governor of New York state.

Cornwall S. Roe was a prominent man in Milton for a number of years. He died out West only a few years since. His parentage was unknown, as he was picked up from the water at Cornwall when a babe, his father and mother being drowned by the capsizing of a boat. The little boy was bundled up in a blanket and floated.

Ship carpentering was carried on by Philip **Caverly** on Dog street, Milton, at an early date.   He married a widow by the name of McElrath, and bought the farm where Luther Caverly now lives.   He used to buy wood of Wilhelmus DuBois, and got some big bargains, because Wilhelmus' land was entailed, and he would not bother to measure the wood, saying that as it was entailed he didn't care who got it.

LATTINTOWN FIFTY YEARS AGO.

At the beginning of the present century Lattintown village was the principal centre of the town.   More business was transacted than in Milton or Marlborough village.   The inhabitants had not yet learned that the Hudson river was the great backbone of the state, and that live towns and cities must be located close to its banks.

In those days there were in Lattintown two hotels and a still.   Mechanism of all kinds was carried on, there was a school ; men came there to look for work ; law suits were carried on ; there was horse racing, and sometimes pugilistic encounters and the like.

The village derived its name from a man called Lattin (or Lattin?) whose origin and history has been almost forgotten. Jacob and John Lattin lived here and afterwards moved to Esopus.   A man of the same name visited Marlborough nine years ago, in the endeavor to trace his ancestry, but learned very little.   It is probable that much might have been discovered if the burying ground near —— Odell's had been undisturbed, but as many of the stones had been carried away, and used for dairy shelves and other useful purposes, the work of the historian was greatly hindered.

A Scotchman named McElrath was one of the earliest storekeepers.   He kept all kinds of groceries and liquor, and married a grass widow.

Two farmers, one of whom was named Chas. Brown, set up a still and made cider.   They did a thriving business.

A great deal of the land then was set out in apple trees as soon as it was cleared. The cider machine was an odd affair, consisting of a circle, with two large wheels or crushers, on which the boys used to ride, as on a merry-go-round. The cider was afterwards distilled into whiskey.

In 1826 a good hotel was built, and the landlord kept a blacksmith shop, with two journeymen and an apprentice. The local Methodist minister was also a shoemaker and made to order. There was also in the place a harness maker, hatter, tailor, wagon maker, undertaker, tanner and other tradesmen.

Fourth of July was a big day at Lattintown, during its glory, and a revolutionary cannon was freely used. There are still in the village many gates swung by a ball and chain, and it is tradition that the balls belonged to this old cannon.

The Lattintown Baptist Church was established in 1807, and the village knew its highest prosperity between that date and 1825.

Town meetings were held in Lattintown at the house of David Merrit, for many years. These gatherings were quite informal, being more of the character of a meeting of farmers to talk over their mutual interests, than a properly organized legislative body.

The following description of David Merritt's property is taken from an advertisement in the "Political Index," published in Newburgh in 1809 :

"For Sale, a farm situate in the village of Lattintown, town of Marlborough, and county of Ulster, containing about 180 acres of land. Said farm is under the best improvement, excepting 80 acres of excellent wood land. There is on the same a dwelling house neatly finished, containing four rooms and a kitchen on the first floor, and one above 20 feet square. Also about 300 bearing apple trees, a cider mill and house, and two barns, one 32x43, the other 30x40, and other outhouses. The situation is excellent for a public house, being the place where town meetings and the elections have hitherto been held. For further particulars enquire of the subscriber on the premises.

DAVID MERRITT.

December 18, 1809."

Among the residents of Lattintown during the '20s and '30s were Thomas Wygant, grandfather of Asbury Wygant; John Hait, who owned the farm where ———— Odell now lives; John and Lattin Caverly; Chas. Brown, who owned 400 acres where Edward DuBois now resides; James Quimby, grandfather of Samuel Quimby. The Wygant brothers were well-to-do, and owned a good deal of land. Buchanan Lounsbury owned where John Poyer is located. The Purdys owned several hundred acres.

John Bailey, grandfather of Dr. Elisha Bailey, was a resident, and Dr. Bailey taught school in Lattintown when a very young man.

Wm. Lymasen settled half a mile above Lattintown about the time of the Revolution. He died in 1801. His children, Joseph, Peter, John and William all settled in the vicinity. Moses Lymasen, son of Peter, is now living in Poughkeepsie. He fought in the late civil war. The rest of the family are scattered.

Rebecca Drake, a widow, kept store in the village over fifty years ago, and Thos. Warren kept the hotel. Charles Craft was undertaker at the same period. Wm. Lymasen was a tailor, and used to go about in a wagon, and work at people's houses.

Squire Waterous was Justice of the Peace for many years. He was born in 1741, and administered the law for our grandfathers. He had many petty trials. Perhaps the most important one was of the members of a family named Cole, living half a mile above the village. On the occasion in question a hunting dog ran into a hole and brought out a roll of cloth instead of a rabbit. This was identified as having been stolen from Buckley's cloth mill, and Martin Cole was proved guilty of the theft, and served two years in Sing Sing in consequence.

A family named Rhodes was a great trouble to the neighborhood. There were seven or eight brothers of them, who were thieves. For the credit of the present generation let it be said that they left no descendants in the town of Marlborough. Five of these brothers were arrested at one time for breaking and entering a church. All were sent to the State prison in consequence, for periods varying from five to ten years. John Rhodes was a horse thief and got a fourteen years' sentence the last time he was jailed. There was a younger brother of this family named Lewis, who married a lady named Bennett, who was said to be the only decent one of the lot, but he also ended up in State prison.

Benjamin Harcourt was Justice of the Peace at the time of the troubles with the Rhodes family. He also served two terms as Sheriff.

The liquor taverns were much thicker then than now. Everybody drank whiskey, including the ministers. The residents became frightened because there were so many drunkards, about 55 years ago, and circulated a pledge, by which the signers agreed to abstain from whiskey, which was the principal drink. In 1834 a temperance institution was organized in every district in the town. It seems to have been necessary, as the taverns were simply liquor shops, having no accommodations. They were very common, and almost everybody carried a bottle as well.

There was a good deal of dancing in Lattintown, and hops at the hotel were frequent.

As navigation in the Hudson grew with the establishment of steamboats, the river villages of Milton and Marlborough began to draw from the life and activity of Lattintown, which has suffered a gradual decadence, until to-day there is little more than a country cross road left of what was once a thriving village. There is a church, a blacksmith shop, a school house, and a small store. The dwellings thicken at the centre, but all the trade comes to Marlborough and Milton.

THE MEDICAL PROFESSION.

The first physician to locate in Marlborough, of whom there is any record, was Dr. Abijah Perkins. He practiced here before the Revolution, and died in 1776. Dr. Cornelius Roosa practiced here previous to 1814, when he died. Dr. David Lynch died here in 1822. A Dr. Fowler prescribed here about the same time. Dr. Marcus Dougherty and Dr. Nathaniel Deyo ministered to the sick about 1830 or later. Dr. James S. Knapp was in practice here for many years, and died in 1879. Dr. S. E. Hasbrouck succeeded him. Then Dr. J. N. Miller settled here for four years, removing to Highland. Drs. A. H. Palmer and David Mosher are the present resident physicians in the village.

Dr. Benjamin Ely practiced in the town about 1810 and '15, and owned a farm of 85 acres a mile and a quarter from Lewis DuBois' landing.

Dr. William Gedney settled in Milton in 1817, and had a large practice from that time until his demise in 1849. He was Supervisor in 1825. His son, Dr. William H. Gedney, entered the profession in 1846, succeeding to his father's practice. He has now retired. Dr. Theodore Quick and Dr. Wm. B. Pierson each practiced several years at Milton. Dr. Edward W. Carhart is now the only practicing physician in the village.

CHURCHES AND SOCIETIES.

The Presbyterian Church of Marlborough.

In 1763 the following subscription was raised to found the Presbyterian church :

"We, the subscribers, for an encouragement towards building a meeting-house for the worship of God, near the Old Man's Creek, in Ulster County, to be founded in the Presbyterian foundation and government of the Kirk of Scotland, do promise for ourselves, heirs, and assigns, to pay on demand the following sums annexed to our names to those that are trustees of said building, providing that Lewis DuBois does give two acres of land to remain for that use forever.

	£	s.
Lewis DuBois,	15	
Stephen Case,	5	
John Woolsey,	2	
David Brewster,	1	10
Joseph Presley,	0	8
Henry Case, Jr.,	1	8
Benjamin Woolsey,	3	
Lewis Adams,	0	10
Thos. Quick,	0	16
Thos. Woolsey,	2	
Matthew Presler,	0	8
John Jackson,	0	8
John Harris,	0	5
Micajah Lewis,	1	
Phineas Lattin,	1	
James Merritt,	0	15
Michael Wygant,	2	

		£	s.
Joseph Hallett,	. . . .	1	4
George Stanton,	. . . .	1	5
Joseph Cain, .	. . . .	1	10
Urian Mackey, .	. . . .	1	10
Lattery Carpenter,	. . .	1	
John Carmon,	. , . . .	1	
Daniel Thurston, .	. . .	1	
Zachariah Thurston, .	. . .	0	8
William Mitchell, .	. . .	1	
Silas Travis,	. . . .	0	16
Richard Wodey, .	. . .	3	
Benjamin Carpenter,	. . .	2	
Thomas Knowton.	. . .	2	
Eliphalet Platt,	. . . .	2	
Elijah Lewis,	. . . .	1	
James Quimby,	. . . .	3	
Nehemiah Fowler,	. . .	0	16
Alexander Culden, .	. . .	0	16
Jonathan Hasbrouck, .	. .	1	4
		———	
And sixteen others, in all,	. .	73	2

A second subscription, amounting to £17, s. 1, was raised Feb. 25, 1765, to finish the meeting house.

From a centennial discourse by Rev. S. H. Jagger, in 1867, the following is compiled:

On the fifth day of April, 1764, Lewis DuBois conveyed a tract of land to John Woolsey and Stephen Case, as Trustees of this Society. But the Society having come to the conclusion that an acre and a half was sufficient for their use, the lot was reduced to that size. The motives of the donor are thus expressed in the deed of conveyance: "For that paternal love he hath for and towards the propagation of the Gospel of Jesus Christ, agreeable to the Articles of the Kirk of Scotland, in the Presbyterian faith." The uses to which the land was set apart are thus defined: "To build a meeting house on, and for a burying yard, for the use, benefit and advantage of the said Marlborough Society, and their heirs forever." The conditions on which the Society were to hold the grant of land are thus expressed : "Provided always, and it is upon this consideration, that if the said Marlborough Society do from time to time, and at all times forever hereafter, call, choose, appoint, and settle a minister of the Gospel whose principles shall be to maintain, and fulfill, and keep the Articles of the Kirk of Scotland, agreeable to their Confession of Faith." If they should settle any other minister, the deed was to be void, and the land was to revert to its former owner or his heirs.

On this land a small building, about thirty-five by twenty-five feet, was erected, and was so far completed the ensuing summer, as to be occupied for Divine worship. The nature of the building may be learned when it is stated that its whole cost was not more than one hundred and seventeen pounds. The first sermon delivered in it, on the 26th day of August, 1764, was by the Rev. Charles Jeffrey Smith, of Long Island, a graduate of Yale College, who had studied Theology with Dr. Whelock of New Lebanon, the celebrated teacher of the Indians. After laboring awhile with the Indians, Mr. Smith was induced to go to Virginia for the instruction of the slaves. Returning to Long Island to settle his affairs, he went out one morning with a fowling piece and was found dead—by some supposed to have been murdered, by others to have shot himself accidentally. He was but just ordained when he preached here, and died just six years afterwards. He was a young man of much wealth and eminent for gifts and graces, and died greatly lamented.

The first burial in the church-yard was on the 3d day of March, 1764. The 13th day of December of the next year, the congregation chose a committee of five to procure a clergyman, and to provide the means for his support for one year. They secured, accordingly, the service of the Rev. Abner Brush, a member of the Presbytery of New York. He remained with them and was virtually their pastor for several years. On the 24th day of September, 1773, the people secured the services of the Rev. John Mecallah, who was to preach one-half the time at Marlborough and the other half towards Newburgh.

During all this time there was no Ecclesiastical organization in this Society, and the ordinance of the Lord's Supper had never been administered among them. On the 23d day of April, 1775, for the first time, this Sacrament was administered, by the Rev. Nathan Kerr, to Doctor Abijah Perkins, John Woolsey, John Polhemus, John Stratton, Mrs. John Stratton and Mrs. Jehiel Clark. We have no evidence that any Ruling Elders were set apart at this time, or that the ordinance of the Supper was again administered for many years. This Mr. Kerr was the pastor of the Church at Goshen, where he died in 1804, after a long pastorate of thirty-eight years. The Sacrament of Baptism had already been administered to thirty infants. And we learn how much importance they attached to the ordinance when we know that is was made the duty of their Clerk to ascertain and record, in connection with every burial, whether the deceased had been baptized or not. When they were without a stated preacher, as was often the case during the ten years and more of which we have been speaking, they embraced the earliest opportunity to have their children baptized by the neighboring clergymen, who were called in to supply their pulpit. We find in this way the Rev. Francis Peppard, of New Windsor, and the Rev, Wheeler Case, of Pleasant Valley, Duchess County, preaching and baptizing children among them. The celebrated Indian preacher, Samson Occom, spent some little time here, in the beginning of the year 1775, and on 22d day of January, baptized Lewis, the son of Lieutenant DuBois, among others.*

The next ten years embrace the stormy days of the Revolution ; and Marlborough felt their effects beyond many other places, as it was the refuge of an unusual number of Whigs.

---

* Samson Occum was one of the Mohegan tribe, who had been educated by Dr. Whelock at Lebanon, Ct. Shortly after being ordained to the Ministry, he was sent out to England, to raise funds for the education of the Indians. Here he attracted much attention, and drew large audiences to hear him, as the first Indian preacher who had ever visited England. He was successful in his mission, raising about $40,000. And this eventually laid the foundation for the establishment of Dartmouth College. He finished his days as a missionary to the Oneidas.

During all this time, this Congregation was without any stated ministry. depending on the services of such clergymen in the neighborhood as they could obtain, for one or more Sabbaths at a time. Among these were the Rev. John Close, the learned and eloquent pastor of the Churches of New Windsor and Bethlehem, the Rev. John Maffit, pastor of the Church of Goodwill, and the Rev. Andrew King, the witty but dignified, the talented, but not learned, the earnest, faithful and useful pastor of the Wallkill Congregation, for thirty years. The Rev. Robert Annan, of the Associate Reformed Church, also preached here, a man of talents, of ardent temperament, and of decided patriotism ; of whom one of his hearers was wont to say : " A capital preacher and a capital Whig." The Rev. Stephen Gostshins, of the Reformed Dutch Church of New Paltz and New Hurley, supplied the pulpit. They had also supplies from the other side of the river. The Rev. Samuel Sackett, of Long Island, who had been driven from his charge at Bedford, by his attachment to the views of Edwards and Bellamy—which led him to refuse baptism to those who were not in full communion—was one. This man sympathized strongly with the revival movements of that day, which created so much discussion in the Church ; and his monument pronounces him a " judicious, laborious, faithful and successful minister." The Rev. John Graham, for many years stated Clerk of the Presbytery of Duchess, and the Principal of Fishkill Academy, was another. His views of the revival were like those of Mr. Sackett.

The Legislature of the State of New York having passed " An Act to enable all the Religious Denominations of the State to appoint Trustees, who shall be a body corporate, for the purpose of taking care of the temporalties of their respective Congregations." April 6th, 1784, after legal notice, the Congregation of Marlborough met, and chose nine Trustees, viz : Anning Smith, Jonathan Brown, Michael Wygant, Isaac Fowler, Junr., Reuben Tooker, Nathaniel DuBois, Daniel Kelsey, Samuel Stratton, and Wolvert Ecker, Esq. This proceeding was proved, acknowledged, and recorded, according to law. These Trustees chose Benjamin Ely, M. D., Treasurer, Collector and Clerk.

On the 30th day of September following, the Trustees met to transact some business which they would have blushed to record had they not lived in the days of ignorance. It appears that, like most others of that day, they had not learned the evil of lotteries, and they did not hesitate to resort to them to raise funds for religious purposes. They have accordingly left a record of a meeting to settle the accounts of a lottery, which had been " drawn for the benefit and use of the meeting house."

The War of the Revolution, with its disturbing influences, being past, the people appear to have been animated with new zeal to promote the cause of religion, and to secure for themselves a stated ministry. On the 1st day of March, 1786, they commenced a subscription to pay for the services of a minister of the Gospel, who should preach in Marlborough, and in some convenient place in the Precinct of New Paltz. This subscription was signed by ninety men, nearly one-half as many as all the male heads of families, at that time, residin the township. Little more than one-third of the names upon it are now known among us. The sum raised was liberal for that day, and afforded a salary of four hundred dollars to the minister; better than twenty-five hundred at this day.

On the 10th day of June, the Trustees appointed Doctor Benjamin Ely to secure for them the services of a clergyman for one year; instructing him to obtain a man from some part of New England. Some of the leading men of the Society, at this time, were from New England, and their recent supplies had come from that direction. The following ordinance is also entered on the records of the Trustees: " *Resolved*, That no Baptist or Separate Minister be allowed or admitted to preach, in the Meeting House, under any pretence whatever, without the joint and mutual consent of the trustees, or a majority of them, for the time being."

The Rev. Ethan Osborn was the supply obtained by Doctor Ely; and he labored in this place, in connection with

Paltz, probably till 1792. About the same time, also, the house of worship underwent some repairs.

The Congregation, finding itself again without a clergyman, in May, 1792, sought and obtained the services of Mr. Abel Jackson, a licentiate under the care of the Morris County Association. On the 22d day of November following, he was ordained and installed, by that Association. He was the first minister, so far as we can learn, who had a formal installation over this Congregation. On the 1st day of October. 1793, a Committee of the same Association organized a Church of eight members, viz: Jonathan Brown, Cornelius Polhemus, Andrew Ely, Abigail Polhemus, Dorcas Olford, Elizabeth Cropsey, Hannah Ely and Electa Polhemus. Five of these persons, at least, were received by certificate from Churches in Connecticut. This was the first Ecclesiastical organization, of which we have any account; and it was formed in violation of the deed by which they held their Church property. That required them to be Presbyterians, settling only Presbyterian clergymen; they had now become Independents, and had settled a Congregational pastor. Accordingly the Congregation chose a new board of Trustees, and altered their style to suit their new Church connections. Efforts were made to obtain a new and appropriate grant of land, previously given to the Society, but without success. Still, they held the Church property, valued at that time at one thousand dollars, undisturbed; and Mr. Jackson remained their pastor about seven years.

For about ten years after Mr. Jackson left them, the Church was without any settled minister. During this time the pulpit was supplied by Isaac Sergeant, Wm. Bull, Ambrose Porter, Richard Andrews, Joel T. Benedict, and others, all of the same Ecclesiastical order as Mr. Jackson. Mr. Bull, who supplied the pulpit for some length of time, was an Englishman, exceedingly eccentric, and very prolix in his performances. He was a bachelor; and sometimes, in the family where he boarded, continued so long in prayer, at family worship, that all deserted him. At a funeral he was known to protract his address till interrupted and admon-

ished that it would be too dark to bury the dead.   Mr. Benedict is said to have been a man of ardent piety, untiring zeal,
and much eloquence, and to have drawn crowds to listen to
his preaching.

So far there had never been any special awakening of the
Church, but of late there had been a general accession to
their numbers.   The whole number that had been admitted
to the Church, up to 1808, was 71, of whom 53 were still
members.

Being wearied with difficulties growing out of their
Church government, and discouraged about obtaining permanent supplies of their present denomination, in 1809, the
people began to turn their attention again to the Presbyterian Church.   Mr. Jas I. Ostram, a candidate for the Gospel
ministry, under the care of the Presbytery of Hudson, occa-
sionally attended religious meetings among them for some
months.   They also obtained some supplies from that Presbytery.   In April, 1810, they applied, by their Commissioners, Charles Millard and Leonard Smith, to be taken
under the care of Hudson Presbytery.   At the same meeting of Presbytery, Mr. Ostram was licensed to preach the
Gospel, and on the first Sabbath after, agreed to accept a
call from this people, in connection with the Congregation
of New Paltz.   He labored among them as a licentiate till
September, when he was ordained and installed over them
by the Presbytery of Hudson.

The Congregation soon became enlarged, and a few more
were added to the Church.   In October, 1811, a special season of Divine influence began, in this Congregation, and
continued till the following Spring, adding to the Church
116 members.   During the period of this work, nothing
special appeared in Paltz, although within six miles, and enjoying precisely the same means of grace; illustrating most
clearly the sovereignty of Divine Grace, and teaching us
that the Lord " will have mercy on whom he will have
mercy."   About the middle of February, 1820, it pleased
the Lord to visit them with another revival, which added to
the Church 150 more, 90 in a single day, of whom 60 had not
been before baptized.

Being thus increased in numbers, and having enlarged their house of worship to double its former size, in 1827 the Congregation was separated from that of Paltz, the pastoral relation of Mr. Ostram to Paltz dissolved, and his labors confined to Marlborough. Here he continued his labors till March, 1829, when, having accepted a call from the Church in Salina, his relation to this Church was dissolved.

The first bench of Ruling Elders ordained and installed here, in 1810, when the Church was organized in a Presbyterian form, was composed as follows, viz: Charles Millard, Leonard Smith, Allen Lester, Andrew Ely, and Nathaniel Bailey. Of these, Charles Millard departed this life, April 30th, 1827. He was a man of blessed memory; a devout Christian, and ready for every good work. His character, and not wealth, made him a controlling spirit among the people. Andrew Ely was a soldier of the Revolution. Of Allen Lester we have the following record: "He departed this life July 24th, 1834, in the 78th year of his age. He was the first deacon (he was both deacon and elder) in this Church; had lived a useful life and died lamented." We have no doubt, from the business entrusted to Col. Smith, and the fidelity with which he discharged it, that he was a man of worth.

In November, 1829, this Church extended a call to the Rev. John H. Leggett, of Peekskill, and he was installed their pastor the 7th day of January following. Next Spring it pleased God to visit the Church with "a time of refreshing," and it received an addition of more than forty members. Again, in the Fall of 1832, the Lord poured out his Spirit among them, and about forty more were added to the Church. In April of next year, Mr. Leggett, having received a call from the Church at Hopewell, Orange County, the pastoral relation between him and this Church was dissolved. It may seem strange that a revival of religion was followed so soon by such a result. But some awakenings have always been fruitful in such results. Mr. Leggett continued his labors in Hopewell till 1854, when, feeling his health inadequate to such a charge, he accepted a call to the Church in the village of Middletown.

On the 16th day of September following, this Church made a call for the services of the Rev. Leonard Johnson, who was installed their pastor on the 2d day of October, 1833. He labored here a little more than one year, and on the 29th day of January, 1835, his relation to this Church being dissolved, he removed to Triangle, Broome County, where after a long pastorate of nearly a quarter of a century, he died in 1859.

Weary with changes, the people began to turn their minds again towards their old pastor, who had left them seven years since ; and they resolved now to extend to him a call, offering a larger salary than before and seeking to induce him to return. This call he accepted, and was installed again over them in the Spring of 1835. This time, however, his stay among them was brief: being but little more than three years. Yet he left behind some substantial results. He was instrumental in leading the people to erect a cheap parsonage, which has greatly increased the comfort and usefulness of his successors. In July, 1838, Mr. Ostram, having received a call from the 4th Free Presbyterian Church, in New York city, the pastoral relation was again dissolved. Here he continued to labor till 1852, when, under the infirmities of age, he left the city and retired to the village of New Windsor. Here he continues to reside, performing more or less pastoral labor, as his health will permit.

At the time of the division of the General Assembly, which took place this year, this Church was found in the New School body. Accordingly, Mr. Henry Belden. a licentiate of the 3d Presbytery of New York, came among them, and supplied the pulpit from Jan. 1st to April 15th, 1839. At that time he received from them a call, and was installed their pastor the 2d day of May. He continued his labors here about seventeen months, and was instrumental in adding about forty to the Church. But his doctrinal views, and the measures which he adopted, were such that a large majority of the Congregation became dissatisfied, and in October, 1840, the pastoral relation was dissolved. Mr. Belden was afterwards suspended from the functions of the Gospel ministry, by his Presbytery, for want of doctrinal soundness.

Soon afterwards, having received license from Oberlin, he built a Church at Washingtonville, Orange County, of his own order, in which he labored for a short time. Thence he removed to the city of New York, where he still resides.

A portion of this Congregation, who sympathized more strongly with the New School body than others, at this time erected a house of worship in Milton ; and (September 27th, 1841,) certificates were granted to fifteen of these persons, residing in and near Milton, for the purpose of being constituted a separate Church. The remainder of the Congregation appointed delegates to meet the Old School Presbytery of North River, and to renew their connection with that body.

On the 25th day of January, 1841, the Presbytery appointed the Rev. John H. Carle as stated supply of the Church of Marlborough. He continued his labors here till the Spring of 1842, when he went to the Church of Rondout to officiate in the same capacity. After a few years labor in that place, he returned to the Dutch Church, and labored for some time near Canajoharie. At present he is believed to be laid aside by ill health from all active labor.

In the Spring of 1842, the Congregation sent to Princeton for supplies, and were directed by the professors, among others, to Rev. S. H. Jagger, then a licentiate of the Presbytery of Long Island. He commenced preaching here on the 15th day of May, and, on the 27th day of June, the people gave him a unanimous call to become their pastor, which he accepted. He found the Church much divided, owing to the recent change of Ecclesiastical relation, and other things. Many, having deserted their own Church, were worshipping elsewhere. Although, in a short time, most of these breaches were healed, the pastor labored eighteen years without witnessing any extensive revival, and was instrumental in adding but one hundred to the Church during this long period.

At the beginning of his pastorate, the Parsonage was mortgaged for nearly its full value. This debt was soon paid ; and the house, barn and grounds have since been much enlarged.

This ends Rev. S. H. Jagger's sketch of the Church.   Its history since he left the Congregation is too recent to require production here.   The following additional points of interest have been gathered from other sources:

List of pastors of the Presbyterian church: Sept., 1806, Rev. Ambrose Porter was ordained pastor. The subsequent pastors have been Rev. James Ostram, 1810–29; Rev. John H. Leggett, 1830–33; Rev. Leonard Johnson, 1833–33; Rev. James I. Ostram, 1835–38; Rev. Henry Belden, 1839–40; Rev. John H. Earl, stated supply, one year; Rev. Sam'l H. Jagger, 1842–69; Rev. Charles W. Cooper, 1870–75; Rev. Duncan C. Niven, 1875–83; Rev. Charles E. Bronson, 1884.

The elders of the church since organization, 1810: Gen. Leonard Smith, Charles Millard, Andrew Ely, Allen Lester, Nathaniel Bailey, Michael Wygant, Joshua Conklin, Gilbert Kniffin, Daniel Wygant, Jonathan Cosman, Bernard Bailey, Peter V. Fowler, Thomas D. Bloomer, James O. Conklin, Asbury Wygant, Augustus G. Clark, Charles E. Bingham, Charles M. Purdy, and Cornelius D. Bloomer.

In 1869 the old church was destroyed by fire. The present house was built the following year, at a cost of $33,000.

In 1859, some individuals in the congregation engaged in erecting a small house of worship at Middle Hope. The enterprise was one of doubtful propriety, and viewed with much suspicion by many from the beginning; and the result proved that their fears were but too well grounded. It created much jealousy, and led to divisions, till the prime movers of the scheme withdrew from the church and went to Newburgh.

In 1861, a small church of about twenty persons was organized in Middle Hope, being nominally separated from the parent church, but yet remaining in reality part and parcel of it, having their old pastor installed over them.

The Middle Hope congregation was never large, but the Church there survived and had an irregular existence until 1885, when the building was sold to the Methodists. The remnant of the congregation previously returned to the Marlborough Church.

LATTINTOWN BAPTIST CHURCH.

The following is taken from the "History of Ulster County":

The earliest record of the Baptist church at Lattintown to be found in the keeping of the church is the following copy in an old unruled writing-book, with pasteboard cover:

"Record of the Trustees of the Meeting-House belonging to the Baptist church of Lattintown, in Marlborough.

"Lattintown, January 2nd, 1807.

"Church met according to appointment and elected Nehemiah L. Smith, Noah Woolsey, and Matthew Benedict Trustees for said church, to manage the affairs of the meeting-house in Lattintown."

The same ancient book is used by the church to record the annual election of trustees. It remains in a good state of preservation, and contains the names of trustees annually elected (two years excepted) up to January, 1864.

The society was incorporated by a certificate bearing date Jan. 26, 1807. The paper was signed by the officers who presided at the meeting, Matthew Benedict and Richmond Burwell. The trustees chosen were Nehemiah S. Smith, Noah Woolsey, and Matthew Benedict. The proceedings were verified before Judge Jonathan Hasbrouck, and the record attested by George Tappen, deputy clerk.

The next record is found in a deed bearing date Jan. 26, 1808, signed by Thomas Wygant and Elizabeth his wife, whereby, for the sum of £20, the lot of ground on which the meeting-house stands, also the graveyard, together containing half an acre of ground, was conveyed to the trustees of Baptist church of Lattintown.

The earliest record found in the church book states that at a meeting of the church held in the month of May, 1812, Deacon Purser being present with them, made the church a present of this book, it being the one in use at the present time for keeping the records of the church.

From the records it appears that the Pleasant Valley church, situated nine miles southwest from Lattintown, embraced members living both sides of the Marlborough mountains. On the 6th of May, 1812, a meeting was appointed in Lattintown for the purpose of constituting into a separate church those members of the Pleasant Valley church residing on the easterly side of the Marlborough mountains. Elder Lebbeus Lathrop being chosen to preside, stated the object of the meeting, and the importance attached to it. After the cause had been presented, Articles of Faith, previously prepared, were read in the hearing of those present desiring to be constituted into a separate church. Tney individually signified their assent and agreement thereto, and were formally constituted in a separate church, adopting the name of the Baptist church of Lattintown. The right hand of fellowship was given by Elder Lathrop to 24 members present; 5 were subsequently added, making a total membership of 29. A letter was immediately prepared and sent to the Warwick Association, asking admission, which request being granted, the new organization became a member of that body.

On the 23d of May the church extended an invitation to Elder Hall to become their pastor, and a request to that effect was sent to the Pleasant Valley church, of which Elder Hall was pastor. In June following word was received from the Pleasant Valley church stating that their request was granted, and they might expect Elder Hall. In July following the Pleasant Valley church sent Brethren Jones and Edwards to the Lattintown church to inform them that they had revoked their decision respecting Elder Hall, and that they could not spare him, not even for half the time. The church then appointed a committee, consisting of the clerk and four members, to arrange supplies for the pulpit; also, to open correspondence with ministering brethren with a view of settling a pastor. Their house of worship had been completed two years before their organization as a separate church, and in June, 1810, the Warwick Association held its annual meeting at Lattintown, when, the record states, an abundant provision was made for the delegates and their horses.

In September, 1812, Aaron Perkins accepted the invitation of the church, and in November, 1812, commenced his labors at an annual salary of $200, with a positive understanding that if either party wished to rescind the contract, that six months' notice should be given to the other party.

In June, 1813, Elder Perkins was ordained. The church were united with him. He was ardent and faithful, the congregation large and attentive, and Lattintown enjoyed years of happiness, usefulness, and prosperity. There are old people now living in the vicinity whose eyes glisten with delight as they speak of the days and years when Elder Perkins preached in Lattintown, when the meeting-house, with its capacious gallery, proved too small to accommodate the congregation, and those who arrived latest drove up to the sides and ends of the meeting-house and sat in their wagons —there were no carriages in those days—and listened, and loved to listen, to the preached word.

> "Those were golden, happy days,
> Sweetly spent in prayer and praise."

Elder Perkins remained with them as their pastor twelve years, during which time he baptized 160 members. In 1820 an extensive revival took place, when the records show 54 as being baptized. The largest membership during Elder Perkins' pastorate was 128. In the year 1821, Elder Perkins' salary was raised to $250 per annum, as a reward for his services and a token of respect and confidence of the church.

In November, 1824, Elder Perkins received a call from the Berwick Baptist church, in the city of New York, which he felt it his duty to accept, and, after giving the Lattintown church the stipulated six months' notice of his intention, he took his leave of them. The church was next supplied in part by Daniel Hill, who had been licensed to preach. During the fall of 1826, Elder Draper had been introduced to them, and having preached with satisfaction, was called to preach for them half the time, for which services they agreed to pay him $75 per annum, and move his family gratis from the West. His term of service commenced on the 1st of May, 1827. A resolution was adopted by the church that each member shall pay twenty-five cents per quarter for the support of the gospel among us. Brother Conklin was appointed receiver and to collect and pay over the same to Elder Draper. On the 19th of January, 1827, the church passed a resolution that it was improper to take public collections on Lord's day.

During the history of the church thus far the covenant and business meetings were regularly attended to on the third Sunday of each month in the afternoon, when the necessary business of the church was attended to, after which there was a free conference among the members present respecting their progress in the divine life. These meetings invariably commenced and closed by singing and prayer. The same date is still observed by the church for holding their covenant meetings; also, the same custom prevails with respect to commencing and closing their meetings. Their communion seasons have been observed once a quarter, on the Sabbath succeeding the third Saturday in the month.

The records state that in April, 1827, the church met to inquire into the reason " why our Association neglect and even discard the old practice of ordaining deacons," and they by resolution bound themselves to practice as the Association directed.

During the interval, until September, 1831, the church enjoyed peace and some good degree of prosperity under the ministry of Elder Draper. Some few were added each year to the church, of such as felt constrained to come out from the world and be a separate people. Some of those remain with the church to this day, and have continued with the church to rejoice in its prosperity, and to weep between the porch and the altar when clouds of darkness brooded over Lattintown. Among such deserving mention are the names of Sisters Lucy Woolsey and Mary Ann Staples, both of whom in early life embraced the cause of Christ, and who for near forty years past have been unwavering in their fidelity and zeal in their Master's service. Another, a prominent Baptist residing still in the vicinity, came before the church in February, 1813, relating his experience to the church, which being considered satisfactory, it was resolved to receive him as a member after baptism. He requested to be baptized immediately; said he could not wait. It was now midwinter, and extremely cold; the streams and ponds were frozen—no baptistry in those days. The brethren expostulated with him, advised him to wait. Remonstrances were unavailing. The ice—near a foot thick, and making rapidly—must be cut; he must follow his Master's example; and he has lived to see his children and his grandchildren after him buried by baptism in a liquid grave. His consistent Christian life and godly conversation for fifty years have fully attested the sincerity of his convictions.

In September, 1831, Elder Draper requested a letter of commendation, which was granted, and the church was left without a pastor.

Again the church, as usual on such occasions, appointed a committee to wait on Elder Perkins and obtain his views. and get him to recommend a supply, with a view to settling another pastor. Until July following the church was sup_plied by Brethren Bishop and Duxbury, when the church received a letter from Elder Archibald McClay, of Kingston, recommending Brother Hadow, recently from Scotland, to preach for them. After a month's trial, he was invited to settle as their pastor. In September following, a council was called to assemble at the meeting-house on the 10th of October, to ordain him; also at the same time and place to ordain their deacons. Brother Hadow continued as their pastor until Jan. 19, 1833, when the church informed him that in the succeeding spring they should make an effort to obtain Elder Perkins as their pastor, and he might seek some other field of labor. Brother Hadow left the church in May. In the meantime Elder Perkins had been written to and invited to again become their pastor; he declined, and again they were left destitute.

In June following, John Alison—who had been a prominent member of the Presbyterian church at Marlborough, and also a student for the ministry—applied for baptism and

admission to the Lattintown church. He was received, and
also obtained license from the church to preach. During
the next few months he preached to the church with great
acceptance. In the spring of 1834 Brother Alison resigned,
after which a letter was sent to Elder Perkins, inviting him
to settle with them again as their pastor. Elder Perkins
writes them in reply that he must decline, and also that the
church owes him $50.16 for services rendered ten years since.
A collection was taken and the debt was discharged.

On the 20th of December, 1834, the Newburgh church,
situated ten miles South of Lattintown, was constructed ;
the Lattintown church being in a country place, and their
members scattered about the country, many of them residing
nearer Newburgh than Lattintown. Several such, and
among them some of the officers and more prominent members, took letters and joined the Newburgh church, which
greatly reduced the Lattintown church in means, strength,
and members. In the spring of 1835, Elder Powell directed
to them Elder Jeremy H. Dwyer. After hearing him preach,
in June, 1835, the church gave him a call to become their
pastor, which he accepted. During this year several more
members took letters to join the Newburgh and Pleasant
Valley churches, which still further reduced the Lattintown
church.

In the month of August it was resolved to hold a protracted meeting, and Elder Powell was invited to come and
assist Brother Dwyer in conducting the meeting. A committee, consisting of Brothers D. Cosman and N. Merritt,
were appointed to wait on the innkeeper, to request him to
desist from selling liquor during the continuance of the
meeting. He cheerfully complied with the request, and on
the 20th of August, the meeting commenced. It was a busy
season of the year for the farmers ; the attendance was small,
and the prospect gloomy and disheartening. They humbled
themselves in the sight of God, and after earnestly beseech-
ing God to vouchsafe his blessings, they solemnly ordained
their deacons, and concluded, notwithstanding the discour-
aging circumstances, to proceed with their meeting, to labor

and pray earnestly, and leave the result with God. A glorious harvest of souls was the result, in which the surrounding churches also largely participated. On the 2d of September, 1835, thirty-three willing converts repaired to the majestic Hudson, and there, in the presence of many hundreds of spectators, they were buried by baptism in the liquid waves.

Soon after the close of the protracted meeting, Elder Dwyer tendered his resignation, which was accepted by the church, and again Elder Perkins was asked to furnish them with a pastor. In February, 1836, Brother Samuel Barrett received a call, which he accepted. He was young, ardent, intelligent, and pious, and under his watchful care the church steadily grew in grace and strength. They were united, useful and happy. Near the close of his ministry with the church, a large number of members took letters and moved West, where they formed a new and eventually a flourishing church. In April, 1839, Brother Barrett preached his farewell sermon, and went to Port Jervis. After he left, Brother Davis preached for them until 1841. The church at this time was in a low state, but few attending the house of worship. In 1844, Brother David Morris was invited to preach for them half the time. He divided his time between them and the Hyde Park church.

In 1845, Brother S. Barrett was again invited to preach for them. He accepted the call, and again became their pastor. The records state that he preached on the 5th of April, 1846, to a crowded house, and all were happy to hear him again speaking forth the words of life from the sacred desk at Lattintown. The two intervening years the church steadily grew and prospered. In April, 1848, Brother Barrett resigned to take charge of the church at Middletown, Orange county, N. Y., where he spent his remaining days.

In May following, Brother J. S. Adams commenced laboring with them, while at the same time prosecuting his studies in order to prepare himself more fully for the gospel ministry. After he left, in February, 1849, a letter was sent to Rev. J. I. Grimley, who came and preached for them, and in

March was engaged as their pastor. On the 15th of August a council was called, of which Deacon Staples of Lattintown was one, to sit in council and aid in ordaining Brother Grimley. After his ordination, he preached acceptably and profitably to the church until September, 1850, when he resigned and went to Unionville. During the thirteen years up to August, 1863, the church became very much reduced by deaths and removals. Preaching was rarely heard at Lattintown. The members became scattered, the house of worship dilapidated and uninviting. Application for aid to the State Convention was refused or neglected, and it was thought advisable by most members to disband. Meetings were neglected except by two or three sisters (those before mentioned, who still met to pray). The roof of the meeting house had gone to decay, the walls had fallen, the windows were broken, the storms beat and the winds sung their requiem through the old edifice. In August last (1880) a toil-worn missionary was directed that way. He sought out some members (then attending the Newburgh church). They spoke to him of Lattintown as numbered already with the past. He asked to preach for them. They tried to discourage him, but he, neither daunted nor doubtful, appointed a meeting, and once more held out to them words of hope and life. This was Brother Cole, of the Greene and Ulster Mission, and to this as a period, and to him as an agent under God, they took as a new starting-point in their history. In 1863 a committee was appointed by the Central Association to visit the church. A meeting was held in October for the purpose of raising money to repair the house. A subscription-list was circulated, and the members took hold in earnest of the work before them, and complete success has crowned their labors. The old structure has been moulded into a neat, comfortable, attractive house of worship.

Rev. Joseph I. Grimley is acting as the pastoral supply to the church in 1880, the trustees of the church being Gideon Morgan, David Cosman, and Daniel Hasbrouck; William Staples, church clerk.

THE EPISCOPAL CHURCH.

Christ Church, Marlborough, was the third Episcopal church organized in Ulster county.

In 1836 the village of Marlborough contained between four and five hundred inhabitants, many of them descendants of the Dutch and Huguenot families, who were the early settlers of the county. There were also a number of English and Irish families who were employed in the different manufactories, and New Englanders engaged in merchandise and transportation. Many of these people were regular attendants at the Presbyterian and Methodist churches, whilst the others seldom or ever entered a place of public worship. The Rev. Robert Shaw, rector of St. Andrew's church, Waldon, Orange county, whilst visiting some of his old parishoners living near the village, heard of the spiritual destitution of these English families, some of whom had been baptized and made members of the church. At the request of Gen. Gilbert O. Fowler, of Newburgh, he visited them and remained several days, making the acquaintance of the people, fully informing himself of their number and condition.

There were several influential families living in the neighborhood, members of St. George's church, Newburgh, who offered to contribute liberally towards sustaining a mission church, if located in the vicinity. At their suggestion divine service was held in the district school house on Sunday, the 12th day of February, 1837. This was the first public service of the Protestant Episcopal Church in Marlborough.

This service was attended by the people generally; so much interest manifested that a meeting was called. The following named gentlemen were present: Edward Armstrong, of Dans Kamer; Thomas Fyfe, of Hampton; John Buckley, Gabriel Merritt, Leonard S. Carpenter and others of Marlborough. After consultation it was decided to take immediately the initiatory measures to organize a church in the village.

Permission having been obtained to occupy the Methodist meeting house on the two following Sundays, " Public notice was given that on Sunday morning next, the 19th of February, and the following Sunday, the 26th, divine service would be held at that place according to the rites and ceremonies of the Protestant Episcopal Church; all who were disposed were invited to attend, as it was intended to organize the church in the village of Marlborough." At the time appointed Mr. Shaw found a large congregation, most of whom were utterly ignorant of the church and its services. Prayer books were distributed and the people requested to join in the responses. The pages were called as the service proceeded.

Mr. Shaw read the prayers very impressively, the people generally joining in the responses. The sermon was suitable for the occasion and gave general satisfaction. Divine service was held in the same place on Sunday, the 26th, and on Monday, the 27th February, 1837. The male members of the congregation met in the village at the home of Miles J. Fletcher and elected Edward Armstrong and Miles J. Fletcher church wardens, and Thomas Fyfe, Dennis H. Doyle, Leonard S. Carpenter, David E. Fowler, Andrew Oddy, Joseph Hepworth, Richard R. Fowler and William Cushion vestrymen, and they chose the Rev. Robert Shaw rector of the parish, the church is to be known as Christ Church in the village of Marlborough.

The Church was admitted into union with the Diocesan Convention September 26th, 1837. The following spring Bishop Onderdonk visited the parish and confirmed two persons. During the summer divine service was held in the old school house at Hampton. In the fall and winter the congregation again worshipped in the Methodist meeting house. A lot of ground, containing over an acre very eligibly situated a short distance south of the village, was generously donated by Dennis H. Doyle, on which the vestry erected a small wooden structure, 24 feet front and 48 feet deep, with a tower and belfry in the western end, affording sittings for 140 persons, at a cost of $2,500, including the organ and bell. The church was consecrated by Bishop Onderdonk, September 10th, 1839. The Bishop said in his address: "The union in this church of economy with great neatness, I would commend to the imitation of all parishes who would pursue the honest and Christian course of building in strict conformity with their means." At the close of the year Rev. Shaw resigned and accepted a call to Trinity church, Fishkill. The services were continued by the Rev. George B. Andrews, rector of Zion church, Wappingers Falls, and the Rev. William Walsh, of Newburgh, until the following summer, when the Rev. George W. Fash was appointed missionary and chosen rector of the parish.

He entered on his duties July 5th, 1840. He began his work by organizing a Sunday school numbering 35 scholars, who were carefully instructed in the catechism and at stated times publicly catechised in church. His entire time was given to his parish duties. Bishop Onderdonk visited the parish the 28th August and confirmed six persons, and expressed much gratification at the increased attendance and growth of the congregation. The rector of Trinity church, Fishkill, having resigned, it was proposed to the vestry that Rev. Fash be allowed to officiate for them on Sunday mornings, and hold an afternoon or evening service in Marlborough. It was reluctantly consented to. The divided service was a serious loss to the church. It was discontinued at the end of the year.

On resuming the usual services on Sundays, the church was well attended and the rector highly gratified by the presentation of a silver communion service from some ladies, members of St. Mark's church, New York. The vestry being unable to give Rev. Fash a sufficient supporthe resigned the 1st of July, 1843, leaving many warmly attached friends.

The services were continued by Henry Edwards, a candidate for holy orders, assisted by the neighboring clergy, until the spring of 1844, when he was succeeded by Mr. Samuel Hawksley. He was born in England and came to this country whilst quite young with an elder sister and her husband, landing in Philadelphia. They left him there and went to the West. Young Hawksley was aided by the Rev. Dr. Wm. Cooper Mead, Rector of Trinity church, who, placed him at school and afterwards sent him to Trinity College, Hartford, where he graduated A. B. in 1839. He entered the General Theological Seminary in New York in 1840. His close application to study so seriously affected his sight that he was obliged to ask for an extended absence, during which time he visited England, and on his return asked for a dismissal from the Seminary. Soon after he was employed by Mrs. Armstrong as a tutor for her sons. He volunteered his services as a lay reader, which were gladly accepted.

In 1845 he was ordained deacon by Bishop Brownell, in Christ Church, Hartford, and soon after appointed missionary to Marlborough. He now relinquished teaching, and devoted himself to the duties of the ministry. After two years of incessant labor, holding service at different places, baptizing the children, and by his kind and sympathizing disposition, he gained the confidence and esteem of the working people and gathered in the church a congregation respectable in numbers and regular in their attendance.

On Sunday, May 2d, 1847, he was advanced to priests' order in St. George's church, Newburgh, by Bishop DeLancey, of Western New York, and soon after was made rector of the parish. His missionary labors were extended to Milton and Lloyd; afterwards to Stone Ridge and Ellenville, frequently journeying on foot from village to village. In 1850 he organized All Saints church, in Milton; in 1853 St. Paul's church, Ellenville, and had charge of St. Peter's church, Stone Ridge, preaching at each place one Sunday in the month, and on the other Sundays supplying them with lay readers.

These arduous labors had gradually undermined his constitution; his health was so much impaired that he was obliged to relinquish his duties and seek a change of air. He visited the sea shore and returned home somewhat improved in health, but without that buoyancy of spirits for which he was noted. Before he had fully recovered his strength, he resumed his duties, assisted by a lay reader, he reading his sermons seated in a chair in the chancel. The following summer he was again confined to his bed. At the urgent request of his friends he consented to have a physician called. It was then too late. After lingering a few days, he died on Sunday morning, Sept. 2d, 1855. It might not be incorrectly said that he was purely worn out in the service of his maker. An appropriate monument marks his grave, bearing the following inscription :

"REV. SAMUEL HAWKSLEY, PRESBYTER,
Rector of Christ church, Marlborough,
departed this life Sept. 2d, 1855, aged 41 years."
"*Even so saith the spirit, for they rest from their labors.*"

After Rev. Hawksley's death, the church service was suspended for two Sundays. At the request of the wardens Samuel M. Akerly officiated as a lay reader until the following May, when the Rev. James C. Richmond—then living in Poughkeepsie—offered his services. He officiated until the 1st of November, when the services were resumed by Mr. Akerly, who had become a candidate for holy orders. He was frequently assisted by the Rev. George B. Andrews, who at the stated seasons administered the Holy Communion.

On Christmas day, 1857, the Rev. William Walsh, of Newburgh, officiated and administered the Holy Communion to a large number of communicants. The day being very cold and windy, larger fires were made than usual and were carefully secured at the close of the service. About six o'clock on Sunday morning, the 27th, flames were discovered bursting out of the windows and roof. Before assistance could be obtained the church was totally destroyed. It was insured for eighteen hundred dollars.

The present structure was erected on the site of the old church, from plans furnished by Messrs. Richard Upjohn & Sons, of New York.

The foundation was commenced on the 10th of May. The work was carried forward very energetically, and completed the 20th ot October, 1858. The church is a gothic structure, known as the early English, built of brick with substantial hollow walls with brown stone trimmings. It is 29 feet front, 52 feet deep with a semi-octagon chancel of 18 feet deep. On the north side of the chancel is a robing room 10 feet square. The tower is on the southwest corner 11 feet square (intended for a spire 80 feet high from the ground). The entrance is through the tower. The roof is covered with slate. A large window occupies the western end. This and the other windows are filled with enameled glass with stained glass borders. The chancel windows are smaller. The central one has a nicely finished copy of Sir Joshua Reynold's figure of Faith. The interior shows an open finished roof. The seats, pulpit, bishop's chair and altar are black walnut, oiled and polished. The floor, doors and trimmings are of Georgia pine. In the basement is the Sunday school room and in the cellar at the west end is the furnace, so carefully guarded that no danger may be apprehended from it.

The church was consecrated on Tuesday, October 26, 1858, by Bishop Horatio Potter. There were present taking part in the service Rev. John Brown, D. D., of Newburgh; Rev. Christopher B. Wyatt, of New Windsor; Rev. John R. Livingston, of Fishkill; Rev. Joel Clapp, of Cold Spring; Rev. George B. Andrews, of Wappingers Falls; Rev. Henry Anthon, D. D., and Rev. Theodore R. Eaton, of New York, Rev. Archibald M. Morrison, of Brooklyn, Rev. Samuel M. Akerly and Richard Upjohn, the architect, besides a large attendance of the people living in the village and vicinity. After the services were concluded the bishop and clergy and members of the congregation were hospitably entertained at the house of John Buckley, the senior warden. The entire cost of the church including the furniture was six thousand five hundred dollars.

Samuel M. Akerly having been admitted to deacon's orders was appointed a missionary and requested to continue his ministration. On the 1st day of December, 1859, he had the satisfaction of paying off the last and only obligation existing against the church, leaving it entirely free from all incumbrance. He was admitted to priest's orders by Bishop Potter July 21, 1861, after which the bishop confirmed seven persons. In the afternoon he preached in All Saints' church, Milton, and confirmed one person. On the 21st of September, 1861, the Rev. Samuel M. Akerly was unanimously chosen rector of the parish.

At a vestry meeting held December 3, 1861, a letter was received from Mrs. Hester Doyle, offering to give the rear part of a lot adjoining the church containing about half an acre on which to build a parsonage. The offer was accepted and the building commenced in the spring. It is a frame building 40x28 feet, two stories high, commanding a charming view of the river and adjacent hills. It was completed in October, 1863. It cost about $2,600. The last obligation against it was paid November 25, 1865.

On the 1st of June, 1870, John Buckley, the senior warden, died in the 85th year of his age. He had taken a warm interest in the church from its organization, contributing liberally towards erecting the present church and parsonage and served as warden and vestryman for over thirty years.

At the Easter election, in 1875, Rev. Akerly gave notice of his intention of relinquishing his charge. At a vestry meeting, held the 22d of May, he sent in his resignation, to take effect on the 19th of June. Rev. Akerly's services in the parish commenced even before the death of Rev. Hawksley, for whom he frequently read the service, and from that time to the present he had faithfully served the church as lay reader, deacon and priest, and for seventeen years had been their faithful rector, leaving the parish entirely free from all pecuniary obligation. The resignation was accepted with a vote of thanks for his faithful ministration.

On Sunday afternoon, June 13th, 1875, he took leave of his congregation, many of whom were unable to restrain their tears. On Saturday, June 26th, he and his family sailed for Europe, intending to remain abroad several years.

Rev. Geo. Waters, D. D., of Kingston, succeeded Rev. Akerly, entering on his duties the 5th of Sept., 1875. His family retaining their residence in Kingston, he was unable to devote his entire time to the parish. He resigned his charge, to take effect on the first of July, but consented to remain until the place could be supplied. The resignation was received with very great reluctance by every member of the vestry.

A vestry meeting held the 14th of October, 1876, unamimously elected the Rev. John W. Buckmaster, of Elizabethtown, N. J., rector of the parish. He entered on his duties 1st of November, 1877.

Wardens and Vestrymen of Christ Church, Marlborough, from the organization of the parish, February 26, 1837 to 1887.

Church Wardens—Edward Armstrong, Miles J. Fletcher.

Vestrymen—Thomas Fyfe, William Cushion, Dennis H. Doyle, Leonard S. Carpenter, David E. Fowler, Joseph Hepworth, Andrew Oddy, Richard R. Fowler.

These gentlemen organized the parish and were the first vestry:

Edward Armstrong, served as warden for 1837 and '38. Died 1840.

Miles J. Fletcher, warden for 1837 and vestryman from 1838-'41 to 1843 '56. Died 1870.

Thomas Fyfe, vestryman from 1837 to '39, inclusive. Returned to England. Died 1867.

William Cushion, vestryman 1837 and '38. Returned to England.

Dennis H. Doyle, vestryman 1837 to '40. Died 1844.

Leonard S. Carpenter, vestryman 1837, warden 1838 to '47; again warden from 1859 to '74. Died 1875.

David E. Fowler, vestryman from 1837 to '40, and '43 to '48. Died 1879.

Joseph Hepworth, vestryman 1837 and '38. Warden 1839 to '56; again vestryman from 1866 to 1875.

Andrew Oddy, vestryman 1837 to 1856, warden 1857 and '58, vestryman '59. Removed to Connecticut.

Richard R. Fowler, vestryman 1837, again 1841 to 1845.

James Carpenter, vestryman 1838 to '41 '44-'49-'51, 1856 to 1874, warden form 1875 to '87.

Dennis D. Purdy, vestryman 1839 to '42.

Gabriel Merritt, vestryman 1840 to '47, warden 1848 to '53. Died 1853.

Josiah W. Carpenter, vestrymen 1841 to '43. Died.

Frederick Flagler, vestryman 1842, again '57-'58.

John Buckley, vestryman 1842 to '53, warden '54 to 1870. Died 1870.

Benjamin Oddy, vestryman 1846 to '50. Died 1861.

Henry H. Holden, vestryman 1848 to '49.

John Hepworth, vestryman 1849. Died 1853.

John Hoffenden, vestryman 1849 to '51.

Andrew McElrath, vestryman. 1854 and '55.

John W. Barrian, vestryman 1859 and '60.

Nathaniel H. DuBois, vestryman 1854, 1876 to '78.

Ephenetus R. Woolsey, vestryman 1862.

John L. Wygant, vestryman 1864 and '65.

John A. Hepworth, vestryman 1876 to '78.

Daniel Barnes, vestryman 1876 and '77.

Gabriel Merritt, jr., vestryman 1849 to '53.

Samuel M. Akerly, vestryman 1855 to '58.

John W. Armstrong, vestryman 1854 to '63. Died 1870.

Gouveneur Armstrong, vestryman 1864 to '75.

William H. Armstrong, vestryman 1872 to '79, warden 1884 to '87.

D. Maitland Armstrong, vestryman 1878 and '87.

John Buckley, jr., vestryman 1850 to '59, 1876 to '87.

William F. Buckley, vestryman 1875.

William Kelly, vestryman 1850 to 1861. Died 1870.

Marcus D. Kelly, vestryman 1868 to 79, '87, 1861.

James S. Knapp, M. D., vestryman 1852 to 79. Died 1879.

Philip A. Passman, vestryman 1857 to 1871.

Christopher Champlin, vestryman 1859 to 1874.

Isaac Conklin, vestryman 1839 to '48, 1860 to '66. Died.

Wm. Smith Wright, vestryman, '60 to '65. Died '65

William A. Husted, vestryman 1870 and 71, warden '72 to '75.

Rufus R. Skeel, vestryman 1861 to '63.

Charles M. Purdy, vestryman 1863 to '67, 1875 to '87.

Edward Jackson, vestryman 1867 to '75, warden '76 to '79, vestryman '80 to '87.

Charles W. Jackson, vestryman 1879-87

John Storer, vestryman 1879 to '85

George S. Clark, vestryman 1880 to '87.

Oct. 14, 1876, the present rector, Rev. John W. Buckmaster, of Elizabethtown, N. J., was chosen to the parish. He officiates also at All Saints' Church, Milton. His ministrations have been productive of a great deal of good.

James Carpenter became a vestryman of the church in 1838, serving several terms. In 1875 he became a warden. He was also church treasurer for some years, serving the church in all about 44 years. He died the present summer, full of years and full of honor.

ALL SAINTS' CHURCH, MILTON,

was organized in 1850 by Rev. Samuel Hawksley, of Christ Church, as previously stated. Rev. Dr. Brown, of Newburgh, officiated at the laying of the corner stone May 30, 1854, and Bishop Horatio Potter held the consecration service in October, 1859. It has always been in the care of the rector at Marlborough. The first wardens were Wm. H. Gedney and Lee Ensign, the vestrymen Jacob Handley, David Sands, jr., James T. Knapp, Jacob Rowley, jr., Edgar D. Gillis, Smith Wood, jr., L. Harrison Smith and Rich'd Gee.

MARLBOROUGH METHODIST CHURCH.

The history of Methodism in Marlborough has not been properly preserved. Away back in 1798 Luff Smith was a leader in the Marlborough class of the Newburgh circuit. Irregular gatherings were held here from that time to 1825, when the erection of a church building was agitated, and the old frame church on Main street subsequently built and used until 1867, when it was disposed of to the Catholic church in Marlborough, while the Methodists occupied the new church on Grand street, built by them in that year.

Two certificates of incorporation have been issued for this society, one in 1830, the other in 1860. The first one is dated Oct. 20, and the meeting was held in the village school house, James H. Longbotham and Barnabas M. Mapes being inspectors of the election of trustees, who were chosen as follows: Samuel Beebe, James H. Longbotham, Josiah Lockwood, B. M. Mapes and Charles Merritt. The instrument was sworn to before Justice A. D. Soper. The second certificate was executed June 11, 1860, before Justice Isaac Staples. L. W. Walsworth and Enoch Baxter were the inspectors, the trustees chosen being Morey Wygant, Enos Reynolds, John H. Baxter, Washburn Baxter, M. L. Masten, Daniel Decker, David L. Wygant, John C. Rose and Benjamin Rose.

Charles Merritt was the first superintendent of the Sunday school connected with this church, so far as can be ascertained. When the new building was completed, in 1867, Charles D. Brower was the first superintendent. Next came David L. Wygant, who had previously been assistant. George M. Bambart was the next superintendent in 1874. W. H. Reynolds in 1875, Rev. J. B. Hermance in 1876, A. M. Osborn in 1877, and James S. Carpenter in 1878 until the present time.

The church's first organ was procured in 1867, and the organists have been Nettie Osterhoudt, Addie White, Martha Wygant, May Barnes and Hattie Kniffin.

The secretaries of the new church have been W. H. Purdy, James S. Carpenter, W. R. Greiner, W. S. Barnes and Wm. Palmer.

Milton Methodist Church.

Nov. 16, 1812, the Milton M. E. Society was incorporated, the original trustees being Thomas Woolsey, Uriah Coffin, Richard I. Woolsey, Henry Woolsey and Jacob Dayton. The certificate was sworn to before Justice David Staples. The society was only a station in a large circuit until 1858, since which time the pastors have been: 1858–59, D. W. C. Van Gaasbeck; '60, J. A. Edwards; '61–62, J. W. Smith; '63, N. Hunt; '64–65, E. S. Osbon; '66–67, J. Craft; '68–69, D. Phillips; '70–72, P. C. Oakley; '73–74, H. Wood; '75, F. D. Adams; '76–77, C. Palmer; '78, E. H. Roys; '79, J. L. G. McKown, died and year finished by H. Jackson; '80–82, C. C. Miller; '83–85, C. F. Wixon; '86–87, C. H. Snedeker.

The officers of the church in 1887 are: Trustees, Jesse Lyons, J. M. Purdy. Jesse Lester, Jas. H. Crook, Isaac Conklin. Stewards, Jesse Lyons, Jesse Lester, Lewis Bloomer, J. H. Crook, Ethan Parrott, Griggs Rhoades, J. T. Marno, J. M. Purdy, James Clark. Sunday school superintendent, Earl Stone; asst., Ensign Lyons.

Rev. P. C. Oakley, aged 87, has been spiritual father to the village for the past seventeen years, and still possesses full vigor of mind, keeping well abreast of all leading questions of the time.

The church has 100 members, 25 probationers, and 130 Sunday school scholars.

The church building was put up at the time the society was organized in 1812. It has been enlarged and remodeled several times, and is undergoing improvements the present year.

Like the Marlborough church, this society obtained a second certificate of incorporation. It was executed March 18, 1845, the trustees chosen at that time being James A. Disbrow, Isaac L. Craft, James Blockledge, Jacob H. Gillis, and Remos Woolsey.

ROMAN CATHOLIC CHURCHES IN MARLBOROUGH

AND MILTON.

There is no old history connected with the Roman Church in this town. The original settlers of the place were Protestants, and only during recent years has the Catholic body become established here. Now there are two places of worship, at Marlborough village in the old Methodist structure on Main street, which has been rearranged and placed in neat condition; and at Milton in a pretty little church. Alongside the latter is the parsonage, occupied by Rev. James F. Mee, who has charge of both churches. The Church flourishes and grows here, and holds annual fairs and picnics, which are largely attended by all denominations.

MILTON PRESBYTERIAN CHURCH.

The Presbyterian Church of Milton was organized July 12tn, 1841, and the church building was erected during the same year. At the outset there were twenty members, of whom fifteen joined by letter from the church at Marlborough. Rev. M. F. Liebenan was installed pastor of the churches of Lloyd and Milton Oct. 28th, 1841. He remained two years and was succeeded by Rev. W. K. Platt, who also remained two years. The pulpit was supplied by several ministers (among whom was Rev. Sumner K. Mandeville, for twenty years pastor of the Presbyterian church of La Grange, Dutchess county) until March, 1849, when Rev. M. F. Liebenan returned and continued to preach until March 31st, 1867, thus ministering here more than twenty years in all.

He was succeeded by Rev. E. W. Clarke, who had established a boarding and day school in the village, and who preached until Rev. J. H. Myers, D. D., became the minister, April 1st, 1868, remaining until the winter of 1871. Rev. B. F. Wilde followed, remaining until 1876. After him Rev. Duncan C. Niven occupied the pulpit until the spring of 1884, when the church was again served by Rev. E. W. Clarke with others. In April, 1885, Rev. Wm. G. Westervelt came to Milton. April 28th, 1886, he was installed pastor, being the first pastor to serve the Milton church exclusively. The church has enjoyed several seasons of revival, and steadily added to its membership. At present (1887) there are seventy-four members. Financially, for its size, the church has always been strong. During 1886–7, the interior has been redecorated and a fine parsonage property purchased, while the spiritual interests of the church have been greatly advanced.

THE MILTON SOCIETY OF FRIENDS.

The Society of Friends have held meetings at Milton for at least one hundred years. The meetings were first held at the house of Edward Hallock, a minister. In 1789 seven acres of land were bought on the west side of the main road,

a short distance north of the school house, district No. 2.
A meeting-house was built there and occupied for fifteen
years, when it became too small, and in 1804 it was sold and
a new lot bought on the same road further north.   There a
suitable large meeting house was built and occupied until
1828, when, differences of belief having crept in, the church
divided.   The Orthdox Friends being in the minority, left
the meeting-house in possession of the Hicksite Friends.

The number of Friends being now very small, the meeting
was held for two years at the house of Foster Hallock (now
the property of E. W. Watson).

In 1830 the Friends bought a lot of land of Foster
Hallock, and built a new meeting house, which, though it
has been repaired and modified at different times, has done
good service for fifty-seven years.   It had become so much
the worse for wear that in 1886 it was thought best to build
new, and also to change the site nearer the village.   A lot of
land was purchased of James H. Barrett's estate, and a new
meeting-house built, which looks very different from those
erected years ago.   It was opened on the 22d of 5th month,
1887, with appropriate dedicatory services.

Samuel and Anna Adams were ministers who resided in
this vicinity in the early part of this century, and labored
faithfully for the upbuilding of the church here, and also in
many other places.   Hannah P. Fry, a minister of more recent date, will be remembered by many as having served well
her day and generation.

Stephen Taber, also a minister, has attended this meeting
over forty years and is still zealous for the prosperity of the
church.

During the past few years several ministers from other
places have resided here for a short time, their service adding
much to the interest and welfare of the meeting.   Among
these are George Wood, Jesse McPherson and P. Adelbert
Wood, the latter being here at present.   Of late years the
Society of Friends have changed very much the mode of
conducting their meeting.   Singing has now a recognized
place in their worship, and much zeal is shown by a large

proportion of their members in carrying the "good news" of the Gospel to those outside. Within the past fifteen years the number of Friends in Milton has increased more rapidly than at any time previous. There are now about one hundred members of this church, including children.

Knights of Pythias.

Guiding Star Lodge, No. 199, K. of P., of Marlborough, N. Y., was instituted in November, 1883, by John F. Vannort, Grand Chancellor State of N. Y. H. Scott Corwin was the first Chancellor Commander. The Lodge has grown steadily to the present time. For several years they have given annual picnics, which have become very popular. The members are united and harmonious. The present officers of the lodge (May, 1887) are C. E., J. W. Badner; V. C., Harrison Berrian; K. R. of S., W. W. Mackey; P., Joseph Conklin; M. of F., H. S. Corwin; M. of E., F. A. Wright; M. A., William Henderson; I. G., John Lent; O. G., Sherwood Staples; P. C.'s, H. S. Corwin, James Shaw, Wm. H. Newman, W. I. Staples. Geo. A. Badner. The other members are T. F. Kniffin, Moses McMullen, John Galaway, Ira Staples, Wm. McElrath, Wm. Wilklow, John Gladhill, H. H. Baxter, C. W. Jackson, A. B. Masten, G. M. Phillips, John Morehead, J. W. Baxter, Wm. H. McCullough, John Anderson, D. J. Scott, A. Lyons, M. V. B. Morgan, C. DeGraff, Lyman W. DuBois, F. M. Cronk, J. O. Mackey, Henry H. Case, Wm. P. Drake, Ellsworth Berrian, Wm. G. Penny, Edwin W. Barnes, I. S. Rhodes, G. B. Sheldon, P. A. Rion, Thomas Carroll. The lodge is recognized as one of the permanent institutions of Marlborough, and is destined to continue in existence many years.

Advance Lodge of Odd Fellows.

On the afternoon and evening of January 18, 1882, Advance Lodge, No. 490, I. O. of O. F., was instituted in Marlborough, by D. D. G. M., Wm. Prull, of the Ulster and Delaware District, acting as Grand Master, assisted by D. D. G. M., Schofield, of Dutchess District, acting as D. D. G. M.; Past Grand Van Bramer, of Kosciusko Lodge, of Kingston, as G. Sec.; Past Grand Farrar, of No. 18, as G. Treas.; Past Grand Morehouse, of No. 18, as G. Warden; Past Grand Walter Goring, of No. 18, as G. Marshal; Past Grand Wm. Truesdall as G. Inner Guard. The original officers of the lodge, elected and installed on same date, were James Shaw, N. G.; L. McMullen, V. G.; C. W. Frost, R. S.; Clarence Bingham, P. S.; John Rusk, T. At the initiatory ceremonies, and conferring of white, blue, and scarlet degrees, the members of Acme Lodge, No. 469, of Newburgh, assisted.

This lodge which started out with only nine members now numbers over sixty, including many of the influential men of the town. Invitations to its public gatherings are eagerly sought after. The spirit of the membership is full of brotherly kindness and fraternal feeling.

KETCHAM POST, NO. 495, G. A. R.

In August, 1884, Ketcham Post was organized in Marlborough, as a result of the efforts of Hon. C. M. Woolsey, J. C. Merritt, Rev. S. P. Gallaway, C. W. Frost, P. V. L. Purdy, George A. Donaldson, R. Osterhoudt, R. H. Rose, Henry Scott, R. F. Coutant, A. B. Masten and others. The Post took its name from the brothers Edward H. and John T. Ketcham, sons of David Ketcham, who gave their lives for their country, one at Gettysburg, the other in the notorious Libby Prison.

Members of Pratt Post, of Kingston, and Le Fevre Post, of Highland, assisted in the organization of Ketcham Post, and the occasion was made a gala day by the people of Marlborough. At least two thousand people assembled in and near the flag pole at the centre, to hear the speeches. A subscription of $100 was raised to feed the visitors.

Hon. C. Meech Woolsey was the first commander of the Post, and Peter V. L. Purdy now fills that position. The Post annually takes charge of the work of decorating the graves of the deceased soldiers, fifteen of whom lie buried within the limits of the town. They also exercise a care over sick and unfortunate old soldiers, whether members of the Grand Army or not.

The Post holds its meetings each Thursday night, in Good Templars' hall. The membership is not large, and is made up of men from different sections and different companies, no company having been raised in Marlborough, although the town furnished about 175 soldiers for the late war. The Post often holds bean bakes and social gatherings, which are very popular.

MARLBOROUGH'S LODGE OF GOOD TEMPLARS.

March 11th, 1881, the Marlborough, New York, Lodge, No. 351, Independent Order of Good Templars, of the village of Marlborough, was founded. The charter members were Rev. Duncan C. Niven, L. P. Smith, Mrs. L. P. Smith, S. W. Stilwell, Rev. W. T. Brush, Mrs. C. Hanford, Mrs. I. E. Ostram, Miss Olivia Merritt, Mrs. B. F. Bailey, Mary C. Wygant, Mrs. Carrie C. Carpenter, Josephine Carpenter, Benjamin Bailey, Mrs. J. F. Kniffin, M. V. B. Morgan, Mrs. M. V. B. Morgan, E. J. Merritt, W. R. Greiner, John Bloomer, H. Scott Corwin, Jas. S. Carpenter, W. H. Purdy, Enoch Baxter, Benjamin Baxter, Rosa Kniffin, C. D. Bloomer, James O. Mackey, K. D. L. Niven, Lizzie Wygant, Mrs. Melissa M. Woolsey, Mrs. Susan Dobbs, Charles H. Woolsey, J. C. Dobbs, Wm. S. Barnes, Valentine Dobbs. One hundred and eighty-four members have been initiated during the six years of the lodge's history. The highest number on the roll at one time was one hundred and five. When first organized Marlborough lodge met in Hudler's building, later in Shaw's building on King street, and now in Kniffin's block, occupying the hall, which is named after the organization, Good Templars hall.

The first Worthy Chief Templar was Rev. W. T. Brush, Rev. D. C. Niven being Lodge Deputy.

The Good Templars have done a good work in Marlborough, redeeming a number from the thraldom of appetite, and leading many in the path of total abstinence. Though not a beneficial organization the members have more than once extended a fraternal hand to unfortunate members, in one instance contributing $50 to the relief of a member of the lodge in Milton.

Prominent among those members who have stood by the lodge through thick and thin, from its inception to the present time, may be mentioned S. W. Stilwell, Linus P. Smith and wife, Mrs. J. F. Kniffin, E. J. Merritt and Mrs. Alice Stone. Others have done valuable work at different times, and deserve a share of the credit of building up the Order in Marlborough.

PROPERTY HOLDERS.

The following list of the more prominent residents of the town of Marlborough in 1871, was taken from a directory of Ulster County printed in Syracuse in that year. The figures indicate the number of acres of land owned by each.

Akerly, Samuel M. Rev., Marl., pastor of Episcopal Church.
Alberson, John, Marl. ferryman and mail carrier.
Anderson, Edward D., Mil., harness maker.
    "   Francis T., Marl., farmer 22.
    "   John, Mil., fruit raiser.
    "   William, Mil., farmer, leases of Griggs Rhoades, 80.
Archer, George, Marl., machinist.
Armstrong, R. S. Mil., prop. of Milton Iron Works.
Atherton, Charles, Mil., fruit raiser 2½.
Atkinson, Benjamin D., Middle Hope, Orange Co., farmer 75.
Badner, John, Marl. groceries, dry goods and ready-made clothing.
Bailey, Anthony W., Marl., undertaker and fruit raiser.
    "   Elias, Mil., wheelwright.
    "   James, Marl., carpenter.
Baker, Frederick, Marl., farmer 66.
Ball, John B., Mil., fruit raiser 6.
Barnhart, George, Marl., farmer 47.
Barnhart, Jeremiah, Marl., farmer 26.
Barrett, James H., Mil., rectifier of cider, fruit raiser and farmer 84.
Barry, James, Marl., farmer 4½.
Barry, Patrick, Marl., berry raiser 5.
Baxter, Enoch, Marl., farmer 60.
Baxter, John H., Marl., postmaster and dealer in dry goods, groceries, &c.
Baxter, Washburn, Marl., farmer 53.
Berean, Daniel, Marl., fruit raiser 22.
    "   Matthew, Marl., farmer 24.
    "   Samuel, Marl., farmer 126.
Bernard, John, Marl., painter.
Berrian, John W., Mil., farmer 175.
Bilyou, William R., Marl., cooper.
Bingham, Daniel, Marl., farmer 7½.

Birdsall, Andrew, Mil., farmer 15.
Birdsall, Hosea, U. S. steamship inspector.
Bloom, Mary L. Mrs., Marl., fruit raiser 2½.
Bloomer, Cornelius D-, Marl., farmer 140.
" Thomas D., Marl., farmer 80.
Brower, Charles D., Marl., fruit raiser 2½.
Brower, James I. Mrs., " fruit raiser 3.
Brower, William H., " boatman.
Brown, Charles, " farmer and berry raiser 13.
" Daniel M., " berry raiser 1.
" Joseph, Mil., farmer 15.
" Thomas, Marl., farmer 50.
" William, Mil., shoemaker.
Buckley, Margaret Miss, Marl., *(with Mercy T.,)* farmer 60.
Buckley, Mercy T. Miss, " *(with Margaret,)* farmer 60.
Buckley, Thomas T., " merchant and farmer 80.
Carmichael, Hugh, Middle Hope, Orange Co , carpenter and farmer 60.
Carpenter, Celia Mrs., Marl., fruit raiser 1.
" James, " dealer in groceries.
" Leonard S., " farmer 150.
" Peter M., Mil., farmer 23.
" Selleck, Highland, machinist and farmer 86.
" William, Mil., surveyor and farmer 84.
Caverly, Jonathan, Mil., commissioner of highways and farmer 14.
Caverly, Lewis N., Marl., farmer 40.
Caverly, Luther P., Mil., farmer 125.
Champlin, Christopher, Mil., farmer 50.
Chatterton, James I. Mrs., Marl., farmer 18.
Clack, Robert, Marl., farmer 14.
Clark, Augustus G., Marl., fruit raiser 40.
Clark, Francis T., " drover and farmer 100.
" Jeremiah, " farmer 100.
" J. Oscar, Mil., farmer 111.
" Smith M., Marl., farmer 2½.
" William S., " manuf. of slate flour for roofing, fruit raiser
and farmer 7.
Clearwater, Ansom, Highland, farmer 40.
Coe, Isaac D., Mil., farmer 88.
Coffin, Susan Miss, Mil., summer boarding house and farmer.
Col. Pratt House, Mil., Jayhu Dayton, prop.
Conklin, Anna M. Mrs., Marl., grist mill and farmer 145.
Conner, Charles H., Mil., stoves and tinware.
Cooper, Charles W. Rev., Marl., pastor of Presbyterian Church.
Corwin, Samuel, Marl., dry goods and groceries.
Cosman, D. H., " farmer leases 43.
Covert, Cornelius W., Marl., farmer 98.
Covert, Oliver, Marl., miller and fruit raiser 15.
Craft, D. C., " farmer 75.

Craft, ——,   "   Lyons and Craft.
Cronk, Henry, Mil., farmer 200.
Crook, James H., Mil., grocer, freight agent and town clerk.
Crosby, Ebenezer,   "   farmer 2.
Crosby, Levi,   "   blacksmith and farmer 55.
Crough, Patrick, Marl., mason.
Daugherty, Wm. John, Newburgh, Orange Co., brick maker and far-
        mer 9.
Davis, Ferris G., Mil., fruit raiser 1.
Davis, Isaac S.,   "   farmer 4.
Dayton, Jayhu,   "   prop. of Col. Pratt House.
    "   Morgan A., Mil., farmer 200.
    "   Quimby, Marl., farmer 115.
    "   Thomas R., Mil., farmer.
Decker, Daniel, Marl., berry raiser 1.
Degroodt, Arthur,   "   blacksmith and farmer 3.
Denike, Underhill,   "   farmer 2.
Devoe, David, Mil., farmer 180.
Dickey, Robert J., Mil., druggist and notary public.
Dingee, Enoch, Marl., farmer 50.
Drake, Isaac,   "   fruit grower 4½.
DuBois, Asa,   "   farmer 70.
    "   Charles W., Marl., fruit raiser 1.
    "   Edward,   "   fruit raiser and farmer 150.
    "   Edward P.,   "   farmer 50.
    "   Hudson,   "   fruit raiser 3.
    "   James,   "   carpenter.
    "   John,   "   carpenter and constable.
    "   John D.,   "   farmer 39.
    "   Nathaniel H.,   "   retired farmer.
    "   Philip,   "   farmer 5.
    "   Simon,   "   berry raiser 7.
    "   William,   "   farmer 70.
Exchange Hotel,   "   S. H. Kniffin, prop.
Farmers' Hotel,   "   Mrs. Sarah McMullen, prop.
Ferguson, John, Mil., farmer 80.
Ferguson, John D., Marl., farmer 49.
Fisher, John C.,   "   carpenter and farmer.
Fletcher, Oscar B.,   "   farmer 22.
Foster, George,   "   farmer 20.
Fowler, Seymour,   "   farmer 95.
Frederick, Peter, Mil., farmer 1.
Gedney, William H., Mil., physician and farmer 140.
Gerow, Isaac H., Marl., farmer 258.
Gibbons, Edward, Mil., farmer 52.
Goehringer, William H., Marl., carriage trimmer and harness maker.
Greaves, Joseph, Marl., manuf. of dye stuff and farmer 27.
Grimley, J. I., Marl., fruit raiser 20.

Hadley, J. T., Mil., steward of steamer *St. John.*
Hagerty, John, Mil., farmer 130.
Hall, Benson, Marl., farmer 5.
Hallock, George, Mil., fruit raiser and farmer 50.
    "   Isaac S.,   "   prop. of cider mill and farmer 90.
    "   Nathaniel,"   prop. of grist mill and cider mill, and far-
            mer 200.
    "   Phebe Mrs., Mil., farmer 5.
    "   Sarah H. Mrs., Mil., summer boarding house and farmer 4.
Halstead, Phebe, Mrs., Marl., farmer 7.
Handley, Jacob, Mil., farmer 10.
Harcourt, Eli, Marl., farmer 255.
    "   Emma Mrs., Mil., farmer 40.
    "   John W., Mil., farmer, 109.
Hardenburgh, William, Marl., farmer 5.
Harper, Sidney M. Mrs., Mil., farmer 40.
Harris, Charles, Marl., shoemaker and manuf. of essences.
Harris, Isaac L., Newburgh, Orange Co., farmer 60.
Hasbrouck, Solomon E., Marl., homeo. physician.
Haverly, John,   "   berry raiser 7.
Haviland, James,   "   pattern maker and farmer 35.
Hengstebeck, Capt.,   "   prop. paper mill.
Hirst, Jonathan,   "   farmer 50.
Holmes, Elizabeth Mrs., Mil., fruit raiser 18.
Howell, Walter D., Marl., farmer 60.
Hull, Oliver C., Mil., farmer 5.
Hulse, Charles, Marl., (Hulse & Rhoads,) farmer 7½.
Hulse, George E.,   "   fruit raiser and farmer 59.
Hulse & Rhoads,   "   (Charles Hulse and Isaiah Rhoads,) farmer 10.
Husted, W. A.,   "   farmer 30.
Hyde, Sylvan Mrs., "   farmer 3.
Jackson, Charles D. "   butcher.
Jackson, Elisha P., "   meat market
Kaley, Michael, Mil., farmer 60.
Kaley, Michael,   "   fruit raiser 6.
Kelley, James,   "   farmer 25.
Kelley, Robert B., Marl., saloon keeper.
Kenney John, Mil., fruit raiser 8.
Kent, Oliver P., Mil., farmer and fruit raiser 100.
Kerr, Robert A., Marl., farmer 120.
King, George, Mil., looking glass and picture frame maker.
Knapp, James S., Marl., allo. physician, justice of the peace, loan com-
        missioner and farmer 30.
Kniffin, DeWitt W., Marl., manuf. of berry cups and berry raiser.
Kniffin, S. H.,   "   prop. of Exchange Hotel.
Lawson, George W., "   fruit raiser and farmer 60.
Lawson, John E.,   "   fruit raiser 50.
Lent, Sylvanus,   "   farmer 6.

Lester, Jesse W., Mil., farmer 6.
Lockwood, Charles A., Marl., (with Mary Ann).
" 	Eli T., Marl., farmer 65.
" 	John S., Marl., (with Mary Ann).
" 	Mary Ann Mrs., Marl., farmer 45.
Lounsbury, Rowland R., Mil., farmer 73.
Lyons & Craft, Marl., (Jesse W. Lyons and —— Craft,) manufs. of
 	felloes.
Lyons, Jesse W., Mil., (Lyons & Craft) supervisor and farmer 140.
Lyons, William H., Marl., farmer 97.
Mabie, Lewis, Mil., farmer 15.
Mackey, Carmine, Marl., (Mackey & Ventres.)
" 	Daniel S., Marl., farmer 1.
" 	Daniel W., Marl., farmer 20.
" 	Hiram H., Mil., fruit raiser 1.
" 	Isaac L., 	" 	farmer 80.
" 	James Ostrom, Marl., teamster and farmer.
" 	Smith, Mil., farmer 1½.
" 	Thorn M., Mil., farmer 80.
" 	& Ventres, Marl., (Carmine Mackey and David B. Ventres,)
 	manufs. of berry cups.
" 	Wm. Wesley, Marl., cattle dealer and farmer 680.
Maher, Jeremiah, 	" 	farmer 42.
Marston, Hannah Mrs., 	" 	farmer 1½.
Martin, William, Mil., farmer 118.
Masten, Matthew L., Marl., farmer 84.
Matthews, Joseph, 	" 	farmer 60.
McCale, Anthony, 	" 	farmer leases of Eli Harcourt 50.
McCarty, Cornelius, 	" 	berry raiser 3.
McCarty, James, 	" 	farmer 10
McConnell, Francis, 	" 	assessor, farmer 14 and leases 80.
" 	Philip D., 	" 	(with William.)
" 	William, 	" 	farmer 28.
McCullough, Wm. H., 	" 	wagon maker.
McElrath, John, 	" 	carpenter and farmer 45.
McElrath, Thomas, 	" 	farmer 52.
McGowen, James, Mil., farmer 4.
McManus, Peter, 	" 	farmer 6
McMillan, Wm. J., 	" 	stoves and tinware.
McMullen, Sarah Mrs., Marl., proprietor of Farmers Hotel.
Merritt, Henry, 	" 	farmer 100.
" 	James D., 	" 	farmer 50.
" 	Wygant, 	" 	farmer 100.
Millard, J. P. & Brother, " 	(Samuel N.) freighters, forwarders and
 	dealers in lumber and coal.
" 	Samuel N., Marl., (J. P. Millard & Brother,) farmer 1.
Miller, Abraham, Mil., manuf. of boots and shoes.
" 	Christopher Jacob, Mil., hair dresser and dealer in cigars.

Milton Iron Works,   Mil., R. S. Armstrong, prop.
Moore, Edwin,   "   farmer 45.
Morgan, Gideon B., Marl., farmer 90.
Murray, Elizabeth Mrs., Mil., farmer 56.
Myers, J. H. Rev.,   ,   "   pastor Presbyterian Church.
Nevin, Samuel, Marl., blacksmith.
Newman, John, Mil., manuf. of wheelbarrows.
Nicklin, William, Marl., lithographer and fruit raiser 20.
Northrip, Emma Mrs., Mil., farmer 28.
Northip. C. S.,   "   farmer 30.
Norton, James, Marl., farmer 44.
Oakley, Peter C. Rev., Mil., pastor M. E. Church.
O'Connor, Patrick,   "   farmer 92.
Ordway, Charles T.,   "   carriage and sleigh maker and farmer 2.
Ostrander, Wm. Rev., Marl, pastor M. E. Church.
Ostrom, James I. Rev., Marl., retired Presbyterian clergyman.
Palmer, Henry, Mil., farmer 108.
Park, Jesse K., Marl., inventor and manuf. of tracing paper, engineer-
             ing cloth and telegraph paper.
Parmalee, William L., Marl., carpenter.
Parrott, Ethan, Mil., postmaster and general merchant.
Parrott, George, "   saloon.
Parrott, M. E.,   "   dentist.
Patchin, Richard H., (Newburgh, Orange Co.,) farmer 120.
Patten, Eugene F., Mil., meat market.
Peck, Wm. M., Marl., farmer 15.
Pembrook, Isaiah B., Marl., carpenter and fruit raiser 1.
Perkins, Friend W., Mil., (R. D. Perkins & Son.)
Perkins, R. D. & Son, " (Richard D. and Friend W.,) cooperage.
Perkins, Richard D , "   (R. D. Perkins & Son.)
Phillips, Oscar, Marl., farmer 7.
Plumsted, Chas. D., " farmer leases 70.
Plumsted, Henry,   "   farmer 1.
Porter, Henry B.,(Newburgh, Orange Co.)banking clerk and farmer 10.
Porter, John B., Marl , farmer 26.
Poyer, Benjamin, "   farmer 75.
Purdy, Adolphus G., Marl., engineer.
    "   Dennis D.,   "   farmer 50.
    "   George W.,   "   farmer 90.
    "   Hackaliah,   "   farmer 98.
    "   Isaac,   Mil , cooperage.
    "   John M., "   cooper.
    "   Sylvanus, Marl., farmer 50.
    "   William H , "   mechanic.
    "   William J. " commissioner of highways and fruit raiser 30.
Quick, E. Miss, Mil., farmer 15.
Quick, Mary Eliza Mrs., Marl., farmer 27.
Quimby, James, Marl., teamster and fruit raiser 7,

Quimby, John C. Marl., (with Samuel L.,) farmer 55.
Quimby, Samuel L., Marl., (with John C.,) farmer 55.
Rand, Arminda Mrs., (Newburgh, Orange Co.,) farmer 40.
Ransley, James, Mil., fruit raiser and farmer 16.
Ransley, Wm. S., " (with James.)
Rein, John, " ferryman to Poughkeepsie.
Reynolds, Charles B., Marl., fruit raiser and farmer leases 40.
Reynolds, Charles E., " assessor.
Reynolds, Enos, " farmer 24.
Reynolds, Isaac, " farmer 35.
Rhoades, Elijah R., Mil., wheelbarrow manuf.
 " Elizabeth, Mrs., Mil., resident.
 " Jonah, Mil., farmer 15.
 " Lorenzo C., Mil., farmer 3.
Rhodes, Benjamin W., " farmer leases of Mrs. Harriet, 75.
 " Isaiah, Marl., (Hulse & Rhodes,) farmer 7½.
 " James K., " farmer 2.
 " Lewis G., Mil., farmer 32.
 " John L., " farmer 17.
Roe, Benjamin, " fruit raiser 3½.
Roe, Benjamin F., " (P. W. & B. F. Roe.)
Roe, Peter W., " (P. W. & B. F. Roe.)
Roe, P. W. & B. F., " (Peter W. and Benj. F.,) carpenters and
 builders.
Roe, William, Mil., steward of boat Mary Powell.
Rose, Benjamin A., Marl., fruit grower and farmer 50.
Rose, John C., " retired farmer 1.
Rose, Reuben H., " farmer 27½.
Rowley, Daniel, Mil., livery stable.
 " Daniel, " overseer of the poor and farmer 55.
 " Jacob, " groceries, boots and shoes.
Ryan, John, Marl., farmer 46.
Sands, David, " justice of the peace and collector of accounts.
Sands, David Mrs., Marl., fruit raiser 26.
Satterlee, N. B., " hair dresser.
Schultz, Isaac Mrs., " farmer 1.
Scofield, Edgar, Mil., fruit raiser 2.
Scott, D., Marl., (with James D.) farmer 49.
Scott, Henry, " farmer 4.
Scott, James D., Marl., (with D.,) farmer 49.
Sears, Sherburne, Mil., farmer 100.
Sears, Thomas, Marl., farmer 45.
Shaw, James, " stoves and tinware.
Sherman, Isaac, Mil., (with Townsend H.,) manuf. of cider and vinegar,
 and farmer 124.
Sherman, Townsend H., Mil., (with Isaac,) manuf. of cider and vinegar
 and farmer 124.
Sherow, David, Marl., farmer 2½.

Sherow, George, Marl., farmer 56.
Shorter, Benjamin W., Mil., farmer 100.
"   B. Wesley,   " school teacher and farmer.
"   William A.,   " school teacher and farmer.
Smith, Abiah, Marl., (with Hester E.,) farmer 10.
"   Abraham B., Marl., farmer 75.
"   Clark, Mil., manuf. of coffee and spice mills.
"   Daniel, Marl., farmer 77.
"   Evert V., Mil., fruit raiser 20.
"   Hester E., Marl., (with Abiah,) farmer 10.
"   Lewis, Highland, farmer 105.
"   L. Harrison, Mil., dealer in coal and lumber, and farmer 3.
Sommer, John, Marl., shoemaker.
Sparks, J. W. Rev., Mil., pastor Episcopal church.
Staples, Davis S. Marl., farmer 125.
"   Ira,   " saw mill.
"   Isaac,   " insurance and real estate agent, and farmer 8.
"   Jonathan M., Marl., farmer 7.
"   Samuel,   " farmer 200.
Stilwell, Samuel,   " farmer 17.
Stott, Charles E., Mil., druggist in New York.
Taber, Stephen,   " minister of Society of Friends and farmer 115.
Tanner, William, " prop. of Milton Hotel.
Taylor E. E. L., Rev., Marl., Secretary of Baptist Home Mission So-
      ciety and farmer 100.
Terwilliger, John S., Marl., farmer 85.
Thorn, Gershom,   " farmer 65.
Tooker, Charles,   " wagon maker and berry raiser 5.
Topping, Nathaniel S. " carriage maker and farmer 5.
Townsend, W. H. Mil., general merchant.
Tuthill, Sarah Mrs. " farmer 15.
Twoomey, Jeremiah, Marl., farmer 13.
Underwood, Daniel L., " carriage painter.
Vail, Dewitt C., Mil., farmer 100.
VanAmburgh, David E., Marl., butcher.
Van Fradenburgh, David Rev., Mil., Baptist clergyman.
Velie, Ezekiel, Marl., farmer 117.
Ventres, David B., " (Mackey & Ventres.)
Warren, Phebe A. Miss, Mil., farmer 48.
Warren, Stephen D., Marl., blacksmith.
Watson, Elias., Marl., farmer 40.
Watson, E. W., Mil., farmer 1½.
Whitmore, John, Marl., wagon maker.
Whitney, J. F. & Son, Mil., (Oliver B.) manufs. of veneer berry cups
      and baskets.
Whitney, Oliver B., Mil., (J. F. Whitney & Son.)
Williams, Nathaniel, " carpenter.
Williams, W. R., Rev., Marl., pastor of Baptist Church, New York,
      and farmer 100.

Winter, Adam, Marl., farmer leases of B. A. Rose, 5.
Wolley, William D., Mil., farmer 100.
Wood, Caleb, Mil., ferryman and mail carrier.
Woolsey, C. M., " lawyer, member of Assembly and farmer.
Woolsey, David W., Mil., farmer 160.
    "   Eli S.,   "   fruit nursery and farmer 3.
    "   John E., Marl., meat market.
    "   William H., Mil., school teacher and farmer 160.
Wright, N. W., Marl., miller.
Wygant, Asbury, R., Marl., farmer 150.
    "   Augustus   "   farmer 100.
    "   Charles D., Highland, farmer leases of Selleck Carpenter 86.
    "   Clemence, Marl., farmer 160.
    "   Cornelius,   "   farmer 50.
    "   Daniel,   "   farmer 91.
    "   David L..   " blacksmith.
    "   Dennis M.,   " (E. J. & D. M. Wygant.
    "   Edward J., " (E. J. & D. M.)
    "   E. J. & D. M., Marl., (Edward J. and Dennis M.,) fruit raisers
         and farmers 150.
    "   J. Ward, Marl., farmer 100.
    "   L. M., Mil., farmer 50.
    "   Martha J. Miss, Marl., (Misses M. & M. J. Wygant.)
    "   Mary Miss, Marl., (Misses M. & M. J. Wygant)
    "   M. & M. J. Misses, Marl., (Mary and Martha J.)
         dressmakers and milliners.
    "   Mory, Marl., farmer 115.
Young, Charles, Marl., (with Wm. C.,) fruit raiser.
    "   John, Mil., farmer 300.
    "   John H., Mil.. fruit raiser and farmer 100.
    "   Smith,   " farmer 140.
    "   William C., Marl., freight agent, fruit raiser and farmer 95.

DIRECTORY OF OLD RESIDENTS.

RESIDENTS NEAR MARLBOROUGH IN 1763 AND LATER.

The following is taken from an old history of the Town of Newburgh:

"Above Balmville lived Samuel Fowler, the father of Samuel Fowler (of Newburgh), the Methodist minister of the last generation, a very devout and pious man.

"Next were the fathers of Arthur Smith, Esq., and Jehiel Clark. Their fathers purchased their lands together at 17s 6d per acre, and divided.

"Next about these were Gilbert Purdy and Luff Smith. Some of the Purdy lands are owned by Mr. Wood, and lie in the village of Middle Hope. Within a few past years Timothy Wood has erected one of the most beautiful residences on this road. The farms that we have referred to were long and narrow, and generally ran through the patent east and west to the river.

"They are now in a fine state of agricultural improvement—very different in appearance from what they were at the time we speak of. They were located and improvements made on them by the settlers above named as early as from 1730 to 1750,—for at the first formation of the town, in 1763, these names appear on the records; and this district of the country seems then to have been quite populous. During the war Marlborough was quite a village, and some of the Whigs fled there from New York.

"The earliest deed we have seen for a purchase in the district we have been speaking of, was from William Elsworth, of the Precinct of the Highlands, to Samuel Stratton, of the same place, for one hundred and forty acres, dated in 1753. The deed was shown us by Mr. Samuel Clark, of Middle Hope, a descendant of Jehiel Clark, the first settler of that name, and now owns the lands. Mr. Elsworth was not a patentee, but a second-hand purchaser.

"Rossville must have been settled about the same time. This is in Wallace's Patent, which was small—only 1,900 acres. Joseph Penny purchased the whole patent and set-tled it chiefly with his children. He had seven sons—John, William, Robinson, Joseph, Peter, James, Allen, and a daughter, Nelly, who never married.

"Mr. Penny sold two hundred or three hundred acres to Robert Ross, the father of William and Alexander Ross. Mr. Ross was a tanner and shoemaker, and during the war conducted the business to some profit. He first built a house and then established his yard and shop. He subse-quently, and before the war, perhaps as early as 1760, built a stone house, which is still standing, and makes part of the present residence of Mr. Adderton, who owns the family residence. The yard was standing and vats open when Mr. Adderton took possession, since the death of Alexander Ross, and were filled up by him.

"We are informed that no part of the original purchase made by Mr. Penny is in the possession of his descendants. That by Mr. Ross has passed out of his family. If this is true, it is rather singular that so much land—a whole patent —and owned by an individual who had seven grown up sons to settle and cultivate it, should in one century have passed out of the possession of his descendants. We have not met with another case in the county.

"The ancestors of Daniel Tooker, Esq., and of Daniel Mer-ritt, Esq., in this vicinity, are among the oldest in this part of the town; their names are on the records at its early or-ganization. Both seem to have been active and influential men."

RESIDENTS FROM 1779 TO 1788.

From various records are reproduced the following names of old residents in 1779, whose descendants still live in Marl-borough or vicinity: David, Caleb and Josiah Merritt,

Henry Decker, Lewis DuBois, Isaac Cropsey, Adam Cropsey, John, Peter, Lewis and Thomas Quick. These lived
where the village of Marlborough now is, and to the west of
it.

In the vicinity of Milton village in 1779, lived the following: Nathaniel Harcourt, James and Nathaniel Quimby,
John Woolsey, John Young. Wright Carpenter, William
Lyons, Capt. Anning Smith, Jacob Wood, Edward Hallock,
jr., Samuel Hallock.

In and near Lattintown in 1779 lived Edward Hallock, sr.,
Nehemiah Smith, William, Richard, Noah and Jonathan
Woolsey.

In the western part of the precinct in 1779 were located
Leonard Smith, Elisha Purdy, Samuel Merritt, Jacob Canniff, Isaac Lockwood, Alexander Cropsey, Richard Carpenter, John, Philip and Peter Caverly, Joseph and Benjamin
Carpenter.

In 1788 Lewis DuBois was the largest land owner in Marlborough, his property comprising the present village and
some distance north and west. Caleb and Josiah Merritt
each owned a large number of acres south of Lewis DuBois.
Leonard Smith owned land on the Lattintown road. Luff
Smith had property in and west of Milton. John Hall,
Zadok and John Lewis, Isaac Rowley and Jacob Wood also
were landholders in that vicinity. Elijah Lewis owned a
dock and other property near Milton. On the Lattintown
road, south of where Clark's mill now is, Alexander Cropsey,
James Merritt, John Case and Humphrey Merritt each
owned good sized farms. South of them toward Newburgh
were the following property holders: Matthew, Thomas
and John Wygant, Isaac Lockwood and John Bond. Silas
Purdy owned the mill property where Clark & Son now are.
In the western part of the precinct John Hallock, Solomon Fowler, Abel Adams, Nathaniel Hull, sr., owned land.
In the southwest corner of the precinct Samuel Merritt held
a large extent of land. The Caverly's all owned land west
of Milton, John having the most. Leonard Smith, Nathaniel Kelsey and Job St. John had large holdings north of

Milton. Edward Hallock was a large landholder south of Milton.

In 1799 John J. E. Robart was the next largest landowner in the southern part of the precinct to Lewis DuBois. His property was where Africa lane now is. He owned and liberated a good many slaves, who settled in that section and gave the street a name from their fatherland. At Milton Nathaniel Harcourt and Anning Smith were the largest property holders. James Hallock, John Caverly, John Wood and Benjamin Sands were large taxpayers.

RESIDENTS OF MILTON, MARLBOROUGH AND VICINITY IN 1816.

The following is believed to be a tolerably accurate list of the principal residents of Milton, Marlborough and vicinity, during the period from 1816 to 1825. It is compiled mostly from the ledgers and account books of David Sands, sr., who did a large business in Milton, and there were but few people but had some dealings with him during those years. It is therefore the best directory of Marlborough in 1816, which can be obtained at this time:

Darius Ayres, Samuel Adams, Lawrence Alschoff, John Anthony, Loama Adams, David S. Adams, Nathaniel Adams, Peter Alsdorff, David Ayers, Benjamin Anthony, Aickford Armstrong.

Moses Birdsall, John S. Brewer & Co., Matthew Benedict, Jacob Bailey, Edward G. Burger, William Bolton, Oliver Brodhead, Hait Benedict, John Benedict, Daniel Brannan, Townsend Barrett, R. C. & A. C. Brodhead, Conrad Bishop, Isaac Bogardus, Isaac Barton, William Banks, Zachariah Baird, Nicholas Belly, Jacob Bailey, Richard Burger, Jesse Booth, Catherine Bailey, George W. Birdsall, Dolly Booth, Robert Brown, John Bradley, Stewart & Birdsall, Sands Beech, Nathaniel Bailey, Joseph Brown, Obadiah Brown, Charles Brown, Wesley Brodhead, Lewis Booth, Jane Belly, Absalom Barrett, John Brower, A. D. Brower, James

Bunday, C. Bishop & Brown, Caleb Bishop, jr., Isaac Brown, Amos Brodhead, Abraham Black, Joel Baker.

John Caverley, David Conklin, Jones, Conklin & Co., Samuel Cropsey, Peter Crookstan, Uriah Coffin, Peter Coutant, Henry Crawford, John Cropsey, Robert Chambers, Hezekiah Coffin, Abagail Crawford, Elijah Coffin, Haddock Carpenter, David Clearwater, Richard Cole, Augustus Conklin, Charles Craft, Peter Brookstone, John Cole, Mapes Crouse, Samuel Cypher, Thomas W. Cole, Nathaniel Chittendan, Seth Conklin, Nathaniel Clarke, John D. Crook, J. T. Conklin & Co., John Church, Peter Clearwater, Joseph Clearwater, Ebenezer Cooley, John Caton, George Conklin, Josiah Cooper, William Cramer.

Jonathan Deyo, Paul Darrow, Robert Dunn, Theodore Dusenbury, Peter DuBois, Samuel Dusenbury, William Dow, Jacob Dayton, John Davis, Jones Denton, James Dow, Richard DuBois, Samuel Drake, Robert Dillon, Cornelius DuBois, Charles L. Davis, Charles Decker, John Deyo, Benjamin Dunn, Rachael DuBois, Emeline Dowe, James DeMott, Walter Dobbs, John DeGraff, Ephraim DuBois, Stephen Davenport, Joseph Dunn, Caesar and Betty DuBois, Simon Deyo, Amos Dickinson, Wilhelmus DuBois, Henry Dusenbury, John Duffieed, Lavina Davis.

Jeremiah Ellis, Abraham Elting, Thomas Elmendorf, John Easterly, Reuleph Elting, William Eckirl, John Everitt, Derick Elting, David Elting, Jeremiah Ellis, Solomon Elting, Francis Evans & Co., Job G. Elmore.

Benjamin Furman, Charles Field, Isaac Fowler, Henry Frederick, Henry Frent, Thomas Fowler, Charles Frost, Solomon Fowler, Sarah Fowler, Martines Freer, James Fisk, James Fowler, jr., Zachariah Freer.

Henry Gregory, Ferdinand Griggs, Fowler Griggs, Milton S. Gregory, Melchior Gillis, Richard Garrison, Wm. Gidney, Thomas Gill & Co., Daniel Gregory, Isaac Gerow, William Gill, Abram Gutcher, Oliver H. Gerow, Harvey Griggs, John L. Gerow, Jacob Gillis, Caleb Gee, Rachael Ann Gregory.

Stephen Hadley, Thaddeus Hait, James Harris, James S.

Hallock, James Hallock, Hallock & Sherman, Nicholas Hallock, James Hull, Benjamin Harcourt, James Hait, John Hadley, Moses Hunt, Moses Hunt & Co., Foster Hallock, Frederick Hadley, jr., Purday Hadley, James Hughes, Adna Heaton, Amos Hait, Nathaniel Harcourt, Parmela Holmes, Samuel Hughson, Gideon H. Heard, James Hull, Joseph Harcourt, Phillip Hasbrook, Charles Hull, Taber Hull, Jonas Hasbrouck, Israel Haight, Ira John Hait, Harry C. Hornbeck, Andros Hasbrouck, Davis Hoag, Garrett Hasbrouck, Alexander Hallock, Josiah Halstead, Martha Hallock, Jacob Halstead, Levi Hasbrouck, Benjamin Hulse.

H. A. Jenkins, Albert Jenkins, Cyrus Jenkins, Cornelius Jenkins, James Jenkins, John Jenkins & Son, William Judson, William Jennings, John Johnson, Christopher Jaycox.

Jonathan Kent, Nathaniel Kelsie, Joseph King, Henry King, William Ketcham, William Kelsie, John Kelsie, James Kent, Daniel Knapp.

Josiah Lockwood, John LcFever, Jacober Le Fever, Abraham N. LeFever, Jones N. LeFever, Elisha Lester, Ladoc Lewis, Simeon Lawson & Co., Robert Lockwood, Thos. L Lynch, Joseph Lester, John Lowell, Garrett LeFever, Nathaniel Long, Abram Lawson, George W. Lynch, Thomas Lawrence, John Lemunyan, A. & J. LeFever, Andrew Lester, William Legget, John J. LeFever.

Gilbert F. Mondon, Hatfield Morgan, James Malcomb, Alexander Mackey, John S. Mackey, John More, Richard Mondon. William Mackey, Wm. More, Elijah Martin, Johile Miller, Clark M. Mackey, John Matthews & Co., William Martin, Samuel Morehouse, Hester Morgan, David Martin, Francis Mackey, Benjamin Mackey, Thomas Mackey, Selah T. Martin, William Marshall, Isaac Mowl, Hackaliah Merritt, Nehemiah Merritt, Phillip Mackey, Polly Mackey, Charles Merritt, Charles Millard, Sarles Miller, Levi Mackey, Drake Mackey.

Stephen Nottingham, John Noyes, Olly Norton, John Norton, William Newell.

Abel Ostrander, Reuben Ostrander, Carpenter Ostrander, Charles Ostrander, Jonas Orson.

Nathaniel Potter, Henry Perkins, Hannah Perkins, David Phillips, Anson Perkins, Hezekiah Perkins, William and Luther Pratt, Henry Phillips, Samuel Palmar, Henry Palmer, Soper Perkins, Eli Perkins, Andrew Patterson, Elijah Porter, Parmalee & Brown, Daniel Polhamus, Abram Palmateer, Sally Patroit, Francis Pell, Abram Parsol, Miss Mary Perkins.

Henry Quick, Jacob Quimby, John Quimby, William Quigley, David Quigley, Amos Quigley, Daniel Quimby, Lewis Quick, Rosevell Quick, Michael Quimby.

Jacob Rowley, John Rooraback, Jacob Ransom, Uriah Raymond, John Rhodes, Joseph Ransom,-Daniel Russell, Joseph Rhodes, Phillip Rhodes, Nathaniel Reeder, Smith Ransom, John Roe, James R. Russell, John Roe and Co., William Robertson, Phineas Rice, Cornwall S. Roe, Jeremiah Relyea, Benjamin Roberts, Richard Rhodes, Lucas Relyea, William Requa, Lewis Rhodes.

Benjamin Sands, Griggs & Sands, Lydia Smith, David Sands, John Sands, Sylvester Strong, Shepherd & Westfield, Ludlow N. Smith, Matthew Sammons, Samuel St. John, Zadock Southwick, Smith & Bailey, David Soul, George Seaman, James Sammons, Anning Smith, William C. Smith, John Stephens, Jacob Smith & Son, Joshua Sutton, Hezekiah Smith, David Strong, Nehemiah Stephens, Stephen Stillwell, Cornelius Schoonmaker, Nancy Smith, James Sherman, John Sheffield, Charles Stewart, John Stewart, Johiel Seymore, Abraham Soper, George Saxon, Julia Ann Sloop, Henry Sloat, Jonathan Strickland, Anson St. John, George Sparks, William Soper, David Selick, Asintha Scofield, Deborah Smith, Emma Sands, Judah P. Sands, Pardon Sherman, Henrietta Sherman, Abram Sherman.

Peter P. Tice, Jacob Townsend, Jeremiah Tompkins, David Thompson, Israel Terry, Nathaniel Thorne, Peter L. Travis, Ira Terry, Timothy Tilson, Anthony Thompson, Isaac Tompkins, Marinus Terpening, Nathaniel Turner, Benjamin Terwilliger, Nancy Tompkins, Haddens Thompson.

Isaac Underhill, Ann Underhill.

Cornelius Van Curen, Peter Van Orden, Abram Van Orden, Peter Van Demark, Edward Van Demark, Salino Vradenburgh.

Stephen Waring, David Woolsey, Jonathan Wood, Nathan Wolley, Noah Woolsey, Abraham Wolley, Richard J. Woolsey, Henry Woolsey, Richard Taylor Woolsey, Jonathan Woolsey, James Waring, John Warner, James Wygant, Thomas Wygant, Jeremiah Whitney, Wm. Wiltsie & Co., Elijah Woolsey, Mathew Wygant, Maria Warner, Jemima Wilson, Job White, Thomas Warren, Joshua Woolsey, Michael White, Timothy Wood, Stratton Wolley, Ichabod Williams, Elidia Watkins, Stephen Winn, George Worden, Samuel Wright, David Weed, Stephen Wardwell, William Wiggins, Elise Westervelt, Derrick Wesbrouck, Jonathan Wesbrouck, John Wilklow, Miles Wells, Moses Woolsey, Daniel Wilklow.

Hannah Young, Edward Young, Charles Young, John Young, Elias York, Robert Young, Alexander Young, Abraham Young.

OLD FAMILIES.

THE WYGANT FAMILY.

The name of Wygant is closely identified with the first settlement of the Town of Marlborough. The numerous residents of to-day who bear the name are almost all descended from Michael Weigand (as the name was originally spelled, who was one of the original owners of the German patent in Newburgh. He came to this country in 1708, being one of the Palatine fugitives from Germany. Louis XIV of France ordered the Palatine of the Rhine to be devastated. His generals gave the inhabitants three days to vacate. Michael Weigand and family were thus obliged to lose nearly all their possessions, and come to America through the aid of a company. They arrived in this country in 1708, and Michael obtained lot No. two of the German patent, 250 acres in extent, being now part of the city of Newburgh. His family was at this time composed as follows: Michael Weigand, aged 53; Anna Catharine, his wife, 54; children, Anna Maria, 13; Tobias, 7; George, 3. The company which aided them in settling here furnished Michael with tools, viz.: " 1 great file, 1 smaller do., 1 hatchet, 1 jointer, besides several pieces more."

The son Tobias grew up to be a man of influence among his neighbors. In 1727 he entered into a written contract with the Consistory of the Lutheran Chnrch of New York, to have a preacher officiate for them in Quassaick twice a year. In 1725 he became a trustee of the Glebe, and served in that position many years. He became the founder of the Monroe branch of the family. Martin, son of Tobias, opened the principal tavern in Newburgh. He was the first to spell his name Wygant. A cut of his tavern appears in Ruttenber's "History of the County of Orange." His place was a great resort for the loyal during the Revolution. He kept tavern until his death in 1792, without issue.

George, youngest son of Michael, had several children, of whom Michael (2) was the progenitor of the Marlborough families. He was one of the original subscribers to the Presbyterian church, and a trustee in 1785. He served with distinction in the Continental army. He had three sons, James, Michael (3) and John Waring. They all became owners of adjoining farms south of Lattintown and west of Marlborough village.

James Wygant served in the war of 1812, and was for a number of years trustee of the Presbyterian church. He married Philvena Waring, and their children were Clemence, J. Calvin, Eliza, Charlotte Ward and Jane S.

Clemence married Sarah Young, of Palmyra, N. Y., and resides a mile and a half west of Marlborough, on a fine fruit farm. He was for several years a trustee of the Presbyterian church and owns a large amount of real estate in Marlborough and vicinity. His children are J. Foster, Fannie E., Elmer E., Adella W., J. Calvin, Philvena and Clemence, jr.

Eliza married J. C. DuBois, of Highland, now deceased. J. Calvin married Jemima Velie, and lives at Hyde Park. Charlotte Ward married Toomis Velie, of Middle Hope, and is mother to Charles E. Velie. Her husband is now dead. Jane S. married Smith Young, of Milton.

Michael (3) married Althea Carpenter, and was the father of Edward J., Dennis M., John, Elmira, Hattie and Ann D. Edward J. is a prosperous fruit farmer, and raises an enormous amount of Concord grapes for the New York market. He lives where the old homestead was. It was burned some years ago, and many valuable old papers lost to history. Dennis W. is a commission merchant, and does business in New York city. John is dead. Hattie married Phineas H. Lawrence, and Ann D. married Asbury Wygant, also a descendant of Michael (1).

Thomas Wygant was born in August, 1753, and married Elizabeth Bond. It is probable that he was a grandson of

Michael (1). He died in May, 1823, leaving the following children: Barnard, born May 9, 1776, died December, 1850. Matthew T., born October 6, 1777, died October 23, 1851. Rebecca, born June 29, 1779, died October 13, 1871. Michael, born April 8, 1781, died September 13, 1782. William, born February 24, 1783. James, born June 29, 1785. Anthony, born March 8, 1787. John, born April 14, 1789. Martin, born May 27, 1791, died August 19, 1792. Benjamin E., born 1793, died July, 1875. David, born May 23, 1796, died August, 1870. Austin, born December, 1798. Lewis, born December 27, 1800.

The second son, Matthew T., was the father of Martin and Chauncey (who died without issue), and Asbury, Hiram and Augustus, all of whom are now living.

Augustus married Phebe C. Barrett, of Milton, and owns a fine fruit farm on the Lattintown road. Their children are Mari Anna, married to William Harris, and Samuel B.

Asbury married Ann D. Wygant, and lives on Hudson street. He has three daughters, Elizabeth, Mary C. and Harriet.

Hiram is living in Steuben county

J. Ward Wygant is a son of John Waring, and is a fruit farmer, living on Greaves' avenue. He married William Cosman's daughter, H. Elizabeth, and has two sons, William and Howard.

Wm. W. Russell, of N. Y. city, is also a descendant of the John W. Wygant branch.

***

YOUNG.

Alexander and John Young, brothers, were the first of that name to settle in Marlborough. They came about 1760 or 1762, and John settled on what is now the Lyons' place, south of Milton village. The brothers emigrated from England about 1730 or '40, and first settled in Long Island. John Young married Dorcas, daughter of

Edward Hallock.   Alexander married Elizabeth Lawrence, of Northern Ulster.   They had three sons and three daughters, John, Lawrence, Edward, Dorcas, Eliza, and Phebe. The daughters all moved to the West.

Edward, son of John Young, who was born in 1775, married Hannah Halsted, daughter of David Halsted, of Dutchess county.   Her mother was a Cromwell, and a descendant of Oliver Cromwell.

The family were members of the Society of Friends in those early days.   Edward kept a boarding school at one time, but his principal business was farming, and he may be called with propriety the first fruit farmer of Marlborough, since he raised more fruit than his neighbors, and introduced the famous Antwerp raspberry.   Others claim to have propagated this berry before Edward Young, but this is not proven, and, anyway, to him belongs the credit of being the first to market this remarkable berry, and pave the way for the shipment of fruit of all kinds to New York city.

The first Antwerp plants were obtained in a singular way. A friend of Edward Young, who kept a shop in Poughkeepsie about 1834, one day observed a package on his counter, which he was satisfied had been left by a stranger who had visited the shop a short time previous.   He laid the package aside for several days when, it not being called for, he opened it, found some young raspberry plants, and set them out.   They yielded such splendid fruit that he sent for his friend Edward Young, and invited him to take some and raise them.   This was in the fall of 1835.   The plants were taken home by Young, and propagated, much attention being devoted to their culture.   He raised them first near Lattintown.   They proved very prolific, and far ahead in quality of any other variety.   He was laughed at for trying to sell them in New York city, but time has shown his foresight and wisdom.   He died in 1854, and his wife in 1848.

The sons of Edward Young were five in number.   John, the eldest, was born in 1803, and married Martha Sands, of Milton.   They had three daughters and one son, Phebe, Hannah, Henrietta and John Hallock Young, the latter a large landholder in Milton.   Martha died in 1833, and John married second Phebe S. Hallock, of Milton, and had by this union, two daughters and one son, Smith.   J. Hallock Young married a Wolley, Smith married a Wygant, Phebe married Justice Gerow, of Plattekill.   Martha married DeWitt Vail, and Henrietta married a Wolley, cousin of J. H. Young's wife.

David, second son of Edward, was born in 1808, and married a Carman, of Dutchess county, and had two children, Edward and Ann Eliza.   Edward married an Adams and Ann Eliza a Hicks.   David died in 1880.

Alexander Young was born in 1810, and married Deborah Ann Harcourt, daughter of Benjamin Harcourt, and had two children, Marietta and William.   Marietta married Chas. G. Velie, of Marlborough, and resides at the southern line of the town.   William married a Flagler, of Sullivan county, and lives in Hampton.   Alexander has been engaged in fruit farming all his life.   He and his brother William C., spent their best years in developing the fruit industry. Many a day they went among the best class of grocers in New York, inducing them to handle the Antwerp berries. They succeeded, driving a little acrid berry, about half the size of natives, entirely out of the market.

Edward was born in 1814, and married Hannah Haviland, of White Plains, and had two daughters.   She died, and he married second a Frost, of Dutchess county, having a son and daughter by this union.   The son married an Underhill, of Long Island; the daughter is deceased.   Edward died in 1878.

William C. was born in 1815, and married Althea Harcourt, daughter of Benjamin Harcourt, and has three children living, Ann Augusta, Charles and Ella.   Charles married a Peck of Albany.   William C. began business when he was only fifteen years of age.   He had a shoot near the present West Shore R. R. depot, and ran cord wood to the river.   When quite young he and his brother bought the Cornelius Bloomer place, and did well there.   Afterwards he bought the Hampton property in partnership with his brother Alexander, and they were in the fruit business a number of years. In 1858 he sold out to Alexander, and bought the property in Marlborough, where he now resides, establishing a fruit farm. In 1862 he built Young's dock, commonly called the upper dock, giving Marlborough increased facilities for the shipment of fruit. The steamer Queen, of Wappingers Falls, was the first boat to land at his dock. Afterwards the Ann, the Walter Brett, and the present line, comprising the steamers Baldwin and City of Kingston. They carry immense quantities of fruit. In 1884 William C. took his son Charles into partnership, under the style of W. C. Young & Son, and they carry on a large coal, lumber and fertilizer business, in addition to the dock property and fruit farm. Through the efforts of William C. the cut-off road to the dock was built, being the only road of record from the village to the docks, the lower end of Landing street being the property of the West Shore R. R. Co.

John Hallock Young, of Milton, is a fruit farmer, owning between 300 and 400 acres of land. He also raises choice stock. His son Arnold is in business with him, under the style of J. H. Young & Son.

CAVERLY.

This name is associated with the early history of the town. The family was numerous in Marlborough during and after the Revolution. John Caverly was a soldier in Capt. Belknap's Newburgh company in 1776, together with a number of others from New Marlborough. At that period there were four other Caverlys resident in the precinct besides John, viz.: John, jr., Philip, Joseph and William. In 1799 we find eight Caverlys on the pathmasters lists: Philip, Latting, Richard, John, Joseph, Nathaniel, Peter and John (2d). Philip was the grandfather of Jonathan Caverly, now residing west of Milton village. He carried on ship building at the foot of Dog street, Milton. He first settled in Lattintown, and owned a farm there where he lived and died, as did also his son Lattin Caverly, being the same place that Jonathan Caverly owned until 1868, when he removed to Milton, where he now resides, his oldest son Luther P., occupying the old homestead at Lattintown. Jonathan was the son of Lattin.

In 1810 John Caverly was Town Clerk.

FOWLER.

The Fowlers are of English descent, and of good family, one of the ancestors being Sir Thomas Fowler, who lived in 1630. The oldest branches of the family in this country are supposed to be direct descendants of William Fowler, of New Haven, magistrate, who flourished there in 1637.

The Fowlers of Marlborough and Middle Hope trace their descent from Joseph, a first settler at Mespat Kills, L. I., in 1665, supposed to be a son of William, the New Haven magistrate. Joseph had a son William, and he a son

John Fowler, son of William, born at Flushing, Long Island, 1686, died at Newburgh, 1768. He had five sons—1, Samuel; 2, Isaac; 3, John; 4, James; 5, Nehemiah.

Samuel, (1) born 1720, died 1789. Married Charlotte Purdy, and had 7 children :

1, Mary,   Married George Merritt ; died 1799.
2, Elizabeth,   "   Samuel Clark.
3, Charlotte,   "   Daniel Gedney.
4, Martha,   "   Reuben Tucker.
5, Abigail,   "   Abel Flewelling.
6, Gloriana,   "   John Fowler, (nephew of Samuel).
7, Samuel, born 1757, died January 22d, 1830.

Samuel (7) married, first, Rebecca Gedney, and had 3 children :
1, Purdy,   married Charlotte Tooker and had 6 children.
2, Mary,   "   George Wandel.
3, Charlotte.

Samuel (7) next married Mary Clapp and had 5 children :
4, Henry,   married Eliza Ann Thorne.
5, Rebecca,   "   George Grone.
6, Electa,   "   Dr. James Smith.
7, Samuel,   "   Susan Phillips.
8, Charlotte,   "   Henry Cox.

It is said of Samuel (7) that he was for 40 years a minister of the M. E. Church. His home near Newburgh was the cradle of Methodism in the town of Newburgh. He was the first located preacher in the First Methodist Church, of Newburgh, (now Trinity M. E. Church) in 1820.

Samuel (1) and Isaac (2) came from Rye, Westchester Co., and purchased part of the Harrison patent of Gomoz, in 1747, being the lands now owned and occupied by Peter V. B. Fowler and M. W. DuBois, and east to the Hudson river.

Isaac (2), son of John, married Margaret Theal, and had one son, Isaac, jr., born April 3, 1746.

*Isaac, jr.—*About 1770 Isaac, jr., married Martha, daughter of Charles Tooker, and settled at the Dans Kamer, where the Armstrong heirs now own and live. They had one child, but both mother and child died of small-pox and were buried in Marlborough in March, 1771. He next married Glorianna Merritt, in 1773, and had 8 children as follows:

1, Caleb, born February 8th, 1775; died March 8, 1826.
2, Martha, married Stephen Taber, died leaving no issue.
3, Dr. Charles, lived and died in Montgomery.
4, Gilbert, died at about 20 years of age.
5, Nehemiah, born 1784, died 1853, in Plattekill, Ulster Co.
6, David, lived and died in Gennessee, Livingston Co.
7, Dr. Francis, lived and died in Ohio.
8, Dr. Isaac, settled in Ohio, and was drowned in the Muskingum river, when quite young and unmarried.

Isaac Fowler, jr., was a military officer during the Revolution. Several of his descendants live in Middle Hope and a few in Marlborough. Among them the sons of Caleb— Peter V. B., Jacob V. B. and Isaac Fowler.

The third wife of Isaac Fowler, jr., was a Mrs. Owens, maiden name Furman. By this marriage were born Furman and Mary, who were both married in Sharon, Conn. Mary married a Mr. Gay. Isaac Fowler, jr., died in 1825, and was buried at Sharon. His widow and children removed to western New York, where his daughter still lives. The son died respected and esteemed by all who knew him.

Caleb (1), married Catharine Sebring, a granddaughter of Isaac Sebring, and had 11 children.

In November, 1804, Caleb Fowler had a gathering of his neighbors for a wood drawing frolic. Some of the logs were cut from a tree which had killed the chopper who cut it down, a man named Hoffman, from Esopus. Nobody wanted to draw these logs, so 'Underhill Merritt, (father of Daniel Merritt, a connection of the ancestors of the Marlborough Merritts) volunteered to draw the load. While walking beside the team he caught his feet in the lines, was thrown under the wheels, an arm broken in two places and his head crushed so that his brains bespattered the road. When the others came up he was quite dead.

Caleb lived at Middle Hope. He was born February 8, 1775; died March 8, 1826. The following are his children :

I. Peter V. B., born February 20, 1800; died 1875. He married Eliza DuBois, of Fishkill, and had four children : 1, Henry D., born 1827, and lives on the old homestead in Middle Hope; 2, Abram D. B., born 1830; died 1854; 3, Caleb Gilbert, born 1835; died 1879; 4, Peter D. B., born 1844; died 1855.

II. Caroline, married James E. Slater and had five children : 1, Elizabeth; 2, Anna; 3, James; 4, Sebring; 5, Frank.

III. Dr. Gilbert S , born 1804; died 1832. Had no issue.

IV. Ann Catharine, born 1806; died 1833. No issue.

V. Amelia, married William D. Weygant, and had one child, Theodore Weygant, now in Portland, Oregon.

VI. Martha B., died in infancy.

VII. Margaret, died young.

VIII. Mathew V. B., married Elizabeth F. Seymour, and had one child, James.

IX. Jacob V. B. settled in Newburgh, and married, first, Susan Brinckerhoff; second, Mary J Currie. Had two children : 1, Catharine, who married Dr. Avery; 2, Helen C., unmarried, resident in Newburgh.

X. Elizabeth, born 1819; died 1836. No issue.

XI. Isaac Sebring, living in New York, married Mary L. Powell, granddaughter of Thomas Powell, and had four children : 1, Robert Ludlow, a lawyer, resident in N. Y. city; 2, Thomas Powell, a lawyer, resident in N. Y. city; 3, J. Sebring, died young; 4, Lulu.

Nehemiah (5). He was the fifth son of Isaac, jr. He lived and died in the County of Ulster, near the western end of the Town of Marlborough. He was a well-to-do farmer. He was married four times, first to Hannah Sears; second, to Elizabeth Mackey; third, to Hannah Coutant, and fourth, to Phebe Van Tassel. He had eleven children:

1, Benjamin, born 1805.
2, Isaac, born May 6, 1808.
3, Francis, born January 20, 1810.
4, Samuel, born October 15, 1812.
5, Stephen B., born July 17, 1814.
6, Tamer Ann, born December 19, 1816.
7, Elizabeth, born June 17, 1819.
8, Caroline, born December 23, 1821.
9, Daniel Wesley, born May 11, 1825.
10, Peter C., born December 22, 1827.
11. Catharine E , born February 7, 1835.

I. Benjamin was a successful lawyer in N. Y. city.

II. Isaac married Elizabeth Griggs, and had three children: 1, Seymour, dead; 2, Mary; 3, Louisa, dead.

III. Francis married twice, first, Sarah J. Owens; second, Betsey St. John Had eight children : 1, Samuel, died Sept. 19, 1885; 2, James Wm.; 3, Gilbert; 4, Charles; 5, Mary Jane; 6, Margaret Ann; 7, Hannah; 8, Phebe.

IV. Samuel, married Elizabeth Halstead, and had three children : 1, Mary Ann, now dead; 2, Catharine Jane, now dead; 3, Samuel N.

V. Stephen B., married Mary Ann Presler and had eight children: 1, Charles; 2, George; 3, John; 4, William, now dead; 5, William; 6, Mary; 7, Ellen; 8, Sarah Ann.

VI. Tamer Ann, married James Underhill and had five children: 1, Hannah E.; 2, Jane C.; 3, Mary; 4, James; 5, Henry.

VII. Caroline, married John R. Terwilliger, and had seven children: 1, Agnes; 2, Hannah J.; 3, Susan; 4, Mary F.; 5, Caroline; 6, John E.; 7, Stephen B.

VIII. Elizabeth, married James H. Ferguson, and had three children : 1, Charles; 2, Reuben; 3, William.

IX. Daniel Wesley, married Lucretia Terwilliger, daughter of William R. Terwilliger, of Plattekill; died May 19, 1874, leaving three children: 1, Nehemiah; 2, William; 3, Anna. Nehemiah is a successful lawyer at the city of Newburgh, N. Y., and is Justice of the Peace. William C. (2) is a minister of the gospel, living and preaching at Livingston, Montana. Anna is married, residing at South Norwalk, Connecticut.

X. Peter C., had six children: 1, Phebe E.; 2, Isaiah P.; 3, Elias O.; 4, Rachel Francis; 5, Eugene J.; 6, Hannah Elizabeth.

XI. Catharine E., married John Ellison; removed many years ago to
Missouri, and died May 14, 1882, leaving four children : 1, Irene ;
2, Francis ; 3, Milton J. ; 4, Estella.

Daniel S. Fowler, of Marlborough, is the grandson of John
Fowler, who settled near Cedar Hill cemetery. John Fowler
died in 1859, leaving a son Daniel Fowler, who lived at
Roseton. His other children were Anna, Glorianna, Matil-
da, Martha, Jane, Charlotte, Henry, Samuel and William
The children of Daniel are Daniel S., Barbary, Rachael
A., Matilda, Orrin, Kate, Eleanor, George and Daniel S. The
latter is the only one living in Marlborough.

The following branch of the Fowler family settled in Marlborough in 1840 :

Jeremiah (3), of Rye, son of William (2), of Flushing, settled at Rye,
Westchester County ; died 1766. He left the following issue :

Fourth Generation.

1, David, born 1728 ; died 1806.
2, Jeremiah, died 1793.
3, William.
4, Sarah.
5, Elizabeth.
6, Mary.
7, Reuben.
8, Anne.

Jeremiah (4), son of Jeremiah (3), had five children :

Fifth Generation.

1, Gilbert, of Harrison.
2, David.
3, Marcus.
4, David.
5, Abigail.

Gilbert (5), son of Jeremiah (4), had seven children :

Sixth Generation.

1, Ann,   buried at Town of Rye, Westchester Co.
2, Woolsey,   "   "   "   "
3, Hannah,   "   "   "   "
4, Abigail,   "   "   "   "
5, David, died 1882 ; buried at Middle Hope.
6, Richard, died 1886, at Holly, Orleans Co., N. Y.
7, Phœbe, died 1887.

David (6), son of Gilbert (5), was a merchant in New York, until 1840,
when he removed to Marlborough, Ulster County. He was a farmer,

and an influential citizen. He held the office of Supervisor of the Town of Marlborough. He in later years moved away and died in 1882, and was buried at Middle Hope. He had eight children:

SEVENTH GENERATION.

I. David H., of New York city.

II. George W., of Newburgh; has three children: 1, Lillie; 2, Ida; 3, Fred.

III. Woolsey R., of Brooklyn; has three children: 1, Gracie; 2, Marian; 3, Justin.

IV. William H., a prosperous merchant of Newburgh. Has one child, Clarence.

V. Sarah Ann, now dead.

VI. Phœbe A., wife of Charles Harcourt, deceased.

VII. Mary E., wife of John S. Purdy.

VIII. Emma E., now dead.

SOPER.

William Soper moved to Marlborough in 1810, coming from Shawangunk. He was in the slooping business, and had a store, living where Townsend's hotel is located. He was justice of the peace and supervisor from 1820 to 1824, also in '38 and '39. He transacted a great deal of legal business, drawing up papers, etc., although not a lawyer. He married Eleanor Dickinson, of Shawangunk. Their children were: Abram D. and William Soper, both of whom became lawyers, one dying in Virginia, the other in Wisconsin. Nancy Mary, who married a Hanford, and went to New York, afterwards to Ohio, where she died. Emma, married Curtis Woolsey Northrip (father of C. S. Northrip). Charlotte, married Nathaniel Clark, lived in Milton, and is buried there.

Abram D. Soper was postmaster in Milton in 1830. Wm. Soper also held the office, and when politics changed turned it over to his sister, Nancy Soper. The office was then located where E. W. Pitcher now has a flower house.

Following is a copy of the commission granted William Soper as a coroner for Orange County, now in the possession of C. S. Northrip, of Milton, his grandson :

"The people of the State of New York, by the Grace of God free and independent : To all to whom these Presents shall come, greeting. Know ye, that we have constituted and appointed, and by these presents do constitute and appoint William Soper, gentleman, to be a Coroner of our County of Orange, with full power unto him to use, execute and enjoy all and singular the power, jurisdictions and authorities to the said office belonging or appertaining. To have and to hold the said office of Coroner for our said County of Orange, together with the Fees, Profits and Advantages to the same belonging, unto him the said William Soper, for and during the term of one whole year, from the date hereof.

"In testimony whereof, we have caused these our letters to be made patent, and the great seal of our said State to be hereunto affixed. Witness, our truly and well-beloved John Jay, Esquire, Governor of our said State, General and Commander-in-Chief of all the Militia, and Admiral of the Navy of the same, by and with the advice and consent of our Counsel of Appointment, at our city of Albany, the seventh day of April, in the year of our Lord One Thousand Seven Hundred and Ninety-Eight, and in the Twenty-second year of our Independence.

"Passed the Secretary of State's office, the 20th day of April, 1798.

JASPER HOPPER, D. Sec'y."

Attached is a great wax seal, three and a half inches in diameter, and half an inch thick, with a rising sun depicted in the centre, the word "Excelsior" underneath, and "The Great Seal of the State of New York" carved above.

NORTHRIP.

Zephaniah Northrip was a nephew of Noah Woolsey, an

early settler in Milton, and came from New Jersey when a lad, and was brought up by his uncle. He married and had two children : Rebecca, who married Eleazer Gedney, of Orange County, and Curtis Woolsey Northrip, who was born in the house where Benjamin Allen lives, near C. Meech Woolsey's. He farmed in his younger day, and then went to New York city for nineteen years, returning to Milton in 1846, and taking up farming again.

C. S. Northrip, son of Curtis Woolsey Northrip and Emma Soper, resides about one mile south of Milton village, and follows fruit farming. He served one term as justice of the peace, and is a trustee of the Presbyterian church.

HARCOURT.

The Harcourt family is said to have been originally a Norman family, and under the name of "de Harcourt" to have entered England with the victorious cohorts of William the Conqueror. Since that time the family has been an influential and prominent one in many parts of England, and is prominently represented to-day in Oxfordshire and Berkshire.

Richard Harcourt is believed to have been the first of the family to settle in this country, and first located at Oyster Bay, Long Island. About the year 1754 he removed to Marlborough, where he purchased a tract of land comprising about one thousand acres, lying between the villages of Marlborough and Milton, and extending west to the Lattintown road. His homestead was where Jesse Lyons now resides. He was commissioned "One of Her Majesty's Justices for the Colony of New York." He occupied a prominent place in the town and drew many of the early deeds and papers for his section. His wife was Mercy Latting, and his children were Nathaniel, Hannah, Esther, Ann, John and Mercy. His remains were interred in the burying ground at Lattintown. Nathaniel, the eldest son of Richard, was born in 1748, and by law of primogeniture the estate of his father descended to him alone. The latter, however, he voluntarily divided with his brother John, and both remained in town. Nathaniel married Mary, daughter of Joseph Carpenter, one of the first settlers of the town. He died June 13, 1823, and his wife May 3, 1839, aged 88 years. They had children: Sarah, Mary Deborah, Richard Joseph, Benjamin, Nathaniel and Mercy. Mary became the wife of David Baker, of Saratoga County; Deborah married John Pinkney, of Dutchess County; and Mercy married Cornelius DuBois, of Marlborough. All of the sons settled in town and died there. Nathaniel Harcourt, though not a public man, wielded a wide influence in the town, and held a number of precinct and town offices. He was notoriously loyal to the patriot cause during the trying days of the Revolution, and contributed liberally to the support and encouragement of the Continental army, in which, though of weak condition, he performed some active service at West Point. He was bitterly opposed to the Tories of his section, held no part nor lot with them, and was possessed of great firmness of character. He was strictly fair in all his dealings, honest and conscientious, and died in 1823.

Benjamin Harcourt, son of Nathaniel Harcourt, was born in Marlborough on Nov. 3, 1788, and passed the earlier years of his life upon his father's farm. His educational advantages were such as the district schools of his locality afforded. Upon attaining manhood he engaged in agricultural pursuits upon a portion of his father's farm. In 1828 he purchased a farm of 407½ acres in Lattintown, and occupied it until his death, on Dec. 14th, 1866. Mr. Harcourt, aside from his farming pursuits, was an influential man in the town and county, and engaged extensively in other business enterprises. In politics he was a Democrat, and held various offices of trust and responsibility. He was justice of the peace for several years, supervisor of the Town of Marlborough in 1826, 1827, 1828, 1829 and 1831, and in November, 1831, was elected sheriff of Ulster County, serving his full term. While a member of the Board of Supervisors he purchased the ground for the county poor house, and furnished it throughout. He dealt extensively in real estate, was drover and cattle dealer, had an interest in the transportation business on the Hudson, and passed an active, earnest and industrious life, enjoying meanwhile the respect and esteem of all with whom he came in contact. He was one of the trustees of the Methodist Episcopal Church at Lattintown, and a regular attendant of the Presbyterian Church of Marlborough. When twenty-one years of age Benjamin Harcourt was united in marriage to Eleanor, daughter of Matthew Wygant, of Marlborough, who died Feb. 18, 1862, and by whom he had seven children, Sarah, Deborah, James Clinton, Eliza, Charles A., Althea and Eli.

Sarah lived in Hampton, Orange County. Deborah married Alexander Young, and had two children, William and Marietta Y., who married Chas. G. Velie.

James Clinton was a resident of Marlborough, formerly engaged in farming, and has filled the offices of assessor, school commissioner and town clerk, and was supervisor of the town in 1854, 1863 and 1880. For the last thirteen years of his life he was engaged in the freighting business with William C. Young, at the upper landing. He died Sept. 22, 1882. His wife was Helen, daughter of Abraham Wolley, of Lattintown, who died on March 8th, 1859.

Eliza E. married first Lewis Griggs, second Henry C. Griggs, and lives in Washingtonville. She had one son by her first marriage, James C. Griggs, who keeps the Morgan House, Poughkeepsie. By the second marriage was born Etta, who married and settled in Washingtonville.

Charles A. was a farmer in early life. In 1850 he married a daughter of David Fowler. He was afterwards in the shoe business in Newburgh, with David Bradley, and by himself. In 1868 he engaged in the furniture business, becoming a member of the firm of Peck, Van Dalfsen & Co., of Newburgh, then located near the corner of Water and Third streets. For more than twenty years he was a prominent business man in that city. At one time he represented the Fourth Ward in the Common Council, and occupied other responsible positions. He was taken sick with a tumor

The History of Marlborough. 169

in the stomach in 1885, and died in March, 1887, in Poughkeepsie, and lies buried in Cedar Hill cemetery, in Middle Hope.

Eli is a farmer and fruit grower in Marlborough. Aside from his farming pursuits he has held minor offices of trust and responsibility. He taught school in 1853, in district No. 8 for one year, and is now district clerk, having held the office for twenty-three years in succession. He has been commissioner of highways of the town for six years, is one of the trustees of the Presbyterian Church, and clerk of the present board. When twenty-four years of age he was married to Mahala, daughter of William Cosman, of the town of Newburgh, Orange Co., by whom he had three children, Annie, Benjamin and Crawford. Annie is the wife of Eugene, son of George W. Lawson. Benjamin married Carrie, daughter of William J. Purdy. Crawford married Hattie, daughter of George Gardner, of Plattekill.

THEODORE HANFORD

Was born in Marlborough, Dec. 6th, 1823, his boyhood being spent on the farm of his father. At the age of 16 he went to Newburgh, with Powell & Son, to learn the cabinet making trade, and while there he united with the Reformed Church. Having completed his trade, he went to New York city and worked at it until the gold fever partially developed itself in 1849, when he started for the gold fields. Arriving at San Francisco he traveled for the mines, and at once commenced active operations. Being successful, he soon had an interest in several of them. He remained in the gold district four years, experiencing all the incidents of miners' life from handling the pick to the position of overseer and superintendent of several mines. Having completed his work in California he went to Australia. There he delved in the soil for two years more, with his usual success, and at the end of that time he started for his native home.

Having secured ample means to travel he now visited nearly all parts of the globe that are interesting to an inquisitive traveler, and making the entire circuit of the world, he returned to New York in March, 1856.

Using his own words, his wild oats were sown, and it was time to turn his thoughts on a future home. To this end he formed the acquaintance of Catharine, the daughter of John Howell, of Newburgh. This friendship ripened into an engagement of marriage, which took place Sept. 3, 1856. Soon after he entered into partnership in the commission business under the firm name of L. Thorn & Co., where he represented the company until 1875, when he withdrew from the partnership.

In November, 1881, he was called to join the silent majority. He died respected by all who knew him.

BLOOMER.

Thomas D. Bloomer was a grandson of William Bloomer, who resided on the Dans Kamer farm before and during the Revolution. William Bloomer married Rachel Cosman, by whom he had seven children. The eldest, John, became a blacksmith and a farmer, and married Martha Denton, of Fostertown, and had three children: William, Thomas D. and Sarah. William went to Seneca Co., where he died in 1841. Sarah married Samuel Halsey, and died in 1855. Samuel D. died on his farm at Lattintown, July 31, 1887, being eighty-two years of age. Until sixteen years old he resided on his father's farm, but at that period engaged as apprentice to Oliver Cromwell, a tanner of Canterbury, Orange County. Having finished his apprenticeship at twenty-one years, he returned to farming, joining his father in the purchase of the Dans Kamer farm, and afterwards the "old Bloomer farm," just south of Marlborough. In 1839 he purchased a farm at Lattintown of William D. Wygant, the property being the old Lattin homestead, after which family the village was named. There he spent the remainder of his life.

November 18, 1835, Thomas D. Bloomer was united in marriage with Mary, daughter of Cornelius DuBois. They had six children, four of whom are living: John, Cornelius and William, fruit farmers, and Mary, wife of Charles A. Wolley.

Thomas D. Bloomer was a active Presbyterian, and an officer of that church for fifty years. In 1856 he served the town as supervisor. He was a man widely known and respected.

William Bloomer was also supervisor of the town for several terms. Cornelius is an officer of the Presbyterian Church.

THE WOOLSEY FAMILY.

William and John Woolsey were brought up in Dutchess County, but came to Marlborough some time prior to 1760. John Woolsey's name appears among the contributors to the fund raised in 1763 to build the Presbyterian Church in Marlborough. William Woolsey was an ensign in the Continental army. He left a son, Richard I., who married Chlorine Woolsey, his cousin. Their children were David, Thomas and John, who all lived and died in this town. David married Lucy T. Meech, of Westfield, Mass. Their children were George, William, Richard, C. Meech, Mary and Ellen. William and Richard lived in Milton, but are now dead. Mary married John Atkins, and went to Cornwall, where she died. Ellen is the wife of Ira Wood, and lives in Cornwall. C. Meech is a lawyer, living in Milton. He has been honored with many public positions, from justice of the peace to the state legislature. At present he represents the town in the Board of Supervisors.

Richard Woolsey, of Marlborough, ancestor of Peter V. L. Purdy, John Ed. Woolsey, Mrs. John Lawson and others, is thought to have been a brother or cousin of William and John Woolsey.

William Woolsey (2) married a cousin, Chlorine Wool-

sey, and settled in Jersey City, and had children—David,
Thomas, John and Electa.

PURDY.

Among the early families who came to Marlborough none
perhaps did more to interest and urge the speedy settlement
of the town than the Purdys.   The Purdy family, according
to a partially written genealogy, came from Yorkshire, England, and Francis Purdy was the first to come to this country.   He settled in Fairfield, Conn., and died there in 1658.

John Purdy was the first of the family born in this vicinity.
He was the second son of Joseph and grandson of Francis,
of Fairfield.   He owned land and lived until death at a
point near the village of Tarrytown, N. Y.   Five children
were born to him, three boys and two girls.   The boys,
Joseph, Elisha and Nathaniel, occupied the land set aside for
them by their father in Marlborough, and grew up to be
men of acknowledged ability.

From the genealogy of the family it appears that Elisha
Purdy married Mehitable Smith, a daughter of Rev. John
Smith.   Nine children were born to him as follows: John S.,
Thomas, James, Hattie, Challie, Elizabeth, Winfield, Nancy
and Diner.   Elisha lived for a time in Middle Hope, Orange
County, but soon returned to his early home, locating near
the present village of Marlborough.

Of the immediate descendants of John S. Purdy (who was
the eldest son of Elisha), Daniel D. Purdy, who occupies a
handsome cottage on Grand street, in the village of Marlborough, is the only survivor.

JAMES S. KNAPP, M. D.

A prominent physician and a well known and respected
citizen of lower Ulster for many years was Doctor Knapp,
a native of Orange County, born May 17, 1824.   He pursued

the study of medicine under Dr. Houghton, of St. Andrews, afterwards graduating and receiving his diploma from the medical college of Castleton, Vermont, one of the oldest institutions of the kind in this country. He commenced the practice of the profession in 1846, in the village of Milton, and some six years thereafter removed to the village of Marlborough, where he soon attained a high position as a physician. He died Sept. 23d, 1879, after a continuous practice in this town of more than thirty-three years. He was a member of the Episcopal Church, and for many years was an officer of Chri t church, of the village of Marlborough. Dr. Knapp also served a term as justice of the peace of this town, and was for a time the U. S. Loan Commissioner.

Of dignified deportment, hospitable and social disposition, he had many friends. To them and his patients his death was indeed a loss. In 1850 Dr. Knapp married Eliza Roe, of Milton, who survives him, as do their four children, three daughters and one son. A kind husband and father, and a domestic man in the true acceptation of the word, his chief delight centered in his family.

LOCKWOOD.

Major Lewis DuBois had a daughter named Margaret, who married Daniel Lockwood about 1775. He came here from Connecticut. She was widowed and married again to Gen. Nathaniel DuBois, (a distant relative) residing in Newburgh. By her first marriage there were four sons, Lewis, Daniel, Eli T. and Charles Lockwood. Eli T. Lockwood, sr., was born April 14, 1800, and married Ann Eliza DuBois, Jan. 4th, 1826. By this union eight children were born: Margaret, Daniel, Eli T., jr., Ann Eliza, Charles, Sarah Jane, Eugene V. and DuBois. Of these three are now living in Marlborough: Sarah J., married to Francis T. Anderson, and Eli T. Lockwood, living on Hudson street. Mrs. Ann Eliza Butterworth, resides in Brooklyn, and Chas. W. Lockwood in Orange County. Eli T. Lockwood, sr., was born in the family homestead, on South street, in 1800. He followed farming, and died in 1848. His son, the present Eli T. Lockwood, was for many years a steamboat engineer, but now resides in the handsome residence on the Terrace, built by him in 1885. His children are Mary Ella, married to Thomas Russell, proprietor of the large bookbinding establishment in New Chamber street, New York, and Daniel Lockwood, who lives on the old homestead.

———

SANDS.

The first settler of this name in Marlborough was Benjamin Sands, who came here some time between 1760 and 1770, from Dutchess County. He was related to Samuel Sands, who was clerk of the Precinct of Newburgh in 1763. He bought about one thousand acres of land, of the Hallock family, located where the village of Milton now is. He resided north of where the Presbyterian Church now stands, and the old house is still in existence, being occupied by Mrs. Conklin. Benjamin married Amy Hallock, daughter of Edward Hallock, of Milton, and they were blessed with a numerous progeny as follows:

I. David Sands, married first a Hall, aunt of Hon. L. Harrison Smith, of Milton; second, Sallie M. Booth, of Campbell Hall, Orange County; and third, a Townsend, a glass manufacturer, still living, at an advanced age, in Philadelphia. Rachel also died there a few years ago.

II. Sarah, lost at sea.

III. Phebe, married Ebenezer Bull, of Hamptonburgh.

IV. Esther, married Daniel Erl, of Turners' Station, Orange County.

V. Rachel, who married first, a Barker, of Poughkeepsie, and as Rachel Barker became a famous Hicksite preacher. She married second a Dr. Moore, of Philadelphia.

VI. Emma, married first, Dr. Wm. Gedney, of Milton; second, Nathaniel Harcourt, of Marlborough. She is still living in Poughkeepsie.

The children of David Sands by his first marriage were:

I. Oliver H., died in the employ of the Government Navy Yard, Brooklyn, where he was superintendent of the paint department.

II. Catharine, married first, James Stewart; second, Elliot Brockway, a pioneer settler of Port Huron, Mich., deceased in 1854.

III. Judah P., died in New York city about twenty years ago.

The children of David Sands by his second wife were:

IV. George W., married Sarah, daughter of Robert S. Lockwood, of Marlborough, and died in 1863.

V. Matilda B., died in Milton in 1883, single.

VI. Rachael B., married Oscar Clark, in Milton; died in 1886.

VII. Walter Sands, married first; Sarah, daughter of Richard DuBois, second, ——— ——— , living in Poughkeepsie.

VIII. David Sands, married Phebe, daughter of John Lawson, and resides on North Main street, Marlborough.

IX. Sarah A., single, died in Marlborough in 1886.

X. Alfred B., went to Staten Island in 1859, to collect $300, and never was heard of afterwards.

XI. R. Montgomery, lives at Maiden Rock, Wis.

XII. Horace B., still living.

David Sands, sr., lived in the old house on Sands' dock, Milton, which is still standing. His land extended to within about 15 feet of where the West Shore R. R. depot now stands. He was a ship carpenter, kept a store, and ran a sloop to New York. He was a busy man, and his ledgers, now in the possession of his son, David Sands, jr., show that he had dealings with nearly all the residents in the neighborhood in the early part of the present century.

David Sands, jr., was born in 1827, and has spent the greater part of his life in this town. He has followed fruit farming, and was a school teacher in his younger days. For a number of years he administered the law in the justice's court in Marlborough, earning the title of 'Squire Sands.

In 1886 he bought the property on North Main street, where he now resides, and remodeled it into the present commodious dwelling. He traces his descent on his mother's side to Sarah Wells, who, when a girl of sixteen years, became the first settler of Hamptonburgh. She married Wm. Bull, ancestor of the wife of David Sands, sr.

BINGHAM.

Thomas D. Bingham came from Wetchester County, and settled in Marlborough several years before the dawn of the present century. At first he lived with Dr. Fowler. In 1793 he married Elizabeth Purdy, and settled on the place now owned by Enos Reynolds, on what is now Bingham street, deriving its name from him. He began his married life in a log house about one hundred yards west of the house in which Reynolds now lives. The present house was built by him in 1795 and '6, and is still in good condition. He had three sons and one daughter. John was born in September, 1795. The others were David, Finetta and Charles. All three of the sons died in 1825 of typhus fever.

Finetta married Jeremiah Clark, and died in Marlborough, December 6, 1886, the 85th anniversary of her birth.

John married Elizabeth Bloomer, and died when about thirty years old, leaving an infant son, Charles E. Bingham, now an elder of the Presbyterian church, and father of John W., Clarence and Charles E. John W. is a nurseryman ; Clarence married Melissa Kniffin, daughter of Samuel H. Kniffin ; Charles E. removed to Livingston Manor, Sullivan County, where he is engaged in the jewelry business.

David lived in Marlborough and had three sons, Thomas, Jeremiah and Daniel. Thomas is living west of Newburgh. He has a son, John F. Bingham, a resident of Delaware, and prominent in railroad affairs.

JOHN JOSEPH ALEXIS ROBERT.

This gentleman with the long name was resident in Marlborough from 1798 to 1813, when he returned to his native country, France. He is spoken of in the "History of Ulster County" as a genuine aristocrat. The title is hardly a correct one. He was a quiet, well-behaved gentleman of some means, who owned several slaves and resided where Isaac Hall now lives, keping a store, and running a nursery. He was short and pussy in appearance, and well liked by his neighbors. He drove a handsome span of brown horses. In his house was a big old-fashioned parlor, where he often entertained company. He had a large swinging apparatus to keep the flies off his dinner table. Iu 1813 he sold his farm here and gave his slaves their liberty. To one of them named Figaro he gave five acres of ground, stipulating that he should pay for it in chickens and turkeys. The fowls were never called for. The house where Figaro lived still stands, being occupied by Philip DuBois. Robert then returned to France, where he had a wife living. From an advertisement of Robert's in the Political Index of Newburgh, dated Sept. 17, 1810, he states that he had fourteen years experience in the nursery business, and had discovered that it was a great mistake to transplant trees in the spring, the proper time being from the 15th to the 30th of November.

BUCKLEY.

The Buckley, or Bulkley (sometimes spelled Bulkiley) family are of ancient origin, settled in Cheshire in the early part of the twelfth century. They afterwards scattered far and wide, some settled in the Isle of Anglesea, some in Ireland, Haughton in Bedfordshire, Cheadle and other parts of England. The Rev. Peter Bulkley, who came to America, was a descendant from the Haughton branch. He was a clergyman of the Church of England, rector of Odell, in Bedfordshire, and was silenced by Arch-Bishop Laud for non-conformity, whereupon, says Cotton Mather, "he sold a goodly heritage and came to America in 1635." About the same time his brother Nathaniel, in company with a large number of non-conformists, emigrated to Holland to escape the persecution they were subjected to under the rigorous administration of Arch-Bishop Laud.

John Buckley, a descendant of Nathaniel, was born in Stuttgart, in the kingdom of Wurtenberg, in 1755, where he received a liberal education, and in compliance with an old law of the kingdom, which compelled every young man to learn some mechanical trade, he chose that of a carpenter and builder. He came to America with Gen. Reidesel, and landed in Quebec June 1, 1776, accompanying him all through Gen. Burgoyne's campaign, which ended in the surrender of his army at Saratoga, October 17, 1777. They were all sent prisoners of war to Boston. Soon after he left the army he commenced working at his trade in Tewkesbury and Lowell; in 1780 he settled in Jaffrey, New Hampshire, where he purchased a farm; in 1785 married Margaret Dunlop, eldest daughter of Hugh Dunlop, one of the early settlers of New Hampshire, by whom he had five sons, all born in Jaffrey : John, James, Samuel, Frederick and William. All settled in Jefferson Co., N. Y., except Frederick, who went South. John was born in 1786, and worked with his father, a carpenter and builder, who was engaged in building in Boston and Cambridge. He left his father's employ in 1805 and went to Providence, where he learned the trade of millright and machinist, and was for several years in the employ of Brown & Amory and Samuel Slater, who is justly called the father of American manufacturers. In 1809 the Pleasant Valley (Dutchess Co.) Manufacturing Co. was chartered and he was engaged by the company to superintend the construction of their great water wheel and running gear. In 1811 the Cornwall cotton factory was incorporated and employed him to superintend the construction of their machinery. He remained in their employ until 1815, when he purchased a carding and spinning mill and a small farm in Marlborough. The mill he converted into a woolen factory, making broadcloth and satinets. In 1855 he changed his factory into a cotton mill, and continued the business until the commencement of the civil war in 1861, when he ceased manufacturing and retired from active business. He died at Marlborough June 1, 1874, aged 84 years.

In January, 1814, he married Phebe, youngest daughter of James Thorne, by whom he had six children: John, born Oct. 23, 1814; Thomas Townsend, born July 11, 1817; Margaret, born March 21, 1819, died March 13, 1872; William, born Sept. 7, 1821; Mercy Townsend, and James, who died in infancy.

Thomas Townsend Buckley died in Brooklyn, February 6, 1887, in his 70th year. He was a prominent merchant in New York city for many years. He began business at the age of fourteen in a store in Marlborough. A little later he went to Newburgh as clerk, and when eighteen years old went to New York city and engaged in the wholesale dry goods business. In the course of a few years he became largely interested in the importing and jobbing trade. In 1874 he retired from active business, spending his summers at Marlborough and his winters in Brooklyn. He married Amelia A., daughter of William R. Thompson, of New York. In his younger days he traveled in the West, becoming unusually well informed on a great variety of topics. He held many important positions during his career, having been vice-president of the Bank of the Republic, receiver of the Atlantic & Pacific R. R. Co., director of the Metropolitan Gas Co., and Home Insurance Co. He was one of the executive committee of the great Sanitary Fair of 1864, and was a member and patron of historical and art societies. At his death the New York papers all devoted considerable space to his obituary. His remains lie interred in Greenwood cemetery.

MERRITT.

The Marlborough branch of the Merritt family are descendants of George Merritt, who was born in 1702, and came to Newburgh in 1747, dying there Feb. 2, 1750. He

was married to Gloriann̄a̍ Purdy, who died Sept. 13, 1765.
Their children were George (2), Samuel, Caleb, Gabriel,
Josiah, Humphrey, Elizabeth, Jane, Glorianna.

Three of these sons subsequently settled in Marlborough
about 1775. One of them lived on the farm which Chas. G.
Velie now owns, and another on the Carpenter farm, where
Isaac Hall now lives, and which at one time belonged to J.
J. E. Robert, the slave holder. Josiah was the third brother,
and the only one who has descendants living in the town.
He settled on the place now owned by Thomas Buckley,
and engaged in farming. He was a man of sterling qualities,
and a hard worker. He married twice, first to Annie Purdy,
by whom he had five children, Gabriel, Josiah, Nancy, Althea and Esther Ann. His second wife was Rachel Sherwood, and their children were David, Joseph and Phebe.
He had a slave named Priscilla, who married a slave called
Peter Milden. Figaro Milden was born of them, and he and
his mother received their liberty from Josiah at his death.

Gabriel Merritt was born in 1777, and served in the war
with Great Britain in 1812 and 1814. He held several offices in the town, being at one time a constable, a justice of
the peace for 20 years, and poormaster for some years. He
married Rebecca Whitmore, from Westchester county. His
death took place in 1853.

Their family was large. Eliza died young. Rachel, married Wm. Kelly, and is now living in Marlborough. Her
children are Elizabeth, Marcus D., the builder, and Harriet
Amelia, married J. H. Elting, of Highland, now deceased.
Esther Ann, married Wm. P. Flewelling, of St. John, N. B.
James D., is a fruit farmer, now living in Marlborough, married Delia Moore, of N. Y. city. His family are Mary E.,
who married George Clarke, and resides in Milton; Susan
R., living in Marlborough; Ida S., living in town; William H.,
a civil engineer, living in Arizona; Robert W., who has a
fruit farm adjoining his father's. Edward A., married Emeline Kniffin, of Marlborough; Rebecca Jane, died a few
years since. Mary died young. Gabriel, jr., married Mary
Flewelling, and settled in St. John, N. B. Charles W., married Mary Lane, of New York.

Nancy, the second child of Josiah Merritt, married Mobury Carpenter (see Carpenter.) Esther married Zephaniah Northrip. She was grandmother to Henry Northrip, of Orange Co., Zephaniah, of Newburgh, and Justice C. S. Northrip, of Milton. Althea married John Brower, father of Miss Charlotte A. Brower, of Marlborough. David I., married Sally Cropsey. Both are now deceased. Phebe married Andrew Cropsey. Joseph married a Miss Wood, of Orange county.

Josiah married Betsy Demott, and settled north of Milton nine years afterwards. They left several children, among them, John Merritt, living in New Paltz, a younger son lives in Catskill, and a daughter who married John Yelvington, of Poughkeepsie.

Edward A. Merritt, son of Gabriel and grandson of Josiah, is still living in Marlborough at the age of 69 years. He was for many years a carpenter and builder, having led a busy life. He now resides on West street, Marlborough.

John C. Merritt, eldest son of Edward A., keeps a large dry goods, grocery and general store on Western avenue. He was postmaster for ten years, takes a lively interest in local politics, and is a prominent Republican.

Charles E. Merritt, the second son, is treasurer and assistant superintendent of the Mackey-Bennett Cable Co., in New York city. The other children are Henry, who died three years ago, at Whitestone, L. I., where he was engaged in business. P. Elting, associated with his brother John C. in the mercantile business. Marcus D., who is in the hardware business in San Francisco; Lizzie A. married Frank Conklin, son of James Conklin, of Middle Hope. She lives in Minneapolis. Mary K., and Frank E., who is in the commission business in New York city.

BROWER.

Charles N. Brower came from Poughkeepsie about 1830, and bought the Lymasen farm, near Lattintown, which he afterwards sold to Levi Crosby, blacksmith, moving to Main street, Marlborough, where he built two houses, now the property of Charles D. Brower. He was a descendant of Mrs. Annike Jans, claimed to be the rightful owner of Trinity church property, St. John's park, and other valuable property in New York city. He married Mary Doty, of Massachusetts, a lineal descendant of Capt. John Ward, of the Mayflower. Their children were Jane E., Charles D., Sarah Ann (widow of Cornelius Valentine), James I., and Rosetta, wife of W. L. Parmalee. Jane E. married a Doty, and moved to Croton, died in New Haven, Conn., and is buried in the old Presbyterian cemetery in Marlborough. Charles D. is a fruit grower, living on the corner of West and Bloom streets. James I. lives in Kingston.

CLARK.

Jeremiah Clark was a man of much force, who left a strong imprint on the locality where he lived and died. He was a Presbyterian in religion, a Democrat in politics, a shrewd judge of men and means, and a hospitable and popular man. He represented the Second Ulster District in the State Legislature in 1860. He was the father of Samuel C., Charles B., William S., Augustus G., Elizabeth A., Jeremiah, John F. and Julia Clark.

George S. Clark, of Milton, belongs to another family, being the son of J. Oscar and grandson of Nathaniel Clark, who came from Cornwall in 1817, and purchased the old homestead, on the Farmers' turnpike, still in the possession of the family.

QUIMBY.

The Quimbys were among the early settlers of Marlborough. Levi Quimby and his sons James and Isaac came here before the Revolution. Also Zadok and Enos Quimby.

They settled in the western part of the town, where Samuel L. and John Quimby now own. The present residents of the name are descended from James, who left a son James, father to Samuel L. and John. Samuel L. was supervisor of the town in 1885, is an ardent Democrat and owns a large fruit farm.

COLMAN.

One of Milton's most public-spirited men was Samuel Colman. He started the wheelbarrow factory there in 1844, and for many years was prominently identified with every good work and enterprise in the locality. He was an elder in the Presbyterian Church, and a strong advocate of the temperance cause, ever ready to lift his voice against the traffic, and assist in elevating his fellow men. On one occasion he bought all the liquor there was in the tavern at the dock, and poured it into the street. His son, S. O. F. Colman, was associated with his father in the wheelbarrow manufactory, and in 1855 married Anna M. Newman. In 1875 S. O. F. Colman withdrew from the factory, and went to Poughkeepsie, engaging in the hardware business. In 1879 he removed with his family to Syracuse. His eldest son died in 1883, another son is married and living in Chicago. He has also a daughter, resident in Syracuse.

BELLY.

Following is the chronological table of this old family which is connected with the early history of the town :

John Belly was born in the year of our Lord 1753, November the 29th, died 12th of April, 1824.

Magdalane Coutant, his wife, was born March the 5th, 1755; died February 8th, 1845.

Elizabeth Belly was born December the 4th, 1779.

Mary Belly was born March the 11th, 1781; died in '82.
Nicholas Belly was born March the 30th, 1782.
Nathaniel Belly was born Sept. 11th, 1783.
Jacob Belly was born Oct. the 29th, 1785.
Jane Belly was born February the 24th, 1788.
Mary Belly was born March the 15th, 1790.
Susannah Belly was born June 16th, 1792.
Martha Belly was born May 17th, 1794.
John Belly jr., was born January 19th, 1797.
Bernard Belly was born May 29th, 1800, and departed this life the 20th
  of January, 1802.

BROWN.

Thomas Brown, born in Bristol, England, in 1817, married
a Boyle, engaged in mercantile business, and emigrated to
Marlborough about 1835, securing a homestead on the Marlborough mountain, where he farmed.   He left four children,
Charles H., Thos. P., William and Mary.   William has
moved away.   Charles married a Scott.   Thos. P. and Mary
occupy the old homestead on Mount Zion.

HURST.

The original settler of this name was Jonathan Hurst,
born in Yorkshire, England, in 1800.   He married a Brooks,
engaged in farming and manufacturing.   In 1826 he came
to Poughkeepsie, and four years later to Marlborough, engaging in John Buckley's factory.   He died in 1857, leaving
four children: Josiah, John, Martha and Elizabeth.   Elizabeth died a few years ago.   Martha married H. J. Bye.

OTHER PROMINENT MEN.

Daniel S. Tuthill, son of Congressman Selah Tuthill, published the "Pioneer" newspaper in Milton from 1829 until

his death in 1833. Though he only lived to twenty-seven years of age, yet he was one of the most active business men of the locality. His remains are interred in the old Presbyterian cemetery at Marlborough.

Jesse T. Conklin was a representative man in Milton fifty years ago. He was supervisor in 1830.

Miles J. Fletcher was a man of much prominence in Marlborough in the thirties. He kept store here and was supervisor in 1836 and '37.

Stephen and Joshua Case lived here a hundred years ago, and were buried here. They exercised a large influence in public affairs. Stephen was town clerk from 1778 to 1783.

Dr. Benjamin Ely was a man of strong character, and a slave holder. He owned a large farm west of the present village and practiced medicine. He was town clerk from 1784 to 1790, and lived here for many years. He was a soldier in the Revolution, and fought at Bunker Hill.

Samuel Stilwell came to Marlborough in 1851 from Stone Ridge. He kept store for four years, and then followed fruit farming. Only his later years were spent in Marlborough. He was an active member of the Methodist Church, and was a class leader. He held several public positions of honor. In 1880 he died, leaving considerable property. He was a man of broad views, and contributed liberally to the construction of both the Presbyterian and Methodist church buildings. His son, S. W. Stilwell, occupies the old homestead on Main street.

THE FRUIT INDUSTRY.

Marlborough is known to the outside world principally through her fruits, which have attained a wide celebrity in New York, Philadelphia and Boston markets. Located in the centre of the Hudson valley fruit section, Marlborough possesses the very best soil and the most fertile slopes of the whole territory. More fruit is shipped from this town than any other point on the Hudson, and the place justly claims precedence in all points connected with the raising of small fruits.

GRAPES.

Concord grapes are raised in immense numbers, though all other good varieties have their footing. It may be of interest here to trace the growth of grape growing in New York. The first grape vineyard in the state was planted by John Jacques, at Washingtonville, Orange county. The first vines planted by him were Isabellas, and they are yet living and bearing every year. Dr. Underhill, of Croton Point, planted his vineyards soon after.

William Cornell, of Clintondale, was the first to plant grapes in vineyard form in Ulster county. These were Isabellas, procured from Dr. Underhill in 1846. Soon after Jacob Heaton, Alexander Palmer and William Kniffin, all of the town of Plattekill, started vineyards. This was before the Concord, Diana or Delaware were known. These varieties were introduced on the Hudson by A. J. Caywood, then of the town of Plattekill. He first planted the Diana in 1853, the Delaware in 1854 and the Concord in 1855. George Lawson, of Marlborough, is believed to have been first to plant the Concord in this town, about twenty-five years ago. Since that time grape growing has steadily increased. It is estimated that three thousand five hundred tons of grapes were shipped from the town last year.

While the Concord is most largely raised, being the grape for the million, many other varieties are grown, some of which promise some day to supplant the popular Concord. The Niagara and Pocklington are among recent candidates for favor.

A. J. Caywood & Son have introduced several varieties, among others the Duchess, Poughkeepsie Red and Ulster Prolific. The Poughkeepsie Red is a cross between the Delaware and Iona, and possesses the peculiar quality of possessing nothing offensive to the taste, but may be chewed down, skin, seeds and all with relish. It is very hardy.

The Ulster Prolific was first fruited fifteen years ago, and is deep red in color, compact in cluster, of fine flavor and about the size of the Concord.

PEACHES.

Peach raising has had a large run in Marlborough, though the fruit is not grown as much now as a few years since, it having been demonstrated that this climate is too cold, and that a good peach crop cannot be obtained but once in three or four years. When there is a good crop of late peaches, however, the prices received are enormous, five and ten dollars a basket being top figures. Many growers have made money out of peaches, and many have lost, and the uncertainty of the crop reduces rather than increases the number of growers.

THE FAMOUS ANTWERP RASPBERRY.

THE FAMOUS ANTWERP RASPBERRY.

The growing of small fruits for market began in the town of Marlborough with the introduction of the Hudson River Antwerp. This variety was brought in by Edward Young, in 1836, as described in the sketch of the Young family, in a previous chapter of this work. In the spring of 1837 plants were brought here from New Rochelle, Westchester Co., by Thomas H. Burling, and planted in the garden of his son-in-law, Nathaniel Hallock, and grown for family use for some years. Edward Young was the first to introduce them to market, and to him and Alexander and William C. Young are present growers largely indebted for demonstrating the profit to be derived from marketing berries and small fruits generally. The Antwerp was the best and most profitable berry ever known, but the variety is now almost run out, becoming more scarce with every season. Other berries have come in to take its place, the most prominent being Caywood's Marlborough raspberry.

Other small fruits are largely raised here, strawberries and currants ranking next to raspberries. Blackberries are beginning to be introduced, and promise to be profitable. One prominent variety has been originated in the town by A. J. Caywood & Son. It is styled the Minnewaski blackberry, and is of large size, glossy black in color, with a tender core. Indeed, the Caywoods have originated so many good new fruits that Marlborough is becoming almost as widely known as a source of new fruits as it is for the successful growing and large production of the same.

THE MINNEWASKI BLACKBERRY.

STATISTICAL.

Marlborough derives its name from John Churchill, the famous English general, Duke of Marlborough, born in 1650, died in 1722. The town lies in the southeastern corner of Ulster county, and is eight miles in length at the west, with a river front of five and three-quarter miles, extending three and a half to four miles west of the river. It includes the villages of Marlborough and Milton, and the hamlet of Lattintown. The superficial area is given in the supervisors' report for 1877 as 14,300 acres. In 1870 the assessed valuation was $379,811. In 1886 it was $974,015. The average assessed value per acre is $40.

The boundaries of the town are described in the revised statutes as follows:

"The Town of Marlborough shall contain all that part of said county, bounded easterly and southerly by the bounds of the county; westerly by a line beginning on the line of the county, two chains and seventy-five links east of the north corner of a tract called the Five Patentees, and running thence on a straight line northerly to the most easterly bounds of the land heretofore of Robert Tift, where it joins the Town of New Paltz; and northerly by a tract granted to Lewis DuBois and partners, called the New Paltz patent."— Revised Statutes, vol. i, page 219.

In 1860 the population of the Town of Marlborough was 2,776; in 1865 it decreased to 2,733. In 1870 it was 2,974. By 1875 it had gained eleven souls, the figures being 2985. The estimated population in 1887 is from 4,500 to 5,000, of which the village of Marlborough comprises 1,200 to 1,500.

In 1701 there was not a house in what is now the Town of Marlborough. In fact there was only one in the whole Evans' tract, and that was near Cornwall. From the time

Capt. Bond settled here in 1712, the place has increased rapidly, the greatest growth being made during the past five years, since the West Shore & Buffalo R. R. was opened.

Following is the list of Supervisors, who have represented Marlborough at the county seat:

1772, Lewis DuBois; '77, Benjamin Carpenter; '78-79, Elijah Lewis; '80, Anning Smith; '81, Lewis DuBois; '82, Stephen Case; '83-89, Anning Smith; '90-94, Ebenezer Foote; '95-97, Stephen Nottingham; '98-99, Cornelius Drake; 1800-11, Benjamin Ely; '12-16, Nehemiah L. Smith; '17, David Staples; '18-19, Richard I. Woolsey; '20-24, William Soper; '25, William Gedney; '26-29, Benjamin Harcourt; '30, Jesse T. Conklin; '31, Benjamin Harcourt; '32-33, Abram D. Soper; '34, William D. Wygant; '35, David W. Woolsey; '36-37, Miles J. Fletcher; '38-39, William Soper; '40, Lewis W. Young; '41-42, Robert S. Lockwood; '43, David Fowler; '44-45, William Martin; '46, John D. Crook; '47, Cornelius Carpenter; '48, John D. Crook; '49-50, Lee Ensign; '51, John D. Crook; '52-53, William H. Gedney; '54, James C. Harcourt; '55, William H. Gedney; '56, Thos. D. Bloomer; '57, William H. Gedney; '58, Robert Beebe; '59, William B. Pierson; '60, Cornelius Carpenter; '61, William B. Pierson; '62, Jesse Lyons; '63, James C. Harcourt; '64-71, Jesse Lyons; '72-73, William Bloomer; '74, William H. Gedney; '75, William Bloomer; '76, Townsend M. Sherman; '77, Eugene F. Patten; '78, Townsend M. Sherman; '79, Eugene F. Patten; '80-81, James C. Harcourt; '82-84, C. Meech Woolsey; '85, Samuel L. Quimby; '86-87, C. Meech Woolsey.

The early settlers of Marlborough received their mail through the Newburgh post office. About 1825 a weekly mail was delivered here. The postmasters have been Daniel J. Russell, Miles J. Fletcher, Robert B. Mapes, Dr. Jas. S. Knapp, Samuel Corwin, Dallas DuBois, Chas. T. Jackson, John H. Baxter, John C. Merritt and M. V. B. Morgan. Milton first had a mail in 1828. The postmasters were Abram D. Soper, Wm. Soper, Calvin Bulkeley, David Sands, Earl Stone, Ethan Parrott, Fred H. Smith.

Marlborough was represented in the State Legislature in 1843 by William Soper; 1853, L. Harrison Smith; 1860, Jeremiah Clark; C. Meech Woolsey, 1871–72.

BUSINESS INDUSTRIES

AND BUSINESS MEN.

The village of Marlborough in 1877 is a thriving place, and contains probably fifteen hundred population within a one mile radius of the centre. About seventy-five business concerns exist here, and most of them are progressive and enterprising. The constant improvements made on every hand indicate that Marlborough is a growing village, and will soon be incorporated. The location is advantageous to growth, being midway between Newburgh and Poughkeepsie. Business men have not been slow to appreciate these advantages, and the influx of new residents and new industries is steady and healthy.

The following alphabetical resume of the men who carry on business, and how they do it, may serve to illustrate the character and extent of the trade now carried on in Marlborough. These are in no sense advertisements, nor are they introduced in this work for any other purpose than to demonstrate to non-residents that the business interests of Marlborough are considerable, and compare very favorably with the condition of the place as portrayed in preceding pages:

B. B. Apgar, who runs the flour and grist mill on Landing street, came to Marlborough from Whiteport, in 1885, and has managed the mill successfully. His two sons assist him in the business.

Edwin W. Barnes established a boot and shoe and hat and cap store in the Kniffin block in April, 1886. He came from Middle Hope, being already known to a large number of citizens. His business is now regarded as a fixture, and a decided addition to the village. Mr. Barnes is a taxidermist, and has fine cases of stuffed birds and animals in his store. The tops of shelves and other prominent places are also adorned with stuffed birds in appropriate positions.

John Badner has the honor of being for fifty-three years a merchant in Marlborough, a record in excess of any other tradesman. He has witnessed a great many changes, and a long and steady growth of the town. When he opened store here the "Terrace" was nothing but open fields, mostly devoted to grain, with a few patches of wood. Four new streets, each half a mile long, have been laid out there during his experience as a boot, shoe and clothing merchant. He has a wide acquaintance, and can discourse quite eloquently of Marlborough, and the many changes which he has witnessed. During the summer he makes a business of furnishing berry pickers to the fruit growers of the vicinity, and many Germans flock regularly to his place for employment as soon as the season opens.

George A. Badner is son of John Badner, and leader of the Marlborough Cornet Band, and also plays in Lent & Badner's orchestra.

John W. Badner keeps a restaurant and pool room on Main street, and has a large custom. He has been established four or five years.

Jacob Berean is a contractor for mason work and lathing and plastering, and the many new houses going up keep him busy.

George Brundidge has carried on the watch and jewelry business for a year or two, having his headquarters in Gordon's drug store.

John Bingham has a nursery and does a considerable local trade in fruits and berries.

S. F. Burgess took the furniture business of C. B. Redfield the latter part of 1886. He is a practical man, having had twenty years' experience in the manufacture of furniture.

Carpenter's store was established in 1843, ranking second in point of age. The business was started by the grandfather of James S. Carpenter. The trade has been that of a general country store, selling a variety of staple articles. In 1886 the store was enlarged and improved, and a meat market added. The proprietor constantly adds new features, and aims to keep everything in the provision line ;

also selling coal and plows. He advertises largely and drives trade on modern principles.

Thos. E. Carroll conducts the harness store at the junction of Main and King streets, which was long and successfully run by W. H. Goehringer. He is a newcomer who has made a good impression in Marlborough.

A. J. Caywood & Son have extensive nurseries south of the village of Marlborough. They make a specialty of producing new varieties of fruit, and have attained a wide celebrity for some varieties, noticeably the Ulster Prolific, Dutchess and Poughkeepsie Red grapes, Minnewaski blackberry, and the Marlborough raspberry. The firm have about sixty acres in fruit, and probably are experimenting with as many new varieties of fruit as any concern in the country. Their trade is mostly foreign.

Caywood & Wardell are a new firm in the nursery business, established in 1887.

Walter J. Caywood & Co. are dealers in paints, oils, varnishe:, etc. The firm handle a considerable quantity of varnishes and stains of W. J. Caywood's own production.

W. S. Clark & Son are proprietors of the mill a mile and a half west of Marlborough, one of the oldest mill sites in town, being on the same spot as Silas Purdy's mill, where town meetings were held during the last century. They have long been established, and have a high business standing.

Charles H. Cochrane established the Marlborough Progress in July, 1885, in connection with M. F. Applegate. The newspaper and job printing business started by them has proved a success. Applegate retired in 1886, and Cochrane conducted the business in the second story of Kniffin's block until August of the present year. The paper was started four pages in size, seven columns to a page, and has been enlarged several times. The present proprietor, Egbert E. Carr, came from Rome, N. Y., where for twenty-one years he edited the Roman Citizen. He has re-christened the paper "The Marlborough Record."

H. Scott Corwin is the Southern Ulster correspondent of

the Kingston Freeman, and also contributes to the Orange County Farmer and several New York papers.

Samuel Corwin is a real estate and insurance agent, and a great deal of property passes through his hands.

Sam'l Corwin's Sons conduct the dry goods, grocery, carpet, hardware and general store business, established by their father in 1860. They advertise largely, and deal in a great variety of goods, and keep a model store, on the principle that people will not go out of town to buy when they can do as well at home, and that it pays to keep a full line in the country as well as in a city store. H. S. Corwin and Edward Corwin compose the firm.

Henry Covert is the only licensed veterinary surgeon in the village. He has all the trade in sick horses and cattle. He is also the inventor of an ointment for sores and wounds on animals, which has acquired some local reputation.

Mrs. Libbie Craft keeps the only millinery store in the place, being located on Main street, having been established about four years.

Patrick Crough is a mason and builder, and has all the contracts he can handle.

George Davy is a mason, and has fulfilled contracts on some of the finest residences in and about the village.

Eldorous Dayton, attorney at law, has recently opened an office in Marlborough village. He also has an office in Milton.

A. Dimick DuBois, contractor and builder, is putting up new houses all the time.

Abner Fuller's harness store in McMullen's building, on Main street, was established the present year, is tastefully fitted up, and promises to be a success. He has come to stay.

J. F. Hensey runs the only tonsorial establishment in town, keeping an assistant. He also sells tobacco, cigars, and gent's furnishing goods.

Maurice Hudler's fruit and confectionery store on Western avenue has been established about five years. He furnishes refreshments to parties, entertainments and festivals, and manufactures ice cream on a large scale.

Chas. W. Jackson is agent of the Poughkeepsie Transportation Company, on the lower dock. He is also town clerk, having held the office several years.

Charles-H. Kniffin opened his grocery and news store four years since. He sells all the popular papers. The telephone office is located in his store, connecting with both Newburgh and Poughkeepsie.

Samuel H. Kniffin is proprietor of the Exchange hotel, the oldest hotel building in the town. A large extension was made to the building the present year, and the arrangements compare favorably with those of hotels in places of greater population than Marlborough.

J. O. Mackey runs a stage line to the West Shore R. R. depot, and also meets all passenger boats and carries the U. S. mail. He began business in June, 1883, and met the first train run on the West Shore line. Previous to that date he ran a stage line to Newburgh.

W. H. McCullough has a wheelwright shop in Western avenue, where he repairs wagons, sleighs, etc. He has been established some years.

Moses McMullen is the proprietor of the Farmers' hotel, on Main street. The buildings are extensive, including a pool room, bowling alley and rifle gallery.

A. B. Masten, house and sign painter, has his headquarters in the basement of Shaw's building, on King street. He is a veteran in the business.

Elmer E. McNamee has the Main street drug store, having purchased of C. W. Frost in 1886. He keeps a full stock of drugs, paints and fancy articles.

Jesse R. Masten is a contractor for painting. and executes numerous large contracts.

M. L. Masten's bakery on Western avenue, is an old established institution. A wagon is run, delivering over a considerable territory.

J. Carlton Merritt, proprietor of the large dry goods, grocery, hardware and general store, on Main street, has been established twelve years, succeeding John H. Baxter. He had the post office in his store for nine years prior to

1886. He is agent for the National Express Co., and does some banking business. His store is one of the first in the place.

Merritt & Kelly are contractors and builders, and have built some of the finest dwellings in Marlborough. Edward A. Merritt and Marcus D. Kelly compose the firm.

J. C. & G. H. Milden have a livery stable, and do all kinds of teaming and hauling, and run a stnge in the summer season. They also cut ice from Milden's pond in the winter, and deliver to owners of small ice houses.

M. V. B. Morgan has a meat market on Main street, and is also postmaster, taking the office by Cleveland's appointment in 1886.

David Mosher, M. D., is a physician of the allopathic school, who settled in Marlborough five or six years since. He started the drug store now owned by Everitt & Gordon.

Milton Munday runs an express to Newburgh Wednesdays and Saturdays, and has his headquarters in Penny's store. He is also an insurance agent.

Wm. H. Newman has the tin and stove store, and does roofing, guttering and spouting. The business was started by James Shaw.

A. N. Palmer, M. D., has practiced medicine in Marlborough for nine years. He is also a justice of the peace, and is serving second term as school trustee.

Isaac R. Penny bought the retail boot and shoe business of Stillwell & Smith three years ago, and in 1886 removed his store to its present location on Western avenue. He carries a large stock of footwear, especially in rubber goods.

Chas. E. Reynolds, carriage maker and wheelright, has been known to the public of Marlborough for years. He occupies the old stand on Main street, and is busy all the year round.

Isaac Reynolds, boot and shoemaker, north of the post office, does custom work and repairing.

Philip A. Rion, undertaker, has been established about four years. He furnishes modern appointments, and directs a large number of funerals.

John Rusk, attorney at law, has been settled in Marlborough for nine years. He is also a notary public and insurance agent. He does a large business in the settling of estates, etc.

John Rusk, jr., is justice of the peace. Office with John Rusk, sr.

G. B. Shelden is station and National Express agent at the West Shore R. R. station.

Stephen D. Warren, blacksmith, located on Western avenue. He was for several years at the shop on the Lattintown road, a mile and a half west of Marlborough, but took the shop in the village the present year. His custom is extensive.

John E. Woolsey is proprietor of the Western avenue meat market. He drives a wagon through the country in the summer months, and furnishes the village trade from his market.

N. W. Wright has a flour and grist mill on West Landing street, being assisted in the business by his son, Fred. Wright. The mill is a very old one, being the same run by Spence & McElrath as a woolen mill sixty years ago.

D. L. Wygant has a blacksmith shop on Main street, and does a great deal of horse shoeing and general jobbing.

William C. Young & Son are proprietors of the upper dock, dealers in coal and fertilizers and agents for the Rondout line of steamboats. Their trade is extensive.

MILTON BUSINESS MEN.

Edward Anderson is the house and sign painter of Milton, having executed some of the best work in the village. He is also blackboard artist in the Methodist Sunday school, where he has rendered useful service for several years. Politically he is a Democrat, and has held the office of collector two terms. He is the Milton correspondent of the " Marlborough Record," and compiles the news for the village.

James H. Crook came to Milton and started in the grocery business at the dock in 1862. He was also agent for the Rondout boats for a number of years. In 1882, when the West Shore R. R. line was cut through the dock property he was forced to move, and W. H. Townsend built him a large store about 150 feet west of the old stand. He continued there until 1884, when he built the commodious store which he now occupies on the main street. Meat and poultry have been added to the grocery stock. J. H. Crook is a native of the town, having been born about a mile west of Marlborough village, October 9, 1833. He has been a life-long Democrat.

C. J. Depuy carries on the blacksmith business in the village of Milton, having come here in August, 1876, and purchased the business of John Galaway. He has built up a considerable trade, and has a constant supply of new work and repairing.

Robert J. Dickey came to Milton from Poughkeepsie in 1860, and bought the drug store of Dr. Pierson. He is a native of Newburgh, and a brother of Nathaniel, Wm. D. and Joseph Dickey of that city.

William A. Goehringer in 1880 saw that there was an opening for a stove and tinware store in Milton, and supplied the long felt want. His business has proved successful, and a confectionary and ice cream store has been added.

C. J. Miller, tonsorial artist, came to this village from Germany in 1866, and opened a barber shop and cigar store, which are of more than ordinary pretensions for a place of the size. He has customers from a radius of several miles.

Nolan & Spratt opened their grocery on the 14th of July, 1886, being the successors of Friend W. Perkins, who followed Jacob Rowley. These young men are natives of the town, and having a large acquaintance command a good trade. They deliver orders anywhere in the vicinity and are up to the times.

Eugene Foster Patten came to Milton December 29, 1870, as successor to J. O. Smith, in the butchering and meat market business. When he took the place the trade was

small, but under his management it has become quite large.
A few years since he enlarged his market to secure more
room, and recently he built a new and large ice house on
the property of Nathaniel Hallock. Seven men are constantly employed by him, four of whom are kept busy
slaughtering for the New York market. In politics Eugene
F. Patten has always been a Democrat, and is local leader
in his party, having served as supervisor, collector and other
honorable positions.

Albert Pattison carries on the wagon making and repair
shop of Milton. He came from Matteawan to this place in
March, 1878, and has secured a good patronage. His work
is superior, and the best wagons and sleighs in the village
are of his make.

Ethan Parrott is one of the oldest business men in Milton.
He commenced business on the dock, in connection with his
brother-in-law, James H. Malcolm, in the year 1854. And
he has carried on the mercantile business here since then
with the exception of the year 1863, when he was engaged
in the grocery business in the city of Poughkeepsie. Returning after one year he purchased of the estate of the late
Luther Pratt the property on Main street, where he has ever
since been engaged in the mercantile business. Besides his
store business he held the office of postmaster for fifteen
years, and he was also town clerk for one year. In 1860 he
he was elected school commissioner for this Assembly District by a large majority, holding the office for three years,
and again in 1881, he was appointed by Judge Lawton to
the same office to carry out the unexpired term of Dr.
Bauscher, who resigned the office to take charge of a school
at College Point, Long Island. In the same autumn he was
again elected to the office for three years by a large majority.
As a public officer he has always given general satisfaction.
He has been a leading member of the Methodist church for
over forty years, and has held the office of steward for over
thirty years, and most of that time has been recording
steward. In his early years he was a successful school teacher in Ulster and Dutchess counties. Besides paying strict

attention to his business, he has found time for literary im-
provement, being well acquainted with the most popular
authors, and always interested in the study of English litera-
ture.   In 1846 he married Julia Ann Malcolm, who died in
May, 1887, leaving six children: Dr. Malcolm E. Parrott, of
Brooklyn; George E. Parrott, of Highland; Dr. Walter E.
Parrott, of Catskill; Mrs. Dr. C. J. Wood, of Wappingers
Falls; Mrs. George P. DuBois, of Milton, and Mrs. DeWitt
H. DuBois, of Highland.

Justice Wm. S. Ramsley has an office in the village, and
dispenses the law therefrom.   He has been justice of the
peace several years.

W. H. Townsend runs a store at the dock, and another at
the centre of Milton, the latter being the one occupied by
Jacob B. Townsend previous to 1867.   He does a large
business in grain, flour, etc., owns considerable property,
and is a prominent member of the Presbyterian church.
His son, W. H. Townsend, jr., assists him in his business.

C. Meech Woolsey has an office in Main street.   He is an
attorney at law, town supervisor, etc., and does a great deal
of public business.

INDEX

CARPENTER (Continued)
  15 James 14 15 20 87 91 127
  137 126F James S 15 128 194
  Jas S 134 Joseph 14 25 26 97
  147 167 Josephine 134 Josiah
  W 15 126F Julia 14 16 Lattery
  106 Latting 14 15 Leonard 14
  15 Leonard C 15 Leonard S 15
  99 125 126 137 126F Leonard
  Wright 15 Luff 14 Margaret A
  15 Margaret Ann 15 Maria D
  15 Mary 14 17 167 Mary A 15
  Mary E 16 Moab 91 Mobury 14
  15 181 Mowbray 91 98 Nancy
  181 Nehemiah 10 25 27 Peter
  M 137 Rebecca 15 Richard 16
  17 25 59 147 Ruth 14 Sarah 14
  Selleck 137 William 15 16 137
  Wright 14 20 25 147
CARR, Egbert E 195
CARROLL, Thomas 132 Thos E
  195
CARY, Adaline S 21 Annie M 16
  George L 16 Hannah Ellen 21
  Helen M 21 Iona 21 Maria 21
  William Woodward 21
CASE, Absalom 25 Henry H 132
  Henry Jr 105 John 147 Joshua
  185 Stephen 25 58 105 106 185
  191 Wheeler 108
CASSIDY, Henry 28 Jos D 28
CATON, John 149
CAVERLEY, John 149
CAVERLY, Cecelia 15 John 90
  102 147 148 158 159 John 2nd
  158 John Jr 158 Jonathan 137
  158 159 Joseph 25 158 Lattin
  102 Latting 158 Lewis N 137
  Luther 100 Luther P 137 159
  Nathaniel 158 Peter 25 147 158
  Philip 100 147 158 Richard 158
  William 25 158
CAYWOOD, A J 186 187 188 195
  Walter J 195

CHAMBERS, Robert 149
CHAMPLIN, Christopher 16 137
  126F
CHATT, Chas 30
CHATTERTON, James I 137
CHITTENDEN, Catharine 21 L S
  22 Nathaniel 149 Nath. W 21
CHURCH, John 149
CHURCHILL, John 190
CLACK, Robert 137
CLAPP, Joel 126D Mary 159
CLARK, 147 A G 13 Augustus 30
  65 Augustus G 116 137 182
  Charles B 182 Charlotte 164 E
  W 99 Eleanor 20 Elizabeth 159
  Elizabeth A 182 Finetta 176
  Francis T 137 George S 182
  126F J Oscar 137 182 James
  129 Jehiel 25 26 58 108 145
  Jeremiah 66 137 176 182 192
  John F 182 Julia 182 Nathaniel
  164 182 Oscar 175 Rachael B
  175 Samuel 145 159 Samuel C
  182 Smith M 137 Symon 51 W
  A 30 W S 86 195 William S 66
  137 182
CLARKE, E W 130 George 180
  Mary E 180 Nathaniel 149
  Symon 49
CLEARWATER, Ansom 137 David
  149 Joseph 149 Peter 149
CLINTON, 11 Charles 53 Gen 10
  George 10 20 99 Gov 26 James
  9
CLOSE, John 109
COCHRANE, Charles H 195
COE, Alexander 30 Isaac D 137
COFFIN, Elijah 149 Hezekiah 149
  Susan 17 137 Uriah 128 149
COLE, 102 Brother 124 John 149
  Martin 102 Richard 149
  Thomas W 149
COLLIER, Oscar 30
COLLINGWOOD, 66

WOOLSEY (Continued)
Elijah 152 Elisyabeth 84 Ellen
171 Ephenetus R 126F George
25 171 Henry 128 152 J E 87
John 25 105 106 108 147 171
172 John E 144 199 John Ed
171 Jonathan 25 147 152
Joshua 152 Lucy 120 Lucy T
171 Mary 171 Meech 134
Melissa M 134 Moses 152 Noah
117 147 152 165 Remos 129
Richard 25 59 147 171 Richard
I 128 171 191 Richard J 152
Richard Taylor 152 Thomas 57
128 171 172 Thos 105 William
25 26 147 171 William H 144
Wm 99 Zephaniah 25
WORALL, John 84
WORDEN, George 152
WORDIN, John 29
WRIGHT, Benajah 60 Curtis 65 F
A 132 N W 144 199 N Woolsey
92 Samuel 60 152 Wm Smith
126F Woolsey 9 62 65 98
WYATT, Christopher B 126D
WYGANT, 12 157 Adella W 154
Alathea 15 Althea 154 Ann D
154 155 Anthony 155 Asbury
102 116 144 154 155 Augustus
144 155 Austin 155 Barnard
155 Benjamin E 155 Bernard
27 Charles C 29 Charles D 144
Charlotte Ward 154 Chauncey
155 Clemence 144 154 Clemence Jr 154 Cornelius 13 144
Cornelius W 66 D L 199 Daniel
116 144 Daniel L 128 David
155 David L 144 Dennis M 15
144 154 E J 144 Edward J 15
144 154 Eleanor 168 Eliza 154
Elizabeth 117 154 155 Elmer E
154 Elmira 154 Fannie E 154
George 154 H Elizabeth 155
Harriet 15 155 Hattie 154

WYGANT (Continued)
Hiram 155 Howard 155 J
Calvin 154 J Foster 154 J Ward
13 144 155 James 152 154 155
Jane S 154 Jemima 154 John
25 26 147 154 155 John B 88
John L 126F John W 155 John
Waring 154 155 L M 144 Lewis
155 Lizzie 134 Mari Anna 155
Martha 128 Martha J 144
Martin 58 153 155 Mary 144
Mary C 15 134 155 Mathew 152
Matthew 25 53 85 147 168
Matt. T 155 Michael 15 25 105
109 116 154 155 Michael Jr 54
Morey 11 Mory 144 Mrs Asbury
15 Phebe C 155 Philvena 154
Rebecca 155 Saml B 155 Sarah
154 Thos 25 102 117 147 152
154 Wm 25 155 Wm D 170 191
YELVINGTON, John 181
YONGE, John 59
YORK, Elias 152 Wm 29 30
YOUNG, Abraham 152 Alexander
8 14 89 152 155 156 157 158
168 188 Althea 157 Andrew 25
Ann Augusta 157 Ann Eliza
157 Arnold 158 Charles 144 152
157 158 David 157 Deborah 168
Deborah Ann 157 Dorcas 17
155 Edward 152 156 157 188
Eliza 156 Elizab. 156 Ella 157
Hannah 152 156 157 Henrietta
156 157 J H 157 J Hallock 157
Jane S 154 John 16 17 144 147
152 155 156 John H 144 John
Hallock 156 158 Lawrence 156
Lewis W 12 98 191 Margaret R
12 Marietta 157 Marietta Y 168
Martha 17 156 157 Phebe 156
Phebe S 157 Robert 152 Sarah
154 Smith 144 154 157 W C 158
William C 95 144 157 158 168
188 199 Wm 89 157 168